The Hungry Mind

The
Hungry Mind

THE ORIGINS OF
CURIOSITY
IN CHILDHOOD

SUSAN ENGEL

 Harvard University Press

Cambridge, Massachusetts · London, England
2015

Library of Congress Cataloging-in-Publication Data
Engel, Susan L., 1959–
The hungry mind : the origins of curiosity in childhood / Susan L. Engel.
pages cm
Includes bibliographical references and index.
ISBN 978-0-674-73675-7 (alk. paper)
1. Curiosity in children.   I. Title.
BF723.C8E54 2015
155.4'133—dc23   2014028454

For Sagaponack

Contents

The Hungry Mind

Prologue

MY CURIOSITY ABOUT curiosity began in a classroom. I was working with a group of teachers in a small experimental school, trying to help them identify their educational goals for the year. As so often happens when educators have gathered, in the years since No Child Left Behind, the teachers were railing against standardized tests for elementary school children. They were adamant that the number of division problems a child could solve, or the number of words spelled correctly, didn't measure what they were trying to teach. I asked the teachers to expand. What *were* they trying to teach, if not spelling, division, paragraph comprehension, or knowledge of historical events? They launched into a variety of answers. But there was one thread that ran through everything they said: "the desire to learn," "an interest in new knowledge," "an eagerness to find out," and "curiosity." Ahh, I thought. The government wants children who know things and can do things, while teachers want children who are curious. But do they think that what happens in their classrooms actually makes children more curious? The idea simmered around in my head. A few months later, I was wandering around the streets of Minneapolis, during the biennial meetings of the Society for Research in Child Development. In the midst of all the talk about experiments, coding systems, and statistics, it dawned on me that we are a society that measures what we value and values what we measure. If we measure computation and vocabulary, that is what we'll teach. And if there's something else we value more than computation and vocabulary, then we'd better figure out how to measure it. If curiosity is an important goal of the educational process, then that's what we should be measuring. Aha, I thought. I'll come up with a curiosity measure. Famous last words.

That was over ten years ago. Since then, all kinds of intriguing challenges have stood between me and that imagined curiosity test. I needed to get a better sense of what children do and say that might count as expressions of curiosity. I realized I had to find out if in fact it increases or decreases as children get older. I discovered I had to wrestle with the question of whether curiosity is best thought of as an internal and stable characteristic of the individual person, or something that expands and diminishes in any of us, depending on the situation. I needed to find out if the urge to know was simply a function of someone's intellectual ability. I realized I had to find out what might link a baby's curiosity to the curiosity of an adult scientist, or any adult, for that matter.

As I delved further and further into the research, and began to collect my own data, a developmental picture began to emerge. This book offers my view of how curiosity develops. But during my years of research, another, less rosy picture came into view as well. I began to see that children's curiosity was squelched in schools. And I also saw that several commonly held myths and preferences were silently abetting this squelching process. (1) Most people, including teachers, implicitly believe that some children are curious and others are not. They don't think of curiosity as something they can actively nurture or instill in all their students. (2) Though most people say that curiosity is a good thing, when it comes to choosing between curiosity and compliance, the educational system pitches toward compliance. (3) Many people think that nice teachers encourage curiosity and mean teachers do not. But in fact, encouraging curiosity has little to do with how nice a teacher is.

In telling my developmental story, I will argue that what begins as a robust characteristic, possessed by all normally developing babies, becomes more fragile, and begins to show the fingerprint of a child's experiences—with her parents, in her home, and at school. This developmental account, in other words, helps explain why a quality that is ubiquitous in toddlers is hard to find at all by the time children are in elementary school. Yet, ironically, it is clearer than ever that curiosity is the linchpin of intellectual achievement. People who are curious learn more than people who are not, and people learn more when they are curious than when they are not. The fact that these two statements are different, and both true, makes it even more important to figure out what prevents schools from encouraging curiosity, and what we might do about it.

A word about the rabbit hole that conversation with teachers led me down. Ten years ago, when I began my investigations, I found to my gleeful dismay that there was very little research on the topic. It made me gleeful because I had stumbled upon something that begged to be examined empirically and hadn't been investigated to death. I was dismayed that such an important quality had been relatively neglected by the fields of developmental and educational psychology. How, I wondered, could we know so little about something so important? However, in the ensuing ten years two things happened to change this—one in the field, and one inside my head.

There has been a burgeoning of empirical interest in the development of curiosity and its close cousin, interest. Obviously I wasn't alone in realizing we needed to know more. The topic is now bubbling up in journals and conferences.

At the same time, I now see that actually a veritable ocean of data addresses the topic, though little of it is framed as work on curiosity. It turns out that curiosity is so important to children's development that it is a strand of a vast array of research. Studies that look at attachment use exploration of the environment as a dependent variable. Studies that aim to identify the roots of school achievement have found that being inquisitive is both a predictor and a cause of later academic success. Research on intelligence includes response to novelty as a key component. In other words, several of the most central lines of research about child development depend, in one way or another, on looking at curiosity. One could say it is so important it is practically invisible. My aim here is not to provide an exhaustive account of all the possibly relevant research. But in trying to trace the development of curiosity, I have drawn on a wide range of research, often by people who probably never thought of their work as being relevant to the topic. I have tried to construct an empirically compelling story about how curiosity develops. And I hope this story will lead the reader to some ideas about how we might encourage curiosity in school settings.

A brief explanation about the shape of the chapters to come: Each chapter contains three converging stories—a story about me, a story about the nature of curiosity, and a story about its development in children. Though my argument is based on observation and research, part of what is so fascinating about curiosity is how tangible and memorable it can be in one's day-to-day life. The experience of feeling curious is worth paying attention to, in childhood as well as adulthood. I wanted to convey, in these pages, some of the texture and specificity of what it feels like to be curious, and I wanted to remind readers that every one of us has a personal history of curiosity. So, each chapter begins with a memory of my own hungry mind from the time I was a little girl until I was grown. And while each chapter tackles a different aspect of curiosity (its ubiquity in infancy, the influence of other people, the role of language, individual differences, and so on), the chapters also follow a progression—starting with babies and ending when children are near adolescence.

I hope my readers will finish the book with three intertwined ideas—a new way of thinking about their own curiosity, an understanding of how curiosity develops, and a conviction that curiosity can and should be central to classroom learning.

1

Capturing Curiosity

WHEN I WAS three I liked to eat bugs. I lived at that time in a tiny, gray-shingled house on the East End of Long Island, New York, in a small village called Sagaponack, which in the Shinnecock language means "home of the big ground nut." All around our house lay acres and acres of potato fields.

I rode a red tricycle, which I used like a scooter because I hadn't yet mastered proper tricycle riding. I'd stand on the ground behind it, bending forward across the seat to hold the handlebars, putting my left foot on the low bar that ran across the bottom back part of the trike, pushing off the road with my right foot. That was in the early 1960s, and I had much more freedom than children do now. I was allowed to tour around the quiet streets of Sagaponack on my own. Besides farm equipment, only a few cars a day would pass through. Perhaps my mother told me to be careful on the road, but beyond that, I was on my own. I had a daily round of visits I liked to make. First I'd go see Mrs. Nichols, who lived in a white-shingled house catty-corner to our gray house. She would let me sit in her big easy chair, and give me a cookie to eat. In those days I only wore dresses, the kind with smocking on the front. But often I'd forget to put on underpants, and with the logic of a three-year-old, I worried that without them I might pee in Mrs. Nichol's chair. Next I'd visit Ruth Hildreth, who lived three houses down from Mrs. Nichols and was our telephone operator. From there

I'd head toward the beach, about eight hundred yards farther down the road, where I probably hoped to find my older sister or brother. But I rarely got that far anyway. As I pushed my trike along the small lane, with the warm tar under my feet, I'd almost always find myself stopping on the road's edge, drawn in by the endless potato fields that lined my route to the ocean. I'd park my bike on the grass and crouch down on the edge of the field, butt dropped down, knees bent and up beside my ears, as only a three-year-old can do, breathing in the sweet aroma of the pesticides that mixed with the dry smell of dirt. I'd watch the small potato bugs crawl busily toward the green leaves of the potato plants that lay in long orderly rows as far as I could see. Potato bugs are larger than ladybugs, but like ladybugs they carry on their backs a dome-shaped shell, crisp and shiny, though theirs is decorated in orange-and-black stripes. I'd watch, mesmerized, as their spindly threadlike legs marched them forward, as if each bug was a small windup toy. Then suddenly, with no reason I could ever detect, two translucent wings would appear out of nowhere, and the potato bug would make its low short flight to a new surface. Inevitably, in a way that seemed similarly without volition, I'd reach down, lift one out of the dirt, and as delicately as a three-year-old can, I'd pop it into my mouth. Then I'd bite. I liked the crunching sensation, and the way its slight vibration felt inside my mouth, just before it died. In retrospect, that was my first deliberate investigation of the natural world. I wasn't hungry, and I wasn't particularly cruel. I was exploring what lay beneath the surface.

Nearly every three-year-old child has that same impulse, not merely now and then, but many times a day. During the first three years of life, the urge to find out defines us. But then what happens? Even the most casual observations of schoolchildren, teenagers, or friends in everyday life lead to the conclusion that as we get older we become less curious. The scientific literature agrees. Studies suggest that when children are between the ages of five and twelve, their curiosity diminishes. But is this a problem?

Most people seem to assume that such a decline is inevitable, if sad. Few researchers have asked why curiosity appears to diminish as children get older. And yet most of us, certainly those who are reading this book, believe that curiosity is enormously valuable. We assume that curiosity underlies many of civilization's most important accomplishments: electricity, the use of antibiotics, and the theory of evolution, to name just three in the Western world. Nor do we think it is only the giants of human history whose discoveries are powered by the urge to know. Most of us believe that curiosity is an essential component of learning. One hears frequent talk about how important it is to make school interesting for children, the value of lifelong learning, and the benefits of a thirst for knowledge. When parents in the United States are interviewed, most spontaneously mention their kindergarteners' eagerness to learn, and often will actually use the word "curiosity" to describe their son or daughter. Moreover, that folk conception is correct. There is overwhelming empirical support for the idea that when people are curious about something they learn more and they learn better.

Given how valuable it is, especially during the process of education, it's odd that we know so little about how curiosity develops. We don't know much about what happens to it during the first twelve years of life, or how parents, schools, and other children shape a child's curiosity. We have been blithely incurious about curiosity.

FEELING CURIOUS

One reason why research on the development of curiosity has been sporadic, at best, may lie in the fact that it is a particularly slippery phenomenon. Take my moment by the side of the potato field. My three-year-old self must have felt an urge to know, but I probably wouldn't have been able to tell you that at the time. Even adults rarely pause and notice their own feelings of curiosity, which are often fleeting, or subsumed by more pressing concerns.

Curiosity begins as a feeling—a stirring, or a sense of mental unrest. Sometimes that feeling is more burning and palpable than others. Most, though not all of us, know what curiosity feels like. But often the feeling is buried amid other thoughts, emotions, and impulses. Because of that, it can be hard to locate or identify the internal experience of curiosity. Even when it's intense and stands out, it is often transitory (though of course not always—any literary scholar who has described a decades-long search to identify the author of a famous text, a historian who has tracked down a seminal relic from a significant past event, a scientist who has labored for years to trace the origins of a particular disease, or the detective who has devoted months to seeking the culprit of a crime can attest to the power sustained curiosity). But for most of us, most of the time, curiosity comes and goes, often causing us to act without our even knowing we have felt it. It is not an easy mental experience to report or record.

Every reader of this book can probably think of a time when he felt curious or saw someone else expressing curiosity (asking a question, taking something apart, reading an encyclopedia). But to measure curiosity requires something beyond intuitive and casual recognition. In order to examine curiosity empirically, one must measure it. And to measure it, one must settle upon a definition. The hunt for a good definition (and with it, a good measurement) does not have a long history.

Daniel Berlyne was the pioneer in this area. The first researcher to study human curiosity experimentally, he defined it as a drive, like appetite or sexual desire. Berlyne argued that just as hunger spurs us to seek food and to eat, and our libido spurs us to seek partners and have sex, when something in the environment tweaks our curiosity, we try to satisfy that feeling by seeking information (Berlyne 1960). He argued that one could measure people's feelings of curiosity by observing their efforts to reduce that curiosity—you could understand the itch by measuring the scratch.

Berlyne based his initial experiments with humans on earlier work showing that when rats are placed in unfamiliar mazes or boxes, they explore the environment. The common understanding of this is that the rats perceived novelty as a threat, and were eager to reduce the threat of the unknown—they explored to reduce danger. But he quickly realized that interpreting the rats' search was harder than people had assumed (Berlyne 1955):

> Most investigations of exploratory behavior in the rat . . . have used the amount of perambulation through maze alleys as the dependent variable. These investigations have yielded many well-known findings, but running through an alley can be motivated by so many different drives and influenced by so many well-known factors that it seems rather an indirect way of revealing what we have called curiosity. Furthermore, whether more running necessarily means more curiosity than less running is a difficult question. Which animal is

showing a greater exploratory tendency, one that explores a large number of objects or areas in a short time or one that spends a long time on a few and so remains relatively stationary. (239)

If it is hard to know what the rat's exploration tells you about its "experience," imagine how much harder it would be to make sense of human search behavior. Berlyne's lamentation about the inadequacy of rats revealed a central feature of curiosity—searching can never be wholly separated from the feeling that leads to the search. On one hand, humans might be easier to study because they could tell you something about why they were searching in a particular way or for a particular length of time. On the other hand, humans are exponentially more complicated than rats. This difference led Berlyne to identify a hugely important characteristic of human curiosity. We exhibit something few other species do—the urge to know about things that have no obvious or utilitarian function. We experience epistemic curiosity. This leads to the truly astonishing breadth of stimuli, topics, and events that seems to trigger the human appetite for information. We not only want to know how to get from here to there, what might be scary on the pathway home, or whether the plant matter before us is edible (all things any decent rodent would also want to know), but we also want to know what happened before we were on earth, how people we've never met are living their lives, how a given building or machine was put together, what caused a friend to behave the way she did, and why a certain novelist stopped writing. Our appetite for knowledge crosses all time zones, geographic regions, and zooms in and out from the grand to the minute. Given the nearly infinite range of things that might spark human curiosity, we cannot look to the stimuli for a definition. However, these endless and dynamic phenomena all have something in common. They all trigger our drive to find out for the same reason—in any given situation, our curiosity is aroused when we are surprised.

In his book *Surprise, Uncertainty, and Mental Structures*, Jerome Kagan argues that surprise shapes our mental life. To illustrate, he describes Nobel laureate Elias Canetti's shock that a group of men had been acquitted of murdering some workers in Vienna (Kagan 2002). A crowd of people gathered to object to the unjust verdict, and the police, in an effort to quell the violence, killed ninety people in the crowd.

Kagan then quotes Canetti: "Fifty-three years have passed and the agitation of that day is still in my bones" (10). We remember things (information as well as events) that rattle our sense of familiarity. Surprise not only etches things in our memory—it leads us, as it did Canetti, to probe the source of surprise. We seek to understand what we didn't anticipate. Curiosity, in other words, can be understood as the human impulse to resolve uncertainty.

Like Kagan, Jean Piaget thought humans were uniquely driven to make sense of their experiences (Piaget 1964b). It wasn't enough, in Piaget's view, to be able to navigate the world—humans, even four-month-old infants, are predisposed to understand the objects and events they encounter. This understanding emerges, in Piaget's framework, as a result of the young child's effort to explain the unexpected. Piaget thought that when young children confront an object or sequence of events that doesn't fit their mental schema, they attempt, however unconsciously, to understand why. Both Piaget and Kagan, like Berlyne, saw curiosity as a fundamental human urge. But they offered two essential additions to Berlyne's conception. First, their definitions stipulate that the internal urge is hitched to the outer world by way of thoughts concerning whatever event, information, or object an individual doesn't expect or understand. And second, both Kagan and Piaget viewed this powerful urge as the engine of early development. As the following pages will show, this second point is key.

WHEN FEELING BECOMES ACTION

So far I have pointed out that curiosity begins as a feeling of surprise, in response to something unexpected. That first feeling can be intense or mild, brief or sustained. Either way, it is, at first, a deeply internal experience. But that is only the starting point. To have any real psychological consequences, that first spark of curiosity must lead to something. When our curiosity is aroused (whether by an unexpected creature, a novel piece of information, or an ambiguous object), we lean in to carefully observe whatever has sparked the need to know. We touch, smell, or listen. As we get older that moment of cognitive arousal may lead to a search through our thoughts or even through books for buried information. The initial feeling of curiosity is pleasurable, but only for a short period of time and only to the extent it can eventually be re-solved (just as hunger pangs feel good when a meal is likely, and sexual arousal feels good when you're about to get in bed with someone). Like other forms of arousal, it is a catalyst for action of some kind or an-other. That action not only is what leads to knowledge—it is the reason we are willing to undergo the cycle again and again. Exploration and inquiry, the behaviors triggered by that first moment, are what interest those who want to study the role of curiosity in the educational process.

When my son Sam was a little boy, he found it hard to wash his hands quickly. He'd turn on the faucet and thrust his hands under the stream. Then, if you were sitting nearby, you'd see him hesitate, study the water as it hit the barricade his hand created, shift directions, and fall from the edge of his palm. That was never enough for him. He'd try tilting his hand at another angle. He'd separate his fingers and then shut them together. He'd lower the water pressure to see if that changed anything. And then he'd begin hitting the water sideways, as if to see just how far he could reroute the stream. Sometimes these small ex-periments lasted only one or two minutes. Other times, he'd be held there, delayed for fifteen minutes, as he tried to understand why the water fell the way it did. The event that led to Sam's actions probably took only a second—the water did something surprising. But what he did in response to that surprise took some time, and was visible for anyone to see. Sam's forays at the sink are just one example of how our urge to know more is expressed with words and gestures. Those actions unfold in real time and space. They provide us with a window on the internal qualities of curiosity, but they also play an essential role in the fate of any given moment of curiosity. Because the minute a person explores, that person's actions are subject to outside influences.

This was illustrated by a spate of studies conducted in the late 1970s and early 1980s, when several developmental psychologists became in-terested in the impact of situation on children's curiosity. They wanted to know whether the look on an adult's face, or the things an adult said, might inhibit (or enhance) a child's exploration. To examine the role of input, these researchers defined curiosity in purely behavioral terms—they were interested not so much in the internal feeling of un-certainty or interest as they were in the act of exploration. For example, they presented children with an unfamiliar object, and measured how quickly the children approached the object, and how thoroughly they explored the object. In one of the more charming and useful examples of this kind of research, Bruce Henderson and his colleagues built what they called a curiosity box. The box had several drawers on each of its four sides, and each drawer contained unfamiliar toys and objects that children could examine, if they discovered them. The basic idea was that the time it took for a child to approach the box, the number of drawers the child opened, and the time the child spent examining the objects within the drawers offered an objective measure of individual curiosity. However, this method (and its implied definition) presents its own limitations. A box of drawers may present more mystery, or greater interest, to one child than to another. Imagine a child who has little interest in inanimate objects but is very curious about living things. The curiosity that child will show in the presence of the curiosity box does not tell you what you would find out if you offered that same child a chance to look at a terrarium. An experiment in which all children are offered the same stimulus overlooks differences in what individual children might want to know about. Children's curiosity is not content-free. Children are most curious when they can inquire about the specific things that mystify or attract them. In everyday life, children choose which aspects of the environment to explore further. A box in a room doesn't allow us to identify the particular topics or materials that a given child actually wants to know about.

However, another line of research offers clues about how curiosity unfolds in children's everyday lives. In the 1920s William and Clara Stern kept a diary of everything their three young children said. A look at the diary shows how frequently their children tried to resolve uncertainty by asking questions (Stern 1924). More recently, researchers like Michelle Chouinard (2007) and Barbara Tizard and Martin Hughes (1984) have documented the endless flood of questions children ask. Questions represent a unique type of search behavior, in that they offer us a window onto the mental experience of curiosity. When children ask questions, we find out something about what interests them, what particular information they are seeking, and what it is that sates their appetite. Yet not all children are garrulous, not all families encourage conversation, and not all settings are amenable to question asking. Language provides a rich window onto a child's need to know, but it cannot tell us everything. We have had a hard time finding out how children search for information when they are not constrained or guided by adults. Luckily, there is a new source of data to help us find out what people do when they are free to search on their own.

Google and its cousins have pushed us once again to realize that curiosity has many faces. Web researchers claim that people engage in two kinds of searches when they use the Internet to find things out: exploratory search, and information seeking (White and Roth 2009). Tracking how people use the web to gain information, it becomes clear that the way we explore hinges on why we explore. To illustrate this important idea, Ryen White and Resa Roth describe George:

> Meet George, a U.S. citizen planning a vacation to the south of France. He has never been to Europe and wishes to experience French culture as an important aspect of his journey. To this end, he wants to rent a villa in a remote village. First George uses a Web search engine to find out whether this is possible. He encounters a website that offers villa rentals in Provence. After investigation Provence and deciding that he likes the region, he looks up villa rental prices and decides that he needs to adjust his goals. The only available villa rentals during his desired travel window are prohibitively expensive, so George decides to book a hotel in Marseille instead. He searches for accommodation with a minimum rating of three stars, studies the websites of a few hotels, decides on a hotel that meets his needs, and proceeds to make a reservation. Following the booking, he needs to investigate transportation options, learn more about French customs and cuisine, and identify sightseeing destinations. He has much to learn and investigate before his trip even begins. (9)

They are making the point that such a goal-oriented, utilitarian search is quite different from the kind in which a person surfs the web with less intention, though perhaps more openness to following unexpected leads. For instance, imagine having a conversation in which you and a friend cannot recall Henry VIII's six wives. You Google "Henry VIII," and while learning about Anne Boleyn, you become interested in the Reformation. Before you know it you've happened upon Mary Queen of Scots, and from there are learning about beheadings. According to web designers, people behave quite differently under these circumstances. They spend less time on each "page" in the more exploratory, less goal-oriented search, but they also cover wider terrain. This mirrors an old distinction between what psychologists have called specific and diversive curiosity. The person who is mildly curious about many things and likely to ask a question in every conversation embodies diversive curiosity. Yet he or she may not push very hard to go deeply into a topic, quickly wanting to move on to the next topic. For that person curiosity is frequent, but short-lived. On the other hand, there are people who feel powerful, sustained interest in a particular topic—furniture making, the galaxy, the Russian Revolution, the physiology of running, or the origins of tea. Such people may find that the more they know about the topic, the more they want to know. At the same time, a person with such specific curiosity may seem completely incurious about many other topics.

WHY WE SEARCH

Any college professor can tell you about the subtle and important differences motivation makes in a student's search for information. This is true of the toddler, the preschooler, and even the twenty-one-year-old. Imagine three students in a college biology course, all reading E. O. Wilson's book on ants, all reading carefully and with concentration. Yet watching them read, or even using a test to assess how much they got out of it, cannot tell the whole story. One student reads the book to get an A on the exam. She has no interest whatsoever in ants, but a great interest in getting a good grade. The second student reads it because she has been fascinated by bugs her whole life and is dying to know more about how they behave and what they are like. She has come to realize that what she can see with her own two eyes is not enough. The third student had no prior interest in bugs, and began reading because she had to for class. But having begun, she is taken aback by the opening paragraph. She had no idea that ants created such complicated social systems. She now feels a great need to know more. The first searches but feels little curiosity. The second is curious because of what she already knows—she has become aware of gaps in that knowledge, gaps she feels could be filled by Wilson's book. The third is curious because her existing schema for ants (simple asocial creatures) is violated when she encounters contradictory information. And that is only the context surrounding their initial surprise.

The studies of people's habits online have allowed us to track certain kinds of exploration in a whole new way. And yet, here we must return to the youngest explorer. Because neither searching for information in order to take a trip, or to simply learn more about an intriguing topic, approximates the curious behavior of the youngest explorers. Imagine a twelve-month-old sitting in the bath with some bath toys. Her rubber duck floats. Her plastic cups float. Then she grabs the plastic bottle full of shampoo off the edge and places it on the water as well. It sinks to the bottom. She pauses, startled. Not what she expected. So she reaches down to the floor of the tub, lifts up the bottle, and tries again. She watches carefully, with slightly suspended breath as it sinks once again. Enough experimentation, and she will have realized something important—not everything floats. In time, with both experience and the input of others, her adventures in the bathtub will lead to two discoveries—that not all objects behave in the same way, and that there are certain reliable facts about the natural world (for instance, that hollow or empty things usually float, and filled or solid things often sink).

Clearly all three types of exploration I have just described have a common underpinning—the urge to find out more. But the circumstances of the search, and the characteristics of the searcher, make all the difference. In the preceding pages I have offered a thumbnail encapsulation of the history of research on curiosity. In describing that history, I have tried to convey what an octopus curiosity is. The somewhat uneven and tenuous history of research has not provided us with an account of how curiosity develops. Yet. But such an account is, I believe, possible, and extremely worthwhile. Moreover, tracing its development can tell us something about its role in education.

Readers may be surprised that I have deliberately avoided providing one exact definition of curiosity in this book. Needless to say, that would be necessary in order to conduct an experiment or set of experiments to investigate a specific question about curiosity. However, such a definition would reduce the phenomenon to something too narrow and static for the richer, more broad-ranging discussion I seek here. As with many of the most interesting psychological phenomena, in everyday life curiosity is multifaceted and dynamic. At the same time, most of us know it when we feel it or see it (and sometimes, though not always, we can quickly recognize its absence). But, in the interests of using research to illuminate curiosity in all its complexity, I do offer some of the more generative (and influential) definitions researchers have used (Berlyne, Piaget, Kagan, and Klahr, to name just a few). Each emphasizes a different aspect, and each points the way to a particular set of testable predictions. Considered together, these definitions converge on a common view: that curiosity is an expression, in words or behaviors, of the urge to know more—an urge that is typically sparked when expectations are violated. That's as far as I will go, for now.

THE DEVELOPMENT OF CURIOSITY

Beginning with the simple idea, common to all the researchers I've described, that curiosity represents an urge to explain the unexpected, which leads to exploration and the acquisition of information, it's easy to see that whatever the internal feeling of curiosity is, it makes us act in certain ways. We pick up objects to look at them more closely, peel things open and take them apart, ask other people questions, read books, do experiments, and wander into unfamiliar situations. In trying to scratch the itch we act in specific ways that lead to discovery, accomplishment, self-expansion, and sometimes trouble. Curiosity leads to all kinds of behaviors, some valuable, some treacherous. In one interview, a mother told me about coming home at the end of the day to learn that her nine-year-old had been setting cotton balls on fire. Was he angry and trying to burn down the house? Was he mischievous and trying to alarm his baby brother? Was he responding to a dare? No. He had read online that water keeps things from burning. So he soaked the cotton balls in water, and then lit a match to find out if what he had read was true.

The risk inherent in exploration may explain why cultures (as well as researchers) have been so ambivalent toward curiosity. It has been seen alternately as the source of all evil (think of Pandora and Eve) and the source of all progress and knowledge (again, think of Pandora, who let hope loose into the world, and Eve, whose transgressions led to the world as we know it). Aristotle characterized it as that which "first led men to philosophize"; Cicero focused on its perils, calling it the "passion for learning" that impelled men who heard the Sirens' song to listen until their death (Loewenstein 1994). In classical China, the intellectual classes discouraged curiosity. Confucius is claimed to have said, "There are three methods to gaining wisdom. The first is reflection, which is the highest. The second is imitation, which is the easiest. The third is experience, which is the bitterest." Much later, William James captured this ambivalence when he identified its dual nature—the "susceptibility for being excited" by "mere novelty," and the "scientific curiosity" that drives people to seek out new information.

And here we come to a paradox. For all the ambivalence societies feel toward curiosity, almost all psychologists and educational researchers view it as a great strength during childhood. Beginning with work done by Berlyne himself, studies have shown again and again that when people want to know, they learn. Inciting children's curiosity is the best way to ensure that they will absorb and retain information. That sounds incredibly obvious. Perhaps its seeming obviousness explains why so little research has been done on children's curiosity at school. We know very little about what makes children more curious or less curious, under what circumstances curiosity can be encouraged, and how to build upon children's curiosity so that they learn well. In other words, how does curiosity develop?

Because whatever its possible hazards, by and large, when curiosity withers and dies, there are serious ramifications. Nowhere is this clearer or more interesting than in the study of children's intellectual growth. Researchers agree that the urge to know fuels mental development. They also know that the curious child learns more than the incurious one, and that when curiosity is aroused, learning is optimized. So, what do we know of the fate of curiosity during childhood?

Studies show that as children get older they ask fewer questions, and explore the physical environment less avidly. Does this mean we all get less curious with age? Some diminishment of curiosity reflects normal development—as babies learn more about the everyday world around them, fewer ordinary events surprise or intrigue. By the time babies become toddlers, they know that a knock at the door means a stranger is likely to come in. When dinner is served, the steam rising off a plate of food no longer fascinates them, and paperclips seem ordinary—most children have given up wondering how one of them would feel inside their mouth. They have become familiar with the routines and objects of everyday life and know, generally speaking, what to expect.

However, once everyday experiences become familiar, some children will begin paying attention to subtler surprises and unexpected details. Other children do not. By the time children are three of four, some will zero in on aspects of life that invite further investigation—why some foods steam and others don't, what the greeting rituals are of the different people who walk through the door, and how many ways you can bend a paperclip without breaking it. It is at this point that the story of curiosity gets complicated and interesting. Because it is between the ages of three and eleven that children seem to either develop an appetite for knowledge and the habit of inquiry, or they don't. It is also during these years that people acquire particular kinds of curiosity—some want to know everything they can about human interactions, others about the natural world. Some tinker, some collect, and some ask questions.

INDIVIDUAL DIFFERENCES

The world offers countless triggers for curiosity, though each of us reacts differently to those triggers. Once when my sons were young I took them to the zoo in New York City's Central Park. We lived in a rural area, surrounded by farm animals, as well as wild animals. The boys were cared for by someone who knew a great deal about wildlife and who talked about everything—a running commentary of observations and questions rippled through their days together, which meant the boys not only interacted with a lot of animals and saw a great deal of animal activity, but had also talked about everything they saw. At the zoo, after seeing the birds and the lizards, we came upon an ancient moss-covered tortoise climbing on top of another tortoise and emitting loud strange moans. The other children's eyes swept across the two lumbering creatures with about the same level of attention they gave all the other fascinating goings on (the brightly colored birds swooping and lighting on the branches of the tropical forest area and the lizards trudging along the ground with their weary pomposity, making their way from one side of the habitat to the other). But my four-year-old son brought a somewhat different perspective with him. He peered in toward the tortoises with laser-like interest, and after a few moments of careful scrutiny said in a loud, intrigued voice, "I know what they're doing, Mom. They're fucking, right? Is that how tortoises fuck?"

His basic knowledge of animals, and his familiarity with zoos freed him to become curious about specific aspects of what he saw. He had seen turtles and tortoises, in the wild and in the zoo. He wasn't so amazed by their mossy backs and slow deliberate crawl. He was a bit mystified, however, to see one crawl on top of the other and moan. He had a script for zoo, and a script for tortoise. That background knowledge is what allowed him to be surprised about what he saw, and want to know more. His experiences led him to a particular kind of curiosity. All the time he had spent with his babysitter, asking questions and hearing answers, led him to ask about the tortoises.

But what beckons one person differs from what beckons another. My friend Scottie Mills cannot pass a patch of grass without wanting to lean down and see what lives among the blades. I cannot sit in a restaurant without swiveling my head around to study, slack-jawed with absorption, the family at the next table. I want to know what they say to one another, I want to know who is married to whom, and I want to see what they order. The author Simon Winchester, on the other hand, has an insatiable need to know about people who write dictionaries and encyclopedias, bone collectors, and those who study other countries—he is curious about those who collect knowledge.

There is also great variety in the frequency and intensity of people's curiosity. Some want to know more about almost everything they encounter, while for others the urge to find out is focused on a few topics about which they have unwavering and infinite interest. For some, inquiry is almost a reflex. Not long ago I returned from a visit to my youngest son's college, where he had just begun his first year. I sat down for coffee with two close friends. I said, "He just loves it there. The tutorial system is so perfect for him." One friend said, with a warm smile on her face, "That's so great." The other said, "How does the tutorial system work?" What seems like an irresistible invitation to find out more to one person may be completely invisible to another.

Finally, not everyone responds to urges in similar ways. I once read that Dolly Parton said, "Whenever I get an urge to exercise, I lie down and wait for it to pass." We don't all sate our appetite for knowledge in the same ways. Watch what happens at the dinner table when a group of friends encounters a word they do not know. All may be interested at first. But only one or two will put down their fork, leave the table, go find the book that might contain the information, and look it up. And now, with smart phones and Google, it is dizzyingly easy to look up almost anything at almost any time. For some people, access to such vast stores of information is addictive and threatens to interfere with life in the here and now. At the dinner table, in the bathroom, at a meeting, or on the bus, each conversation is punctuated by seven pauses for information seeking. But for other people, having all that data at their fingertips has changed little. Their need to know is just not that strong.

Finally, some people have great perseverance for seeking the answer to their question. Working in a family health clinic in the Bay area in California, physician Nadine Burke began to notice how many of her patients, when probed, said that they had suffered extreme stress during their childhoods. She began to think that the conditions of their childhood were causing their adult illnesses. Her need to test her hunch, and get to the bottom of things, led to years and years of investigation, a life's work (Tough 2011). Other people are consumed by a curiosity that seems less urgent, from a practical point of view, but nonetheless leads them to decades of dogged pursuit. The anthropologist Daniel Everett spent nearly thirty years trying to understand the language of the Piraha, in the Amazon jungle (Everett 2009). Some devote their lives to getting an answer to a particular question. For others, a little information easily attained seems to do the trick. Curiosity paired with industry is a whole different phenomenon from curiosity that passes quickly.

We have overwhelming evidence that all babies are born with a great deal of this urge to understand. They carefully watch people and things to detect patterns, they probe anything that surprises them, and they test their budding theories against experience. They are intrepid in their efforts to delve into any mystery that presents itself. And almost everything is, at first, a mystery. Babies put objects in their mouths, try to make things float or bounce, and take objects apart in order to see what's inside, watching carefully when something violates their expectations. These investigations are not merely charming. I will argue that they are the seeds of later learning and many of societies' most important inventions. But I will also argue that curiosity is a fragile seed—for some the seed bears fruit, and for others, it shrivels and dies all too soon. By the time a child is five years old, his curiosity has been carved to reflect his personality, family life, daily encounters, and school experience. By the time that five-year-old is twenty-two, the intensity and object of his curiosity has become a defining, though often invisible part of who he is—something that will shape much of his future life.

But the journey curiosity takes, from a universal and ubiquitous characteristic, one that accompanies much of the infant's daily experience, to a quality that defines certain adults and barely exists in others, is subtle. In the chapters that follow, I'll try to show that there are several sources of individual variation, and each has its developmental moment. Attachment in toddlerhood, language in the three-year-old, and a succession of environmental limitations and open doors all contribute to a person's particular kind and intensity of curiosity. The twenty-two-year-old bears the imprint of all these experiences, which act as a series of layers on which each exploration or question in adulthood rests.

This book is about why some children remain curious and others do not, and how we can encourage more curiosity in everyone.

2

Safe Havens and Expeditions

WHEN I WAS a little girl, our family living room contained two items that called out to me again and again. One was a modern glass coffee table, low to the ground and unusual in shape. I loved looking down and seeing the floor through it. Sometimes all I saw were the wood floor planks with their wide grooves. But other times I would spot a small object under there—a paper clip, a dust ball, a shoe, slightly distorted by the thick glass, and therefore particularly interesting. Almost as intriguing to me was the way the glass top, shaped something like a lima bean, was set on its glass pedestal, which was also curved (this was the early 1960s, and my mother was a fan of modern design). I liked gazing through the top, looking at the way its underside met the edges of the stand. The other alluring item in the living room was a very modern chair, like something out of the Jetsons cartoon. It was shaped like a big cup, with no edges and no seams. Instead of conventional chair legs, the shell-like seat sat on a thick curved wire base. It just begged to be played with. One day, having exhausted my usual explorations, I thought of a new possibility. What if I turned the chair upside down, making the top the bottom, and stood on what would now be the top—the wire frame? I wanted to see what the funny edges that were the armrests would do when set on the ground. I wanted to know what it would be like to try and stand on the wire base. Just as enticing, I wanted to know what the floor would look like when I peered at it through the glass, from such a height. I flipped the chair over and dragged it closer to the wavy edge of the coffee table. I clambered up to the top of the upside-down chair, balancing my feet on the wire base. I was just over two years old, so all of this was accomplished on short legs. Someone called out to me from the nearby kitchen, "Susie, you're gonna fall. Get down from there." But I hadn't yet stood up straight, and I hadn't yet looked through the glass. My investigation was not complete. I heard that voice. But I ignored it. The call of the chair was much louder. I stood up, teetering a little, and stretched my short torso toward the table, intent upon my quest. Then I fell. I don't remember much about the ensuing few hours, except for the moment when my mother was told she couldn't stay in the room at the hospital where I was strapped down, screaming and thrashing, while they removed the glass shards from next to my eye, and stitched me up. The scar is still there, more than fifty years later.

You have to work to keep a toddler from exploring the world around her. Set a typical eighteen-month-old child down on the floor of a room (whether familiar or unfamiliar) and she will energetically make her way from one side of the room to the other, finding things to examine, touch, manipulate, and watch. Jerome Kagan has said that 90 percent of toddlers, brought into a new room, will spend about twenty seconds scanning the environment, and then begin exploring it (Kagan 2002). The curiosity of a toddler is ubiquitous. And it stems from an essential human cognitive mechanism—the tendency to detect novelty.

WHY BABIES ARE SO CURIOUS

A baby's ability to notice change depends on her ability to notice sameness, and that ability kicks in as soon as a baby is born. While behaviorists were once convinced that babies had to devote considerable energy to painstakingly accruing information about the world, bit by bit, the past sixty years have shown that babies come equipped with the cognitive the tools for efficiently and fairly easily creating some order out of their daily experiences. They are quick to detect patterns and make useful groupings of their experiences.

Within days of birth, babies distinguish human faces from non-human faces, the sound of their mother's voice from the sound of other

voices, and men from women (Newman 2005; Easterbrook et al. 1999).
They quickly organize their world into categories. For instance, when
three-day-old infants listened to a recording either of their own cry, or
the cry of another infant, their faces showed greater distress for a longer
period of time when they heard a new unfamiliar cry (Dondi, Simion,
and Caltran 1999). In another study, babies regularly changed their
sucking in a way that produced the sound of their mothers' voice rather
than the voice of a stranger (DeCasper and Fifer 1980). In other words,
right from the start, babies respond differently to things with which
they are familiar than they do to things that are unfamiliar. In the very
beginning, familiarity is compelling. Before they are two months old,
babies put a fair amount of cognitive energy into getting to know certain sights and sounds, often spending more time looking at or listening
to familiar stimuli than novel images or sounds (Hunter, Ross, and
Ames 1982; Rose et al. 1982). This suggests that their first tasks, cognitively speaking, are to make some basic distinctions, and develop
some acquaintance with important sights and sounds (most notably,
their mothers) (Hunter, Ames, and Koopman 1983; Rose et al. 1982;
Nachman, Stern, and Best 1986). But, with the exception of their
mothers, any preference for familiarity is short-lived. By the time babies are nine weeks old they will look only briefly at an image they
have been shown before, and then turn to look at something new
(Hunter, Ross, and Ames 1982). For instance, two-month-old babies look
longer at a mobile with a familiar pattern than they do at one with an
unfamiliar pattern. While some have argued that the early preference
for familiarity reflects the slower processing time of the newborn, it is
equally plausible that it takes babies about two months to have enough
expectations about the world to be surprised by anything. In other
words, babies work to become familiar with things, so that they can
begin to notice novelty. Once this happens, novelty quickly becomes
more compelling than familiarity. Within a few weeks of exposure to
the familiar pattern, Fagan has shown, babies will look more often and
spend longer looking at a mobile with an unfamiliar pattern than one
with a familiar pattern (Fagan 1974; Fagan and McGrath 1981).

By the time babies are six months old, their ability to recognize familiar experiences extends beyond a picture or sound they've seen or
heard before—they begin to look for consistencies in sequences and

more complicated constellations of experience. For instance, when babies are shown two images, one of a smiling face and one of an angry face, and hear the sound of a voice, they look longer (and in most cases with some apprehension) when an angry voice is played while they are looking at a smiling face, or a pleasant voice when they are looking at an angry face (Uzgiris and Hunt 1975; Walker-Andrews and Lennon 1991; Hepach and Westermann 2013).

Voices that do not match facial expressions are not the only events that cause babies to pause, change their breathing, and examine closely. They have similar reactions to a wide variety of phenomena that surprise them in some way. During the first year of life, babies' surprise reflects very complex expectations about the world. Take Karen Wynn's research as an elegant example of this. Babies watch a screen on which a toy duck is projected. Then a second duck is added to the scene. Next, a screen is briefly dropped in front of the two ducks. When it is raised again, within moments, babies see either two ducks, as you might expect, or they may see only one duck, or in some instances three ducks. Wynn has found, again and again, that when babies witness bad math they gaze longer, and their breathing and heart rates change. Their reactions suggest that they expected one and one to equal two, and are surprised when it does not (Wynn 1998). Wynn has used this research to show that babies have some inherent sense of number. However, what it also shows is that babies are interested in the unexpected. Moreover, their sensitivity to the unexpected reaches beyond carefully contained laboratory settings. When a stranger, or someone they don't ordinarily see first thing in the morning, walks into the bedroom, or they hear a novel sound through the kitchen window while eating breakfast, they take note.

Nor is this sense of expectation merely a matter of habit. If it were, you could condition a baby to expect any two things to occur together, and they would be surprised when those things then did not occur together. But actually, there is little evidence that babies show anything more than momentary surprise when two things that have habitually occurred together no longer occur together (Alessandri, Sullivan, and Lewis 1990). In other words, when two events or items are arbitrarily connected through conditioning, children quickly forget the connection. Equally important, babies are surprised by incongruities regarding

events they do not have very much experience with—for instance, surprised when one and one do not lead to two, or when a ball goes behind a screen and doesn't come out the other side (Bower 1974; Wynn
1998, 2000). In short, this early set of expectations is clearly not attained
simply through any kind of habit or conditioning. Rather, babies seem
predisposed, at least for some phenomena, to zero in on the truly important, or essential, aspects of objects and events. In certain cases, they
appear to form "natural" concepts—a sense of what objects belong together, and why they are able to distinguish between criterial and superficial characteristics of an object. So, for instance, babies recognize
many different flying objects as birds—big ones, little ones, bright ones,
and dull ones. That is not to say that young children don't sometimes
mislabel objects (calling a kite a bird, or a cow a dog). We've known for
a long that it is common for toddlers just learning language to over-
and under-extend categorical terms and the concepts those terms represent (Rosch 1978; Anglin 1977). But their mistakes are not random.
Children's under- and overextensions follow a coherent pattern and are
typically based on certain core features (calling a cow a dog because
both are living creatures with four legs). Meanwhile, more recent studies
by Karen Wynn (1998), Susan Carey (2009), and Elizabeth Spelke (1999)
suggest that babies are biologically equipped with certain key concepts,
or at least the means to acquire those concepts at a very young age and
with very little experience. For instance, babies quickly distinguish
between animate and inanimate objects, and would show surprise if
an inanimate object (or a dead animal, for that matter) were to begin
moving around, make living sounds, or breathe. They have an early
grasp of other core qualities too—the difference between animals and
people, between objects and people, and even between broad categories
of objects—for instance, big versus small (Rochat 2001; Muentener,
Friel, and Schulz 2012). All of this is to say that a wide array of research
shows that babies and toddlers are alert to meaningful novelty, novelty that guides them to understand the world around them in ever more
powerful ways.

So far, I have talked only about the baby's ability to grasp the physical world around her—to predict what an object or group of objects
should look like, or what an animal might do (bark, moo, etc.). But babies do not live only in a world of objects. They live in a world of com-

plex social processes, surrounded by people who don't simply follow the rules of the natural world. What about this layer of reality? How much surprises the toddler about her social world?

Here again, the past thirty years have provided us with ample evidence that children quickly and easily detect patterns in the social hubbub that surrounds them. The work of Miller, Galanter, and Pribram (1960), Schank and Abelson (1977), and Katherine Nelson (Nelson and Gruendel 1986) shows that, as with physical reality, children seem to detect and absorb underlying patterns about who does what, and where and when, with the same alacrity they have for learning about contrasts such as few versus many, balls versus trucks, and dead versus living. The speed with which they do this, and the similarity between children in their mastery of such contrasts, suggest that some fundamental rules guide the process by which they construct schemas about everyday events.

Most toddlers, provided even a semblance of coherence and continuity in their everyday lives, quickly seem to use mental scripts to guide their interactions and expectations. For instance, if a baby begins his day by sitting in a high chair, and getting a sippy cup of orange juice, he is likely to show surprise if, instead, he tastes chocolate milk. He'll be even more surprised if one morning a total stranger comes and sits down in the seat that his older brother usually occupies.

However, even at eighteen months, when it comes to knowing what to expect about everyday life, children are still novices. Though most eighteen-month-olds quickly form a breakfast script, a bath-time script, a walk-to-day-care script (or whatever scripts reflect their particular culture and customs), those scripts are fairly spare. It takes time and attention for each child to absorb all the variations that might occur within a script (who gives me my bath, what toys go in the bath, which route we take to day care, whether I ride in a stroller or on my father's shoulder, and so on). Nelson and her followers showed how children learn quickly the difference between the necessary parts of each script (the actors, the goal, the basic sequence of action) and the slot fillers (the objects and actions that can vary from one instance to another). Children are not heedless or casual about these slot fillers. Quite to the contrary, they attend to a lot of the information available. A waffle instead of toast, a grandmother instead of a mother pouring the juice, a large crane on the street when you step outside on your way to school—all these unexpected variables demand attention. They are surprised by important violations of the basic scripts with which they are familiar, and they are often deeply interested in the smaller as well as the larger variations that pop up. By organizing daily experiences into scripts, children also internalize the rituals and values of their specific community and culture. But such scripts are only one layer of the social world.

The baby and toddler must also learn a lot about people—their voices, their tones, their actions, and the subtle dynamics that suffuse most of their human interactions—a cry brings a hug from one old lady, but is ignored by another. Reaching out with your hand toward a desired object (for instance, a cookie or a bottle) and saying a word (*coo-coo* or *baba* perhaps) is likely to get attention, but not from your brother, who seems lost in a world of his own. Toddlers watch for the reactions of those around them, using that information to explain not only why a ball rises or sinks, but also why a certain behavior elicits laughter, and another an angry frown. Here, too, early on children seem to quickly detect and make use of basic patterns, and at the same time be interested in small variations in those patterns.

All of this is to say that during the first three years, children are gathering the material they need to establish, and then enrich, the schemas that help them navigate the physical, psychological, and social worlds. Key to this mastery of pattern and order is their alertness to novelty. This fundamental characteristic of early development explains why toddlers seem practically voracious in their appetite for new information.

FROM WHAT TO HOW AND WHY

But for human babies, as opposed to other species, navigation is just the beginning. At a surprisingly early age human babies show how different they are from the young of other species by attending to differences beyond the bare necessities—novelty that helps them simply survive. They have what is called epistemic curiosity—an interest not only in what, who, when, and where, but why and how. Not only are children between the ages of nine months and thirty-six months eagerly absorbing information about what objects look like, taste like, sound like, can do, and can be done to, they are beginning to try to figure out why things happen the way that they do. They don't always know that they are looking for reasons and explanations, but their behaviors tell us they are.

When babies gaze at an object, or bang it against a hard surface, as they so often do, it is apparent they are trying to take in information about what the object looks like (its shape, its surface, its details, etc.) or what it can do (make noise, knock things over, etc.). But by the time they are twenty-four months, they are just as likely to try to figure out the link between two different actions (for instance, the link between piling the blocks up high and seeing the blocks tumble over, or pulling a lever and hearing a sound).

In Piaget's now famous descriptions of toddlers, he identified the ways in which children act on the objects around them in order to test the causes and effects of various actions. More recently, many researchers have explored this process in experiments—showing that children as young as a year are actively trying to figure out how things work, or, in other words, why things happen the way that they do. For instance, among toddlers playing outside in a children's center, one two-year-old boy rode his scooter toward a hill. Using his feet, he pushed the scooter partway up. But when he lifted his feet, the scooter began to roll backward. He called out to no one in particular, "Why is my scooter going back? Why back?" Having slid down a little, he instantly pushed his way back up, and then, watching his own feet carefully, slid back down. He repeated this about three times, each time lifting his feet in a slightly different way, and then at a slightly different height. He then rode the scooter to a flat part of the terrain and tried lifting his feet, determined to figure out under exactly what conditions the scooter would slide backward. Studies suggest such interest in finding out how things work is common in toddlers. Alison Gopnik and her colleagues gave toddlers an opportunity to get a toy that was set on the other side of a table, by dragging it toward them with a rake. In one or two trials, almost all the babies succeeded, and quickly lost their interest in the toy itself. But they did not tire of using the rake to draw the toy closer, frequently putting the toy back at a distance, just so they could try again. Though the toy became routine to them, they were eager to explore the fact that pulling the rake caused the toy to move. In other words, they wanted to discover the explanation for their success, and those explanations were more compelling to them than simply gaining time with a toy (Gopnik, Meltzoff, and Kuhl 2000).

In one particularly ingenious demonstration that young children actively seek explanations in the phenomena around them, Laura Schulz and her colleagues invited preschoolers to play with a toy machine that lit up and made sounds when activated by beads. When an adult gave the children ambiguous information about which bead would activate the machine and then gave them some time to play with the machines and the beads, their play was clearly aimed at discovering which particular bead (or combination of beads) would make the machine work (Cook, Goodman, and Schulz 2011).

Children not only act on the world in order to understand how it works, but also ask questions that specifically seek explanation (rather than, say, names of things, descriptions, or other straightforward information). Anne Hickling and Henry Wellman, using the CHILDES database, examined everyday explanations provided by four children from the time they were two and a half until they were five years old. During this time the children produced a whopping five thousand explanations (Wellman, Hickling, and Schult 1997). That means that each child was producing causal explanations of everyday events nearly once in every twenty-five utterances. Many of these explanations were biological or physical (as opposed to psychosocial). Wellman has argued that children have three core categories of explanations—one for people (intentions and mental states), one for material and mechanic phenomena (objects falling or colliding), and one for biological events (illness, growth, death). It seems that children not only try to find out how things work, and why things happen the way that they do, but they often are quite explicit in their efforts to construct explanations.

To sum up so far: mothers, fathers, grandparents, babysitters, and day care providers all know that it's hard to keep a child from investigating the world around him. Scientists have shown us that these endless investigations have a purpose—to gather information as a way of understanding everyday life. A close examination of children's encounters with the physical and social world around them shows us that they are not only trying to figure out what is in the environment and what will happen, but also want to know why things happen the way that they do, and how things work. But these investigations aren't triggered simply from within. Opening lids, trying different ways to get the same result with a lever, or a door, finding out how many things you can use a wooden spoon for—these particular behaviors are not preprogrammed to unfurl at every opportunity. They need the right opportunity—a moment of surprise. Once that moment occurs, however small and invisible to the adult eye, investigation is likely to begin. By one year of age, babies have a cognitive repertoire that allows them to actively compare what they expect to what they encounter. For a period of time, most babies behave as if all unexpected events (new objects, new people, new scenarios) require further investigation. There should be nothing surprising about this, nor does it require lots of scientific knowledge to understand: if curiosity comes from wanting to explain what is unexpected, or resolve a moment of uncertainty, then of course babies must encounter hundreds of moments in a day when something they see, hear, feel, taste, or smell is new to them. And in fact, even the most casual observations of babies suggest that babies are curious about many things, much of the time. They regularly encounter disparity between what they already know, based on earlier experiences, and what they don't expect. These unexpected moments can contain the completely new: first time they see a train, watch a balloon pop, encounter a worm, see someone blow out candles, or meet a dog. But just as important are the unexpected sights, sounds, and smells that only deviate from earlier experiences in a slight way (a doughnut rather than toast, grandmother with a new hat on, a bathtub with bubble bath, a toy that makes a loud sound, a different dog from the one they've seen before. The ubiquity of novelty from a toddler's point of view explains why curiosity seems like a universal trait, which functions nearly constantly, in babies between the ages of about six and fourteen months. However, by the time they are toddlers, they are not all equally curious—some continue to detect novelty with enthusiasm, following up with any investigation possible. Some seem startled and fearful when encountering new experiences, and still others seem slightly dulled—as if the discrepancy between what they know and what they encounter doesn't tug at them the way it does other children.

WHAT QUELLS CURIOSITY IN TODDLERS

A toddler who encounters a room that has changed dramatically from its familiar state (new wall colors, a large new piece of furniture) might hesitate at the door, and might take awhile to venture in. However, once comfortable, most babies will eventually want to look around and see what's what. They might even be motivated to explore the particular feature that has changed. However, not all children respond to a big change with eager interest.

What might make a baby incurious? One clue comes from the study of rats. Like humans and other animals, when offered an unfamiliar environment, rats will explore it. Put a rat on a table with various spaces, and he'll sniff, look, scratch, and in other ways actively attend to what he sees. But even to a rat, not all novelty is the same. When Pellow and his colleagues placed rats on a four-arm raised platform where one arm (or path) had no sides, and the other did, the rats preferred the path that was enclosed. Confining them to one of the open arms made them anxious. However, when injected with drugs that reduce anxiety, the rats were more likely to explore the open arms (Pellow et al. 1985). There are two lessons, at least, in this study, for those of us interested in children's curiosity. The first lesson is that even though we may be drawn to novelty (just as the rats are), our appetite for novelty is balanced by our fear of the unknown (just like the rats). The second lesson is connected to the first lesson—anxiety plays a subtle but powerful role in curiosity. When the rats' anxiety was lowered, they were much more "curious" about the open arms. Perhaps they were just more reckless about venturing out onto a surface that had no barriers to prevent them from falling. But the lesson for the study of human curiosity is that our interest in finding out about new or unknown things is tempered by our fear of danger. This has particular significance for understanding how curiosity unfolds in the early years.

Children vary in how timid they are, how attuned to possible threats, and how easily they manage that sense of anxiety in the interests of exploration. Here, Jerome Kagan has been the groundbreaker, showing that a baby's temperament has long-term implications for all aspects of her behavior, including her willingness to venture into the unknown (Kagan et al. 1994). By two months of age, babies take note when an unfamiliar toy is brought into their line of vision. Though they may have been kicking and gurgling happily in their little chair, when a mobile is lowered into their view, they stop everything for a moment—no more babbling, no more kicking. Their breathing and heartbeat change rates. They produce moisture on their palms. Most importantly, they look at the new toy with heightened awareness.

However, within moments, the majority of babies begin babbling and kicking again, though typically they continue to look at the mobile with interest. However, some babies have a very different reaction. Their initial reaction to the new toy doesn't dissipate—what began as a kind of "taking note" response quickly becomes a distress response. Their faces squinch up, they cry in agitation, and then their cries become more intense. Typically they stop looking at the mobile, too upset to focus or be interested in something other than their own internal state. It is not always easy to tell whether they continue to feel distress at the new mobile, or whether they begin to feel simply distressed by their own distress—a kind of cascade of tension. Either way, the temporary pause is no longer temporary—it leads them away from exploring the new toy.

As Jerome Kagan, Nathan Fox, and others have demonstrated, this early predisposition to either encounter new sights and sounds with equanimity or with trepidation and alarm is an enormously stable and powerful characteristic (Kagan and Snidman 2009; Fox et al. 2008). In Kagan's terms, it casts a very long shadow. But we often think of temperament having the biggest impact on a child's emotional and social life. However, given the importance of exploration for intellectual development, it's not hard to see that temperament also casts a shadow over a child's cognitive processes. Over time, this early inhibition might have substantive consequences for a child's interest in the outside world. Given that a core feature of curiosity is not only the ability to detect novelty, but an impulse to explore novel events and objects, children who are distressed or shrink back from new experiences will have far fewer opportunities to sate their curiosity, and may in fact feel it in a more muted way, or less often, because it competes with a sense of tension or fear.

Temperament, it seems, is a powerful source of individual difference in curiosity. From birth, some children may be more likely to explore novel spaces, objects, and even people. Free from the tension that inhibited children feel in the presence of new experiences, uninhibited children have many better chances to gather new information, and to seek explanations for what they encounter. The difference is not only one of opportunity. Uninhibited children may experience more pleasure from their explorations, which in turn makes them more ready to investigate the next time a novel experience presents itself. It should be noted here that some research has focused on the risks of too much non-inhibition (what psychologists refer to as exuberance). These studies suggest that children who are regularly drawn to novelty, but possess few internal restraints, may have specific troubles when they are older (conduct disorder and substance abuse, to name two). But there is a cognitive flip side: given the development of adequate executive control, those who seek novelty are likely to be hungry for knowledge.

How readily a child steps into an unfamiliar room, or explores a new toy, rests in part on his or her temperament. Researchers have long known that one's openness to new experiences is a key indicator of one's personality. Moreover, most people don't change much on this dimension—the baby who is distressed by a new food or a new room is likely to be reluctant to go to a party where there are strangers, try a new sport, or eat an exotic cuisine. The opposite is true as well. Babies who respond with interest to a new playground, an unfamiliar child in the sandbox, or a kind of animal never before seen are likely to be adults who jump at the chance for adventure, eager to attend a new conference, and ready to try a new kind of dancing. Openness to experience is predictive, and stable. Nachman, Stern, and Best (1986) suggested another way in which a child's emotions influence her response to novelty (and hence her readiness to explore the unknown). Arguing that a three-month-old baby's preference for novelty might depend on how pleasurable the stimulus is, they familiarized babies to a toy puppet in one of two conditions. Some babies had a chance to become familiar with the puppet while hearing a friendly, singsong voice saying "peekaboo," while other babies heard the same peekaboo words, but in a flat tone. Babies who heard the singsong voice smiled and widened their eyes in response, while babies who heard the neutral voice studied the puppet and became familiar with it, but showed little sign of pleasure. Both immediately after, as well as one week later, the babies were all given a chance to look either at the familiar puppet or at a new, unfamiliar puppet. Babies who had heard the singsong voice (pleasurable condition) were much less likely to turn and study the novel puppet, while babies who had experienced little pleasure (but no displeasure) while becoming familiar with the original puppet were much more likely to turn and study the novel puppet. Nachman, Stern, and Best used these data to argue that you cannot separate children's emotions from their interest in novelty. This leaves us with an interesting possibility, and a further puzzle: If babies are less eager for novelty when they like, or are attached to, what they already know, why is it that, overall, happy outgoing babies explore more eagerly than negative or dysregulated babies? Though we don't have enough data to answer that question, the researchers' demonstration certainly supports the claim that curiosity cannot be thought of as either a purely cognitive or a purely emotional experience.

One way to explore the link between a child's emotional well-being and his or her interest in the unknown is to look closely at the exploration behavior of children who lack equanimity and social ease—children who are diagnosed with autism. The signature symptoms of autism include a lack of connection or rapport with other people, rigid adherence to ritual behaviors, and extreme distress in the face of unfamiliar experiences or changes in routine. It's not hard to imagine that a child who possessed these characteristics would react to novelty with alarm rather than interest. And yet, some children with autism seek and take in vast amounts of knowledge about particular domains, and can home in on a topic with an almost startling level of focus and avidness. Years ago, I did a case study of a school-age boy with autism who had acquired a vast amount of information about astronomy. He loved to visit the Hayden Planetarium in New York City, and in a journal he kept, he wrote many entries about the stars, the galaxies, and the origins of the universe. There are many such examples in the literature.

Simon Baron-Cohen has argued that children with autism are what he calls "extreme systematizers," interested in finding the patterns that explain how a system works (mathematics, weather, computers, business, a library, and so on). Baron-Cohen contrasts this cognitive style with "empathizers," who are more likely to zero in on the feelings and motivations of other people. He stresses a difference between the orderly, logical nature of phenomena best learned by systematizers and the somewhat less predictable or orderly nature of phenomena most accessible to empathizers (Baron-Cohen, Knickmeyer, and Belmonte 2005). But implicit in his argument is the suggestion that while children with autism are more comfortable with patterns and systems that are predictable and governed by rules, taxonomies, and stable cause-effect relationships, they do in fact seek such information—they want to find things out. This would suggest that their fundamental inhibition and somewhat constricted form of emotional attachment does not limit their curiosity. But do the data support Baron-Cohen's claim? Not fully. In one study, Elizabeth Pellicano and her colleagues (Pellicano et al. 2011) brought both typical and autistic schoolchildren into a "foraging" room—a room with sixteen green spots on the floor, one of which contained a hidden red target. Baron-Cohen has supported his argument about the superior search skills of autistic children by showing that they often conduct very thorough and detailed searches of very small arrays—more skilled than typical children. However, when Pellicano and her colleagues created a more dynamic, complicated, and large-scale setup (the foraging room), more like the real situations in which children often find themselves, the children with autism in fact conducted less thorough and organized searches than did the typical children. In other words, though children with autism may in fact collect information in a very thorough and precise way, within well-defined (and often extremely narrow) parameters, their general proclivity and ability to search more-complex environments are limited. The inhibition and social unease that defines autism may also lead to a lack of exploration, as well as the feeling of curiosity that underlies such exploration. My point here is not to focus on what autistic children may lack, but to provide an indirect form of support for the link between attachment security and curiosity.

But is a child's approach to the world all that drives her level of curiosity? If you took a group of children who had all been classified as uninhibited, or on the far end of that continuum, what is called "exuberant" (Barbaranelli et al. 2003; Schwartz et al. 2003; Fox and Henderson 1999), would they all be equally interested in exploring the world around them? No. Because there is one other stable individual difference that has some role to play in shaping a child's curiosity—namely, intelligence.

Though there is vigorous (and sometimes vituperative) argument about how to measure intelligence, no one disputes the fact that some people are more intelligent than others. Every piece of research and every piece of common sense shows this to be true. Moreover, while intelligence does not account for all variation in measures of curiosity in older children, there is some connection. And why wouldn't there be? A standard way to measure intelligence in infants is to present each baby with some visual stimuli (a photograph of a pattern of objects, for instance) and then measure how long the baby looks at it before turning to a new image. The thinking behind this is that the speed with which the baby processes information can be measured by how quickly the baby tires of something familiar and seeks something new. In other words, the assumption that underlies this well-documented procedure is that babies will want new experiences—that they naturally seek novelty. But recognizing novelty involves processing what is in front of you. The longer it takes a baby to "get familiar" with one image, the longer it will take her to turn toward a new image, or even notice that it is new. This may explain why measures of intelligence and measures of curiosity overlap in older children (a subject to which I'll return in later chapters). Speed of processing is one good stand-in for intelligence—the faster you get to know what is in front of you, the more information you can take in, the quicker you can solve problems, and so forth.

Baron-Cohen's argument is an attempt to show that autistic children are not only rigid (cognitively, socially, and emotionally) and "blind" to what they and others feel, but that they are at the same time often cognitively astute—assiduously looking everywhere for patterns and exceptions to those patterns. The data have not yet really supported this claim. But his proposition is a reminder that interest in exploration rests on two pillars of individual difference—a kind of emotional daring or openness, and the intellectual ability to compare experiences. Though the emotional quality (inhibition, openness to new experience, flexibility) tends to be treated as a categorical one in research, and intelligence as a continuous one, in reality both are somewhat fluid. When it comes to a child's level of curiosity, these two dimensions of an individual both contribute. A child could be extremely open to new experiences, and quite uninhibited, but not all that quick at processing information or comparing versions of experience. And vice versa (hence the kind of autistic child Baron-Cohen has in mind). Taken together these two dimensions help us understand why curiosity seems so ubiquitous and adaptive in infancy, but then quickly begins to take on the characteristics of an individual difference. But intelligence and temperament come from within, are fairly impervious to outside influence, and quite stable. Yet curiosity is, by definition, a dynamic bond between a person's drive to know, and the environment around her. No matter how intrepid or eager for novelty, a child can wonder only about things she encounters. The mind must have a real world to figure out and explore. And exploration is a process—not a moment in time. The act of exploration holds an important clue to the puzzle of why a universal quality seems to become more of an individual difference as children grow up a little.

BASE CAMP: THE TODDLER AS EXPLORER

Babies don't launch themselves into the world of strange people and objects from the abyss—they do what every smart explorer does—they establish a base camp. The flip side to a baby's intrepid exploration is her sense of a safe haven.

We've known for fifty years that a baby's eagerness to throw herself into the world around her hinges, paradoxically, on her sense of safety. She needs an anchor—and the anchor is, typically, her mother.

During and after World War II, John Bowlby, a physician, was overwhelmed by his visits to orphanages and hospitals in London. Though many of the babies were adequately cared for when it came to food, cleanliness, and sleep, many of them were apathetic, small, and in other ways clearly depressed. These observations led him to argue babies required the attention from, and a mutual bond with, one consistent person, an attachment figure. When such an attachment was absent, babies failed to develop properly (Bowlby 1969/99).

His student Mary Ainsworth and her colleagues (Ainsworth and Bell 1970) set out to empirically test Bowlby's insight, and ended up expanding the argument. They found that though all babies who had the chance to form an attachment with a caregiver were dramatically different from those who did not, there were subtle but important differences among even the attached babies.

In order to examine this hypothesis Ainsworth constructed the now famous "strange situation." The strange situation experiment is based on a few key assumptions—that even a brief separation from his mother will cause a baby distress, that the real sign of his attachment is not that expression of distress, but the baby's response once he's reunited with his mother. Most important, for the discussion here, is that a key measure of attachment is how easily and readily a child recovers from a brief separation—how quickly she feels better enough to explore an interesting environment.

The paradigmatic strange situation experiment goes like this: put a one-year-old in a room with his or her mother, some toys, and, in some cases, another person. At some point the mother leaves the room. The researchers note the toddler's reaction to this separation. Then the mother returns. What happens next provides the essential piece of the attachment puzzle: What will the child do when the mother comes back in? Will she break out in relieved smiles and rush into her mother's arms for reassurance and comfort? Will she seem disinterested and aloof? And, for our purposes here, the real question is, will the child then go back to exploring and playing with the toys in the room?

It's by now a well-known story among most psychologists. Many babies in this situation joyfully greet their mother, and, after a quick snuggle, crawl off her lap, happily returning to an exploration of the toys. Those babies are securely attached. But there are some babies who, though they cry when their mother leaves, have a different response when she returns. They might reach up for a hug, or smile with weak relief through their tears. But they don't seem easily or thoroughly reassured. They either stay on their mother's lap, fitfully trying to regain composure, or they wander over to the toys but are too distracted by the need to keep looking at their mother to actually delve into play. These babies were labeled by Ainsworth as insecurely or anxiously attached. They had trouble focusing on their own exploration, distracted by fear that their mother might leave again, or anger at their mother for having left them.

The implication of this work is clear: the quality of a child's attachment has a powerful influence on the vigor and depth of her exploration of the world around her. Those children worried or in some way uncertain about the bond they have with their mother are less likely to make physical and psychological expeditions to gather information.

While a lot of attention has been given to the long-term consequences of early attachment in the realm of social and emotional well-being, less attention has been paid to an equally important idea that emerges from the work: human relationships are a key ingredient in the child's ability to investigate the physical environment. Indeed, a series of experiments has shown that children with greater emotional and self-governing resources do in fact exhibit more curiosity as they get older.

In one longitudinal study, Arend, Gove, and Sroufe (1979) assessed the attachment security of two-year-olds. When the children were between four and five years old, the researchers assessed their ego functioning, self-control, and social comfort. The psychologists were primarily interested in whether the children's attachment style at two predicted their ego functioning at five. But the researchers also happened to measure their subjects' level of curiosity. Each four- or five-year-old child was then brought into a laboratory where there was a box placed on the floor, containing a range of interesting, somewhat unusual toys. Each child was invited to spend some time examining the box and its contents, while an experimenter sat nearby taking notes. We'll return to this "curiosity box" in subsequent chapters, since it plays a small but important role in the history of curiosity research. But for now, let's just consider the measures of Arend et al., and their findings. Children varied in how quickly they approached the box, how many objects they touched in the first ten minutes, and how many different gestures they used to examine the objects. These then became a curiosity score for each child. Children who were rated as more curious not only rated higher on measures of ego functioning and self-control, but also were much more likely to have displayed secure attachments at two. Those two-year-olds who had insecure-anxious attachments consistently took more time to approach the box, explored fewer objects in the box, and explored the objects less avidly (measured by number of gestures).

In one early descriptive study of preschoolers' exploration of objects, the authors simply brought preschoolers into a room where there was an array of toys, five of which were familiar to the children, and one of which was novel. The author, Corinne Hutt (1970), noted that while many children energetically picked the toys up, examined them, and then tried a whole host of gestures and behaviors with them, some children lacked that kind of eagerness and ingenuity. She described these children as inhibited, and noted that when these children played with the familiar toys, they did so in a somewhat "repetitive or stereotyped" manner. "For example, one girl wound the string, which was attached to the truck round and round her finger and then round her foot" (70).

Running through this line of work is a connection that is found elsewhere in the literature—that attachment style and temperament are closely linked. This connection was first identified in the study of nonhumans. For instance, the link is very clear in the work of Henry Harlow, who showed that monkeys raised without an attachment figure are more fearful, and that fear prevents animals from exploring their environment (Harlow 1958). Observations suggest that hunger decreases an animal's exploratory behavior—an animal who has just eaten is much more likely to investigate something new in the immediate environment (Dashiell 1925; Saxe and Stollak 1971). Harlow argued that allowing a monkey to cuddle a figure (animate or inanimate) gave it a sense of comfort that allowed it to relax. This relaxing mitigated the monkey's fear of the unknown and promoted exploration of novel stimuli. In one study examining links between attachment style and exploration, Schieche and Spangler found that avoidant toddlers (those who don't seem distressed when their mother leaves the room, and equally disengaged when she returns) were the least likely to engage in a novel task, or explore new materials (2005).

The experiments and observational studies of babies and animals that I have described show what's going on beneath the surface. In order to appreciate the potent social and emotional context in which a toddler's inquiry unfolds, you can simply watch toddlers who are in a complex and/or new environment.

When my niece Maddie was fourteen months old, her mother and I set her down on the floor to play while we drank tea at the kitchen table and chatted. Next to her were a few toys—a soft ball, some small cars, and a little wagon filled with colored wood blocks. She crawled around, examining the various toys. She lifted the ball and tossed it, but quickly lost interest. She examined one of the cars for a few moments and then deliberately placed it back on the floor. She took three blocks and carefully stacked one atop the another. Seeing that she was happily absorbed, we turned to each other, eager to talk. But all the time we both kept glancing Maddie's way, just to make sure she was OK.

Suddenly I had the vague feeling that something had changed. It's hard to know what was different about her—her still, attentive face, or maybe her closed, uncharacteristically immobile mouth. I said to my sister, "Something's in there. She has something in her mouth." My sister quickly jammed her finger into her baby daughter's soft mouth and pulled out a large carpentry staple. It must have been in the crack between the floorboards. Tired of obvious and familiar objects like balls and blocks, my niece had zeroed in on the more fascinating and unfamiliar object lying in the dust on the floor. Perhaps because it was too small to manipulate with her fingers, she had found another way to investigate it—inside her mouth. Who knows what went on once it was in there? Perhaps she probed the edges of the staple with her tongue, delicately exploring the sharp ends, or perhaps the weight of it on her tongue interested her. Maybe she was waiting to see what we would do when we noticed. I began this chapter with a story about falling on glass. I end with a story of a toddler popping a carpentry staple into her mouth. I hope to have shown that toddlers' reactions to novelty are connected to their sense of fear. As my two anecdotes suggest, danger and risk come hand in hand with curiosity. This is a topic to which I'll return.

In many instances, we think of children becoming more independent of the adults around them as they grow older. They learn to walk and can get places on their own. They learn to talk and can communicate with people who don't know them well. They become more able to function without the security of a loved one nearby. And yet, in the case of curiosity, adults only become more important as children develop. When it comes to finding out about the world around them, toddlers acquire a particularly potent way of using their parents to sate their curiosity. They ask them questions.

3

The Conversationalist

I ONLY REMEMBER two things from my third year of life. The first was my daily trip to nursery school. I rode in a seat behind my mother on her bicycle, traveling from our home on East Eighty-Ninth Street in Manhattan to the school, Madison Avenue Presbyterian, on East Seventy-Third Street. Each morning my mother and I played a game called Red Light Green Light. Each of us, in turn, had to think of a new color light. It would begin simply: Red light, blue light, yellow light. But to this day, I still remember the thrilling moment when I came up with the amazingly subtle and clever "beige light."

My second memory from that time period is less specific but gets at the heart of what happens to curiosity during early childhood. Though my mother took me to nursery school, our housekeeper picked me up at noon. We'd come home together, and she'd give me a peanut butter sandwich and a glass of milk. Then I'd sit under the ironing board while she pressed my family's clothes and I watched TV, which I could see at an angle, from my spot on the floor. We'd talk. I'd ask her questions about what I glimpsed on the TV. I'd chatter away about my morning at school and answer her questions. I'd tell her made-up stories and hope she'd want to know more. Preschool provided a little education. My conversations through the ironing board taught me just as much.

When children are first mobile, their bodies are fantastically powerful tools for investigating the world. They can wander, grab things, climb, build, take things apart, and open things up (Campos et al. 2000). They can test their implicit theories—and they do. They watch one toy sink in the bathtub, and another toy bob along on the surface. Many children, faced with such a puzzle, will spend sustained time trying to solve the puzzle created by that discrepancy. Implicit in their actions are two types of question: what (what happens when I put the boat in upside down?), and why (why do some toys float and others sink?). As all scientists know, answering "what" makes it possible to answer "why."

Their actions tell us they want to know more, and their actions lead them to new knowledge. But by the time most children are three, a sea change has occurred in their pursuit of what and why. They have acquired the cognitive equivalent of a steam engine for finding things out and gathering new information—they have learned to converse. However, from mouthing, climbing, and banging they don't leap directly into the world of questions—they point their way.

FROM POINTING TO ASKING

It's tempting to think that once a child learns language she *suddenly* discovers a new tool for satisfying her curiosity, and with it come new worlds to be curious about. Until recently, that was the unexamined assumption of our developmental accounts—before children have language they act on the world, attempting to discover what things are made of, how they work, and what happens next. In this account, learning language serves as a kind of bootstrap, providing them with powerful new tools that open up the possibility of two related mechanisms—the chance to learn from other people, and the chance to learn about things that cannot be discovered through direct action.

However, the evidence suggests that the path to asking other people questions begins before language. It seems that even before children can talk, they are interested in finding out about aspects of the world that cannot be discovered on their own.

Michael Tomasello and Colwyn Trevarthen have long argued that children use pointing as a way of inviting adults to contemplate objects with them. Their work emphasizes the ways in which children share the experience of objects and events with those around them, and in so doing internalize the cultural valences of those objects and events. In an intriguing new set of experiments, Victoria Southgate and her colleagues show that long before children can put together a question, they use pointing as a way of getting adults to tell them things they want to know (Southgate, Van Maanen, and Csibra 2007; Begus and Southgate 2012). But Southgate and her colleagues have argued that such pointing reveals more than a simple invitation to contemplate together. Children point more often to novel or unfamiliar objects and events than they do to familiar ones. They are also more likely to point when the adult nearby has already proved she is a knowledgeable informant. In one study, an experimenter first demonstrated her reliability or lack thereof by naming objects with which the child was familiar (based on parental report). She either correctly or incorrectly named the familiar objects. Then the infant was shown several unfamiliar objects. Sure enough, babies were more likely to point to the new objects and look at the experimenter when she had proven herself to be reliable and knowledgeable about the names of the objects. These data suggest that babies use adults to get information in fairly refined ways, before they are able to ask questions. They look at parents for information about the world around them, and guidance about how to interpret events. In other words, they are interested in an interpreted world even before they have language with which to represent that world. This means that once a child learns to talk, she is poised to dive into the world of other people's knowledge. Her world is transformed by the acquisition of language, and questions are a crucial piece of this transformation.

THE DAWN OF THE QUESTION

A colleague reports to me that his two-and-and-half-year-old son Kai has a favorite new game. Kai launches the game by yelling, "Question mark!" Then, when he's got his father's attention, he continues, still yelling, "What do I do when I get home from school?"—his name for day care. His father answers, "You play?" Each time, Kai shouts triumphantly in response (and with a touch of relief that his question led to the right answer), "That's right. I play!" Like many toddlers, Kai's discovery of the form and function of questions opens up an ocean of interpersonal and intellectual possibilities.

Baby diaries and recordings of children in their home or out and about with caregivers have, for many years, provided an invaluable source of information about children's early language (Wallace, Franklin, and Keegan 1994). As most psychologists who have kept diaries, or used diary data, will attest, such data provide something no experiment can—a picture of children using language in their everyday lives, to solve the problems that matter to them. In addition, ongoing naturalistic records provide a glimpse of how certain kinds of language use emerge. Diaries have allowed us to trace the emergence of vocabulary, grammatical forms, the acquisition of pragmatic skills, and the transition from categorization to conceptualization, among other phenomena. Looking at a complete record of any individual child's language over a matter of months or years, we can actually see development unfold. These diaries show that during the second year, children work hard to master the question form.

The linguist William Labov and his wife, Teresa Labov, documented all of the language spoken by their youngest daughter, Jessie, from the time she was an infant until she was four and a half years old (Labov and Labov 1978). In one of their papers examining Jessie's language, the Labovs describe all the "WH" (what, when, where, why, and how) questions Jessie asked on one particular afternoon. Their aim was to identify the process by which children might come to master the subtle and quirky syntax of WH questions. They were interested in showing that learning the grammatical rules of question asking takes lots of practice, and does not reflect the hardwiring implied by Chomsky's theory of an innate "language instinct." Though the repetition of questions may signal a need to practice certain tricky grammatical forms (the inversion required for "why" questions, for instance), that's not the only reason Jessie asked so many questions. Jessie's diligence in practicing the question form is paralleled by her persistence in trying to learn about things that seem to mystify her. The record reveals what kinds of things she wanted to know more about.

During one stretch of time on July 16, 1975, when Jessie was three years, ten months old, she asked twenty questions. Interestingly, only two were aimed at finding out what something was: (1) "What's that?" and (2) "What is this?" (It's not clear whether Jessie wanted only to know the name of an object, or whether she wanted some more particular information about the object's function. It is also not clear whether the question "What is this?" was simply a follow-up to the first or referred to a different object.) However, more intriguing than that, the record shows that most of her questions were not that straightforward, nor did they seem aimed at identifying the things in her immediate environment. The vast majority of her questions peeled beneath the surface, to get at more complex or inaccessible aspects of the world. What did Jessie want to know? Some of her questions sought basic information beyond her immediate reach—questions that physical exploration could not have answered—she asked where the chickens were, where Philadelphia is, and where some object in her immediate environment came from. She also asked questions about the physical world that involved abstractions about objects and categories of objects. For instance, she wanted to know whether a peach is bigger than an apricot. She also asked, "What the sun do to snow?" Here it seems she wanted to gain a better understanding of the inner workings of the physical world. Paul Harris has pointed out that even in matters that concern the natural world, children ask grown-ups rather than simply relying on their own interactions with objects (Harris 2012).

The Labovs argued that this stretch of talk shows how much children practice the intricacies of asking questions. If that were their only purpose at this point in development, then once they master it, its ubiquity should diminish, especially where direct experience might suffice. However, the data say otherwise. Even after children have figured out the syntax of inquiry, they continue to deluge their parents with questions about the world around them. Using the CHILDES database, Michelle Chouinard analyzed the questions of four children from the time they were fourteen months old until they were five years and one month of age. The recordings provided a total corpus of 24,741 questions and represent 229.5 hours of conversation. The children in this study asked an average of 107 questions per hour—an extraordinary volume of questions, if you think about it. It means that some of the children were asking more than one question a minute during some or many of their recordings (Chouinard 2007).

Like the Labov's daughter Jessie, Chouinard's subjects asked many questions but also revealed wide-roaming interest in what went on around them. They asked, on average, three times as many questions that were aimed at getting new information as they did questions aimed at getting permission, gaining clarification about ongoing activities, or finding out people's whereabouts. In other words, children seek information from adults not only to help them navigate the immediate world around them, but also to help satisfy their epistemic curiosity.

In a study that complemented her analyses of the language of the four children, Chouinard collected diary data on sixty-eight children between the ages of one and five, drawn from a college campus research-oriented preschool. Parents were asked to keep records of their children's questions for a period of one week. Once again Chouinard found that this wider group of children asked a great many questions. Moreover, like the original four, these children tended to first ask simply factual questions about situations and objects, and then begin asking for deeper kinds of information such as explanations.

Chouinard's analyses of both sets of data show that when a child encounters something brand new, she first gathers straightforward information—"What is it?" "What does it do?" "What is that little piece called?" "Are there lots of those?" "Where do they sleep?" and so on. Even these questions appear to go from immediate and concrete to somewhat more displaced in time and space, just as Jacqueline Sachs pointed out years ago using diary data on her own daughter, Naomi (Sachs 1983).

Once a child has acquired enough information to create a foundation of knowledge, her questions begin to seek a deeper level of understanding. Now she wants explanations—why something worked in a particular fashion, why people behaved one way and not another, why things unfolded in a particular sequence. The sequence of types of questions suggests that children are not asking questions simply to pass the time, dominate the conversation, or keep the adult's attention. Nor are they simply practicing the pragmatics of conversation itself. Instead preschool children use questions to scaffold their own knowledge about a range of topics. Chouinard argues that children use questions to gain information about things that direct experience cannot help them with. They want to know why people get old, why certain foods melt in the sun and others do not, and the like. Frazier, Gelman, and Wellman (2009) analyzed conversations between preschoolers and adults and found that the children, when they got satisfactory explanations to their questions, responded differently from when they didn't. Their data are further evidence that children are not merely asking questions to get attention, or learn verbal forms, but instead are looking to resolve uncertainties and fill out their knowledge. Children's responses show that they care about getting their questions answered.

All of these data also suggest children want to know about things to which they do not have direct access (complex and inaccessible physical processes). However, some of the examples suggest that children are also very interested in acquiring information that is culturally constructed, or at least culturally saturated.

Barbara Tizard and Martin Hughes's work shows how adept preschoolers are in using questions to go beyond the immediate and concrete world around them (1984). In the 1980s they equipped 30 three- and four-year-old girls with smocks in which they had sewn tape recorders. Each child was recorded for two and a half hours at home and for five hours at school. Thus their data set comprised all the conversations that took place during these seven and a half hours for each child. The children asked an average of 26 questions per hour when they were at home with their mothers (one child asked 145 questions during a home observation period). Some 60 percent of those questions were phrased so as to acquire new information or to learn more about something. Tizard and Hughes refer to these exchanges as "episodes of cognitive search," to capture the way in which such exchanges allowed children to expand their intellectual horizons. The following exchange gives a sense of how the children explored topics that went far beyond straightforward facts about the here and now.

CHILD: Is our roof a sloping roof?
MOTHER: Mmm. We've got two sloping roofs, and they sort of meet in the middle.
CHILD: Why have we?
MOTHER: Oh it's just the way our house is built. Most people have sloping roofs, so that the rain can run off them. Otherwise, if you have a flat roof, the rain would sit in the middle of the roof and make a big puddle, and then it would start coming through.
CHILD: Our school has a flat roof, you know.
MOTHER: Yes it does actually, doesn't it?

CHILD: And the rain sits there and goes through?

MOTHER: Well, it doesn't go through. It's probably built with drains
so that the water runs away. You have big blocks of flats with
rather flat sort of roofs. But houses that were built at the time this
house was built usually had sloping roofs.

CHILD: Does Lara [the child's friend] have a sloping roof?

MOTHER: Mmm. Lara's house is very like ours. In countries where
they have a lot of snow, they have even more sloping roofs. Then
when they've got a lot of snow, the snow can just fall off.

CHILD: Whereas, if you have a flat roof, what would it do? Would it
just have a drain?

MOTHER: No, then it would sit on the roof and when it melted it
would make a big puddle. (124) [Paul Harris has a wonderful
discussion of this passage on page 40 of his book *Trusting What
You're Told*.]

A close reading of this conversation shows that the child, Beth, uses
it as an opportunity to puzzle through a series of questions. She wants
to know what a sloping roof is and whether theirs constitutes one; what
purpose a slope in the roof serves; why, if it serves that purpose, the
school's roof is different; and what the consequences are of that difference. Each question builds on her previous questions, and by the time
she has finished this particular cross-examination, Beth has acquired
a surprisingly coherent body of new knowledge.

Moreover, the exchange allows Beth to weave together information
about the physical world with information about the social world. The
fact that water drains off a slanted roof is not socially constructed—it
follows a law of nature. But the fact that different people and groups
have different kinds of roofs points to some culturally specific facts (the
kinds of houses typical of one's region; the fact that in many countries,
houses vary and indicate all kinds of information about the people who
live within; and so forth).

Some of the time, preschoolers seek information that cannot be acquired through direct experience and is also purely social in nature.
For instance, Jessie Labov asks, "Why you said to Daddy you might be
kidding?" "Why we can't wear sandals for walking in the wood?" and
"What you do when you want to be rich?" Here Jessie seeks informa-

tion about cultural conventions. In some places, after all, one does wear sandals in the woods, and interpretations about joking and irony vary from one culture to another. Certainly the means to wealth in a university town in Pennsylvania are not the same as they would be in rural Indonesia, for instance. But she also seeks information about ambiguous and complex phenomena, where it is not clear what the distinction is between cultural and natural principles. For instance, she asks, "Why when a child grows up there's no daddy?"—in other words she seeks information that will close the gap between her construction of reality and the adult reality she discerns through conversation itself. This brings us to one more kind of curiosity that children can only satisfy with questions—not only the unseen, but also the unseeable.

Harris has argued that there are many things children want to learn about that either are hard to see (germs), have no straightforward physical presence (love), are unseeable (the past), or only exist by dint of human imagination (God, Santa Claus). However, the data suggest that even when children can observe and manipulate the physical world, questions offer an avenue for understanding not only what something is or does, but also how it is viewed and treated by others—they want to know about the mediated world.

During the 1920s, William and Clara Stern recorded most of what their three young children, Hilde, Gunther, and Eva, said. In the following conversation, recorded verbatim when Hilde was three years, seven months, she asks what William Stern refers to as a "chain of [causal questions], each reason producing another enquiry as to *its* reason" (Stern 1924, 170). The following conversation took place while the child was looking at a whale in her picture book:

CHILD: What is he eating?
MOTHER: Fish.
CHILD: Why does he eat fish?
MOTHER: Because he is hungry.
CHILD: Why doesn't he eat rolls?
MOTHER: Because we don't give him any.
CHILD: Why don't we give him any?
MOTHER: Because bakers only make rolls for people.
CHILD: Why not for fishes?

MOTHER: Because they haven't enough flour.
CHILD: Why then haven't they enough?
MOTHER: Because not enough corn is grown. You know, don't you
    that flour is made out of corn?
CHILD: Oh, I see.

Hilde goes from asking what the whale in the picture is doing to what it could do, why it eats what it eats, and finally to the world of people and manufactured objects (rolls). Conversations allow children to build knowledge that places the physical world in a cultural context.

Ironically, these examples lend a kind of oblique support to the Piagetian idea that children construct knowledge through their interactions. It's just that the interactions in these examples occur via language rather than physical manipulation, and the data come from what other people say rather than from the characteristics of objects. The examples I have given also show that what a child gets from such an exchange depends hugely on her conversational partner.

When the Sterns and the Labovs were recording their children they had the advantage of having continual access to their young subjects. However, these were no ordinary children—they grew up not only under a microscope, but surrounded by educated, interested, and responsive parents. More contemporary research methods take us beyond the diary case study. Portable microphones, electronic databases, and large-scale studies have allowed us to find out whether children whose parents are not researchers with degrees also use questions to explore mediated and intangible aspects of daily life.

LANGUAGE AS A FINGERPRINT

Though asking questions is a popular pursuit for most two-year-olds, they are not all the same, even on this dimension. Chouinard, for instance, found wide variation between the four children she studied in depth. One of the children, Abe, asked on average 69.6 questions an hour. Adam, on other hand, asked an average of 198 questions per hour. That's nearly triple the number Abe was asking. So, on the one hand, we can see that question asking is a predominant mode of communication for preschoolers—they talk a lot, and they use talk as a way to learn about the world. But within this general characteristic of the age group, it's also possible to see glimmers of individual differences that might, to use Kagan's term, cast a long shadow.

As Chouinard herself acknowledges, the four children whose language she analyzed for her monograph are not exactly representative of the wider population of young children. If we were to conduct a similar analysis of a wider swath of children, what would we learn about the questions they ask? Would we find that there are more Abes or more Adams out there? Would specific characteristics of their home lives provide clues about why some children ask more questions than others?

To answer this question, it helps to consider the developmental backdrop. Most children acquire the components of full-fledged language in roughly the same sequence. Long before children talk in sentences, they point. Then they begin to use one object (a hairbrush) to represent another (a telephone). Next, children everywhere realize that everything has a name, and they begin acquiring new words at a rapid rate. During this burst of vocabulary growth, they begin combining words in orderly ways—in other words they begin speaking in sentences. Though children vary in how quickly they learn to talk, the sequence is fairly universal. And yet, language is, at the same time, one of the all-time great windows onto variation between nations, communities, and individual families.

Children in Shanghai not only speak a different language from children in, say, Minneapolis—they also use language differently. The most vivid example of this comes from research on how children learn to use language to tell stories. Peggy Miller and Heidi Fung compared the ways in which Taiwanese and European-American families socialized their children via personal storytelling. In both cultures adults responded to, commented on, and collaborated with children's efforts to talk about what was happening or had happened. Adults in each culture encouraged their children to emphasize specific forms and styles. But equally interesting, Miller and Fung show that the families in Taipei emphasized the child's role as listener when stories were being told, while the U.S. families tended to encourage children to be the narrators. So, there seems to be stable and meaningful cultural variation not only in what kind of stories children learn to tell, but also in what role they play in telling those stories (Miller et al. 1990; Mullen and Yi 1995).

Nor do you need to cross national borders to find these differences. Families who tell stories for different purposes often live right next door to one another. In her classic book, *Ways with Words*, Shirley Brice-Heath showed that children who grew up in the white working-class community of Roadville in the late 1970s learned to tell stories as a way of imparting morals. A well-constructed story was one that revealed the weaknesses of people and the consequence of those weaknesses. Children heard adults tell stories long before they told any themselves, and in this way began internalizing storytelling "values." Then, as they began telling stories themselves, adults gave them feedback that further inculcated in them the particular narrative habits valued by their community. In contrast, children growing up in the nearby black working-class community of Trackton learned to tell stories as a way of connecting with others. A good story was one that captivated an audience and intensified interpersonal relationships. Here, too, children learned first by observing, and then via the feedback they received (Brice-Heath 1983).

But the impact of individual differences in the way parents talk to, and around, their children starts well before a child can tell a story. By the time children are three, the ways in which their parents have talked to them have already shaped their intellectual futures.

Imagine you are asked to predict the academic fortune of two toddlers you have just met. What information would you want? Three pieces of information would help a lot: the IQ of their parents, their parents' annual income, and whether or not their parents read. When mothers in developing countries are taught to read, even when nothing else about their lives change, the rate of child mortality goes down. Women who learn to read are more likely to get various kinds of health care for their children and to connect to the larger community of institutions (hospitals and schools) in a way that helps their children thrive (Levine et al. 2012). Even within nations, teaching low-income parents to read directly affects their children's welfare. When U.S. mothers learn to read, their children are much more likely to succeed in school. In other words, the impact of reading extends beyond health care and use of government resources. Having a parent who reads changes a child's intellectual landscape.

Hart and Risley compared the language heard by children growing up in poverty with the language heard by children growing up with greater economic resources (1995). Poor children hear far less talk of any kind than children from families with more money (Fernald, Marchman, and Weisleder 2013). And poor children hear a kind of talk different from what children in the middle class hear. Poor children hear mostly what is called "business" talk—comments that tell them what to do ("Close the door," "Get your shoes on," "It's time to go," "Don't touch that, it's hot"). In contrast, middle-class children are far more likely to hear language directed at things that have happened in the past, things that might happen, as well as people's thoughts and feelings ("Did you sing at school today?" "I wonder if all this rain will make the flowers grow," "I think Carey was very sad when her balloon popped, don't you?"). Not only do they engage in conversation with adults more frequently, but each of those conversations is longer, giving them access to a much larger vocabulary, more complex grammar, a greater variety of conversational formats, and simply more practice at discussion.

This early language environment is a strong predictor of school success. Children growing up in poverty hear far fewer total number of words, have a harder time learning to read, and ultimately are less likely to do well in school by the time they are in third grade (Hart and Risley 1995; Fernald, Marchman, and Weisleder 2013). If a child lives with parents who only use words to manage practical tasks, he may struggle to use language for less practical, more contemplative purposes. This goes a long way in explaining the relative difficulty poor children have learning to use language to describe things, construct arguments, and solve abstract problems—in other words the difficulty they have with academic uses of language (Snow 1983, 2010). Catherine Snow and her colleagues have shown that middle-class parents talk to their children in specific ways that seem to uniquely prepare them to read. Among other things, they respond to children's questions in ways that are "semantically contingent"—that is, close in meaning to what the child is focused on. They also subtly demand that their children use the highest level of language of which they are capable (a child who has shown herself capable of asking well-formed questions might be asked to repeat herself if she slips into a more immature form of question asking, for instance), and they consistently prod their children to move toward ever more decontextualized uses of language, a key to literacy. A parent and child might, in other words, have a rich repertoire of language use and yet not include the particular features that form the foundation of literacy. When these features are absent, children are likely to find reading more of a challenge. When they are present, children often learn to read with ease. In one searing example of what children from nonliterate backgrounds miss out on, Richard Wright describes his relatively late discovery regarding the power of the written word. As a seventeen-year-old he borrowed a white man's library card and went to the library to borrow a book of H. L. Mencken's writings, curious about who he was and why he had elicited such fury from southerners.

> That night in my rented room, while letting the hot water run over my can of pork and beans in the sink, I opened *A Book of Prefaces* and began to read. I was jarred and shocked by the style, the clear, clean, sweeping sentences. Why did he write like that? And how did one write like that? I picture the man as a raging demon, slashing with his pen, consumed with hate, denouncing everything American, extolling everything European or German, laughing at the weakness of people, mocking God, authority. What was this? I stood up, trying to realize what reality lay behind the meaning of the words. . . . Yes, this man was fighting, fighting with words. He was using words as a weapon, using them as one would use a club. Could words be weapons? Well, yes, for here they were. Then, maybe, perhaps, I could use them as a weapon?" (Wright 1945, 271)

But nations and income level are not the only sources of difference, when it comes to children's language use. Individual families have something of a linguistic fingerprint, and it's not completely clear why.

Gordon Wells fitted thirty-two children in Bristol, England, with vests in which a microphone had been sewn in. He then recorded their language as they went about their daily lives, from just after their first birthday until the end of their elementary school education. The recordings show that between the ages of one and four, the children engaged in an enormous quantity of conversation while they were at home. But Wells followed his subjects to preschool, recording their classroom language activities as well. He found that children who had many conversations and long conversations at home had an easier time learning to read when they went to school. He did not compare language between economic groups, but was looking only at differences among his working-class British families. So, in fact, the differences he saw seemed to reflect individual family style rather than, say, differences in quantity of toys and access to private space at home, or the amount of parents' leisure time, or level of education. Within one country, and one economic class, children were learning different things about the whys and hows of talking (Wells 1986).

It seems, then, that there is a somewhat different dimension on which families might differ—their use of language to seek knowledge. It's likely that children who hear people describing and explaining things not only learn to read more easily, but also learn that people exchange knowledge through talk.

One of the most interesting findings of Tizard and Hughes, and Chouinard, as well as earlier diarists like James Sully and William Stern, is that children are such dogged question askers. Chouinard shows that children persist when their questions are not answered more than when their questions are answered. In other words, they are selective in their use of questions, and seem to know that a question is a tool for getting information that one actually needs or wants. These observers all show that children are capable of asking as many as ten questions in a row in order to satisfy their curiosity. But not all children get answers to their questions, or are encouraged to probe a topic in depth. Some of these differences reflect broader cultural values. Mary Gauvain and her colleagues have shown that though children from non-Western cultures ask as many questions as their Western counterparts, fewer of those questions seek explanations. The authors suggest that in many non-Western cultures, adults frown upon children trying to find out the whys and hows of life (Gauvain, Munroe, and Beebe 2013). Paul Harris has pointed out that the cultures where children are discouraged from seeking explanations are also the cultures where there is the least access to formal education (Harris 2012). Certainly we know from a broad range of sources that cultures vary in how they view young children's capacity to understand, how children should behave around adults, and what kinds of behaviors are safe or wise to encourage. Thus it is not surprising that questions are not treated similarly in all places. However, whatever cultural beliefs and values underlie adult responses to children's inquiries, those responses have developmental repercussions.

The children described by Hart and Risley, for instance, who hear mostly "business talk" (sit down, pick that up, don't do that) are not getting many chances to ask a series of related questions, probe a topic in depth, or move from one topic of inquiry to another. And it's not only that they are not getting chances to practice such linguistic inquiry. They see little evidence that the adults around them value such inquiry. Though the studies I have described here provide indirect evidence that families differ in their general tolerance of talk, it should be possible to see whether families differ in their use of questions.

To examine this, my student Laura Corona and I asked twelve families to tape-record their dinnertime for five nights in a row. They did not know what aspects of their interactions we were interested in. There was wide variation between the families in the amount of talk that went on during the evening meal. There were also individual differences in how much of that talk consisted of asking or answering questions. One of the things that struck us most about those dinner-table conversations was the variation in how adults responded to children's questions. Some parents answer a question quite directly and then move on quickly to another topic. Others use every question as an opening to a further consideration of an issue.

Compare, for instance, the two exchanges below. The first, between a four-year-old and his mother, is similar to many described by Tizard and Hughes. The child is persistent, dogged even, but not tunnel-visioned—he seems to be using the conversation to expand his understanding of complex phenomena.

CHILD: You said Go away dammit. Why you don't like the crows?
FATHER: Because the crows can get their own food.
CHILD: But why the chickens can't, won't, can't get their food too?
FATHER: Well because we keep the chickens in a pen.
CHILD: But the crows are in the pen. You don't want those crows?
FATHER: Well, the crows can get into the pen, but we built the pen for the chickens because, well because we, we take care of them. We uh, we want, we like to eat their eggs.

CHILD: But we don't like crow eggs right? Right dad, we like chicken eggs, right?

In contrast, the following exchange also integrates information about the natural world with information about the social world, but the parents provide much less complete information, and the child asks fewer questions.

CHILD: Is fish healthy?
MOTHER: Very.
CHILD: How did people get the blood out?
MOTHER: OK, there's a question for Daddy.
OLDER BROTHER: I'm losing my appetite.
FATHER: It's when they clean it, the fish.
OLDER BROTHER: I'm losing my appetite.
CHILD: How do they get their guts out?
FATHER: That's enough. Not appropriate for dinner.

In our study, children who asked a lot of questions had mothers who asked a lot of questions. Of course, the data cannot tell us whether mothers who ask many questions somehow teach their children to ask many questions, whether inquisitive children influence their mothers to respond in kind (a less likely but not impossible causal relationship), or whether some other factor accounts for the pattern. However, the correlation does suggest that question asking is part of a family style, rather than simply linked to individual differences in, say, temperament or personality on the one hand, or wealth and cultural habits on the other.

The variation between families suggests that not all children are learning the same things about questions. Some children hear other people (for instance older siblings and parents) ask many questions. They also see that their family members use questions to get information. These same children, it seems from our data, are likely to get their questions answered. So they not only have a model in front of them of the question asking, but they experience the satisfaction that comes with getting answers to their questions. In many of the diary reports, as well as our own data on family conversations, children are in control of the length of these conversations. In other words, to borrow from Tizard and Hughes, the children are deciding how far to search, in the episodes of cognitive search. It follows that children who get to use questions to find things out, and get to ask questions until they feel satisfied (however temporary that satisfaction may be), are more likely to continue asking questions than children who rarely see people ask informational questions, and are not rewarded with answers when they themselves ask questions.

The idea that children are learning something about the relationships between language and experience finds support from research on the development of autobiographical talk. Studies show that there are clear individual differences in how toddlers and their parents describe the past. Some describe it only for the sake of practical tasks (mentioning where a shoe was yesterday so as to find the shoe today), while other parent-child pairs describe the past for the purpose of thinking more about those episodes—to reminisce. Note that a child might talk a great deal with her parent, but not practice the things that lead to good storytelling: unfolding a sequence of events, conveying a perspective, identifying time and place, and including a high point. Parents who tell stories collaboratively with toddlers, who scaffold this kind of storytelling and regularly engage in storytelling as a way of reminiscing, have children who seem to end up not only telling stories differently than other children, but are more likely to do so under a variety of circumstances (Engel 1995). In this case the amount of talking is not in and of itself the issue—rather, what matters is what kinds of talk parents encourage with their children.

Particular forms and uses of language are intimately tied to certain cognitive processes. The child who practices reminiscing develops what Neisser called an extended self (1988). The child who practices decontextualized language is more capable of decontextualized thinking (Scribner and Cole 1978). Similarly, the child who asks questions that get answered, and hears others asking questions, not only learns to ask questions, but also develops the disposition to wonder about things and to actively seek answers from others. However, not all others are mothers (Hrdy 2009).

THE WIDENING CIRCLE

Just to complicate matters, by the time children are three, most of them, even in cultures that emphasize the nuclear family, spend at least two-thirds of their time with nonparents. This means that children are exposed to a variety of role models, conversational partners, and intellectual resources as they go about daily life. And the response young children get from their parents when they ask questions is not necessarily the same kind of response they get from other adults. We have painful evidence of this when it comes to the storytelling habits children acquire at home. In one of the more searing portraits of language socialization, Sarah Michaels (1991) showed that black children in Boston came to kindergarten armed with one set of narrative tools, while their teachers came expecting a different kind of narrative. When white teachers encountered black children's stories at show-and-tell, they tended to respond in ways that dismissed the children's stories, and, more importantly, failed to offer feedback that might scaffold the children's narrative skills or provide them the opportunity to expand on their emerging storytelling abilities. Michaels offers one example in which a little girl named Deena uses "sharing time" to tell the class a lively story about a trip she made to the doctor's office. Her story is organized as an unfolding plot, in which a string of things happens to her. Her teacher, on the other hand, wants to zero in on the opportunity to explain to everyone what a thermometer is, and how it works. The teacher's insistence in redirecting the story ends up derailing Deena's tale. Michaels's analysis shows that children carry their language customs with them into new environments, and that those environments may or may not support further development.

When you put all the data about children's questions together, the picture is pretty clear—children ask questions to practice the form itself and to get information about the world. When they ask a question, it tells us not only where they are linguistically, but also what they want to know about. The questions tell us something about a given child's curiosity, but they also provide the child with a kind of perpetual feedback loop. Children whose questions get answered are likely to keep asking more questions. That cycle, if Berlyne was right, is self-perpetuating. The child feels an urge to know, she asks a question, the answer satisfies her urge, which makes her likely to use the same route the next time she feels the urge to know something. In this way the child's early question-asking experiences lay down a foundation for her future—she will either experience verbal inquiry as fruitful, or she won't.

The data suggest that while all three-year-olds ask more questions than most seven-year-olds, not all three-year-olds ask questions with the same perseverance or frequency. In other words, at age three we already see not only the first glimmers of individual differences in curiosity, but also a major route by which these individual differences will grow more pronounced.

Children are learning, by the time they are three or four, just how useful, satisfying, and admirable it is to be curious, or risky and troublesome. Riding to school on my mother's bicycle in the mornings, I learned that language was infinitely expandable (there could be a beige light, even if I had never seen one), and that as it expanded, so did my thoughts. I learned that talking was entertaining, and that the bigger my vocabulary, the more fun I would have. Sitting under the ironing board in the afternoons, chatting with my babysitter, added to my intellectual growth. The space under the ironing board was cramped and spare. There wasn't much going on (except for ironing and talk). But the conversations I had with Noonie, day after day, created a spacious vista that went forward and backward in time, and was filled with interesting people, places, and objects of contemplation. My only tool of exploration—a question.

4

Invitations and Prohibitions

WHEN I WAS a child, I had a lot of time on my hands, and I often wandered around aimlessly. I lived in a fairly isolated locale. My stepfather worked seven days a week on the farm. My mother seemed very busy, and though attentive and loving, she didn't actually spend much time with me. It was expected that we children would keep ourselves busy. Of course, during the week, from September until June, I went to school. But after school and on weekends, I had a lot of freedom. When I got restless, couldn't think of what else to do, or felt hungry, I'd go visit my grandmother, who lived on the other end of a short dirt path that ran through the farm. But often, especially on summer days, what would begin as a brief desultory trek would turn into a long and absorbing encounter with something odd or unexpected.

Each mini-environment along that dirt road—my house, the farm, and my grandmother's, offered different enticements. My house had toys, and books, and if my mother was around, someone to talk to. The farm offered a nearly infinite array of things to interest me—potatoes, new or rotting, bugs and worms, horse and cow shit, machines, the black and white men who worked on the farm, dark dank corners of stalls, and the feed bin, just to name a few highlights. My grandmother's house had ladies' magazines, purses and cheap jewelry from her youth, the dogs Prince and Cindy, Thomas the cat, and my grandmother's slow but steady stream of anecdotes and customs from long ago (washing my hair with rainwater we caught in a bucket, pouring Fresca over sherbet as a low-sugar dessert, a pantry filled with odd knickknacks, and a glass by her bed where she kept her teeth at night).

It wasn't only the objects that differed between the house, the barn, and my grandmother's. The people in each of those settings differed, and so did their responses to my interests and explorations. At home, I might be alone, but my siblings or mother might be in some part of the house. Though no one ever paid much attention (all of them busy with their own pursuits), there was clear yet unspoken permission to investigate. I could walk into any room, open any drawer or jar, and especially, I could take any book from the shelf and begin reading. It didn't matter whether it was about sex, murder, music theory, or psychoanalysis. If it was in print, I was free to read it. I also knew that along with all the books in the house there were people who wanted me to read them.

But that sense of passive permission extended to other things besides books. When I was six, my best friend Gwen and I invented a game we particularly loved. The game went like this. One of us would wait in the living room with our eyes closed. The other would scout the kitchen, looking for an exotic food. When the scout had found just the thing, she would call in the victim, who would sit on a chair in the kitchen, eyes closed and tongue out, waiting for a drop or bit of the unknown food. I can remember the tingle of dread and delight as I stuck out my tongue, waiting to see what sensation, spicy, rancid, or sweet, would hit me. I can also remember an equal tingle when I was dropping something onto my friend's tongue, wondering how she'd react at the dollop of ice cream, the pinch of pepper, or the morsel of dog biscuit. The ostensible goal of this game was to identify the food. But of course the real goal was to experience the thrill of wondering whether you would get hot sauce, raw garlic, or honey on your tongue. For the other person, it was the thrill of power. In retrospect, this game, which had nothing obvious to do with finding out more about the world, had everything to do with the enticements of the unexpected and unknown. For about three years we couldn't get enough of this game, playing it every time Gwen came to my house. But here is what was just as memorable: My mother would sometimes come through the kitchen, on her way to phone calls, more errands, or her bedroom. She'd smile, and maybe even ask what we were up to. We'd tell her. Sometimes she came through just as one of us was getting a bit of horseradish or raw clam on our tongue and she could see for herself what we were doing. She never once cautioned us against this. She didn't ask much about it, either. She just seemed to silently approve of our antics, making us feel that our thrill at testing each other was just great. Once when we were playing the game, we found ourselves stirring up a whole batch of the goo one of us had dropped on the other's tongue—some mixture of banana, milk, and some flour. We asked my mother if we could cook some of it and feed it to my baby sister. Sure, my mother replied in a distracted, easygoing way. Why not? We stared at each other, aghast and delighted. And then fed some to my little sister. It was a whole different matter if I asked my mother what a word meant, or what a book on the library shelf was about. That was a sure way of getting her attention, and she always had time to talk to me. I still remember walking up to her during a dinner party of grown-ups and interrupting them to ask her what "hypocrite" meant. I had heard one of the guests using the word, from my perch in the living room. She was glad to turn from the adults to explain a word meaning to me. Other words I still vividly recall asking about include ambiguous, fellatio, peninsula, and facetious.

The farm offered a whole different laboratory. My stepfather and the men who worked with him wanted me to notice the animals, and found endless entertainment in my investigations of their farm world. If I came to them with an injured bird, or wanted to taste the horse food, they were tolerantly amused. If they could instruct, they would. My stepfather had two very different stances toward his environment. Either he animated the natural world as if it were an extension of his own human experience, or he viewed the environment as a set of potential tasks. We'd drive past a dry brown field in August, and looking out the window he'd say, "Jeez, Roost (his name for me), that guy's thirsty." Yet on another day, noticing a dry field, he'd simply explain how to set the irrigation equipment so that it would have the widest possible range. When he wasn't including me in his view of things, he would just enjoy my reactions to the unexpected: disgust at rabbit guts, fear at an angry chicken, or difficulty getting a tractor to start.

Then there was my grandmother, who would happily tell me about her orphaned childhood, or explain to me how they made dinner during the Depression (lots of water and potatoes and one small piece of bacon). I was free to cook things in her kitchen. I could use her recipes and mixes, but I could also make things up—Cheerios and chocolate bits, soda and milk, ketchup and cheese doodles. What I couldn't do is probe the world of the unseen and uncomfortable. I couldn't ask why my step-father and uncle always took the funny papers with them to the bath-room. I couldn't query her about why she rarely walked, preferring in-stead to sit at the kitchen table nearly all day long. I also couldn't ask about things that might take us beyond her somewhat narrow circle of familiarity. I didn't ask her questions about books I had read, or what it meant to be a draft dodger. I didn't ask what the sign on my broth-er's door, "Bury Goldwater," meant, and I didn't ask her what I later asked my biological father—why Truffaut named his movie *Stolen Kisses* when it seemed they were all paid for. Somehow I knew what kinds of inquiry were OK to pursue with my grandmother, and what kinds were not.

By the time a child is four she is a more autonomous and skilled navigator than she was even a year before. While a toddler might sit up and take notice when something other than her daily waffle appears on her breakfast plate, or when a bug crawls across the floor, the pre-schooler is savvier. Given their firm grasp on the quotidian, the curi-osity of preschoolers is more likely to be piqued by a narrower and quirkier, more individualized array of events and objects. Nevertheless, the everyday world of a preschooler is still brimming with mysteries and surprises. And these enticements to explore are still filtered through the attitudes and responses of adults.

Much of the time, at least in contemporary Western culture, no matter what they are doing—playing, accomplishing assigned tasks, watching others, or helping out with chores—children are accompa-nied by adults. Some of the time those adults are directly engaged with them—telling them what to do, collaborating with them, or simply watching over them—and some of the time adults are merely nearby. Children are almost constantly interacting with both man-made things (utensils, tools, toys, clothing, machines, to name just a few) and nat-ural things (trees, bugs, mud, wind, animals). But they encounter both kinds of nonhuman objects through a veil of human attitudes about how one does or doesn't interact with people, events, and things. To understand how this adult influence takes shape, I return briefly to infancy, when parents first begin steering their children toward some experiences and directing them away from others.

MY PARENTS WERE MY DOCENTS

The minute children can explore, whether with their gaze or their body, their parents begin steering them toward some things and away from others. And it is not just the adult who imposes strictures on the baby. By the time babies can crawl, they actively seek out adults as a guide for their explorations. Campos and his colleagues put babies on a clear plastic floor with a shallow visual cliff. When their parent, on the opposite side of the cliff, expressed fear, the babies hesitated, showing concern and caution on their faces. A worried parent kept the baby from crossing. But when they saw their parent smiling, the babies approached the cliff and crossed it with comfort. The invitation or prohibition from the parent seemed much more influential than any inherent risk the baby detected in the physical setup (Sorce et al. 1985; Campos and Sternberg 1981; Campos et al. 2000).

But babies don't only look to their parents for permission to approach or withdraw. They also look to their parents for guidance about how to experience the world around them. Research supports the idea that when babies look at unusual or new objects, they consult the adults around them for interpretive help, what Colwyn Trevarthen called secondary intersubjectivity, and Michael Tomasello and others have called social referencing (Trevarthen and Aitken 2001; Tomasello 1999). In one example of this kind of work, twelve-to-eighteen-month-olds were shown a pair of very strange and evocative objects that resembled somewhat mutant creatures. The experimenter would then focus on one of the toys and express a vivid emotional response of pleasure (a happy "oh," or disgust, "ewww"). Some of the time, the babies could see which toy the adult was responding to, and sometimes they could not. When the babies were then given a chance to interact with the objects, they were more likely to approach the one that had evoked pleasure from the adult. However, they only did this when they could see which toy the experimenter had been responding to. In other words, they were discerning, and wanted to make sure that the adult's response was specifically for the object they were interacting with (Moses et al. 2001).

More casual and everyday observations of infants show how attentive they are to the reaction of those around them. Most adults who spend time around babies have had the experience of watching something abrupt or startling happen (a tower of blocks falling, a door banging, or even the baby falling down). Someone in the room lets out a shriek or gasp, and then the baby begins to cry. Often an adult will actually say, "Don't overreact, and she won't either." And often they're right. When babies look at objects, they quickly look at their parent or another important adult, before looking back at the object. Sometimes they seem to take their cue from the grown-up (is this scary? is this funny?), and sometimes they seem to be inviting the adult to participate in their emotional reaction (I think this is funny, look at it with me). As Tomasello (1999) has pointed out, between about nine and twelve months, babies "begin to flexibly and reliably look where adults are looking (gaze following), use adults as social reference points (social referencing), and act on objects in the way adults are acting on them (imitative learning)" (513). In other words, children not only detect adults' response to things around them, but also are interested in how adults actually interact with objects.

In one powerful demonstration of this, Andrew Meltzoff showed fourteen-month-old babies an adult who bent at the waist to touch his head to a panel, which turned on a light. The babies would imitate this, even though it would have been easier to simply press the panel with their hands. It seemed that the toddlers were more interested in patterning their own behavior on the adult's behavior than they were in simply getting the desired effect. Nor is this simply a case of straightforward imitation. In another experiment, Meltzoff showed toddlers an adult attempting to pull apart a small toy shaped like a dumbbell. Handed a dumbbell toy of their own, the toddlers would, unsurprisingly, imitate the action by pulling apart the two pieces. However, when toddlers watched an adult whose hand slipped as he tried to pull the dumbbell apart, they would enact the full sequence without slipping, as if they were imitating what the adult had intended, rather than what had actually happened. However, when toddlers watched a mechanical robot engage in the same gesture (failed attempt to pull apart the toy) they did not imitate (Meltzoff 1995). Children want to do more than pattern their behavior on the behavior of adults. They seem to want to pattern their intentions on the intentions of those around them. This interest in how others are interpreting the physical world continues as babies grow into children.

When it comes to figuring out how to interpret the world around them, children don't quickly outgrow a dependence on adults. Older children, too, look to adults for clues about when something is scary or when it is not. But emotional reactions represent only one kind of potential response. As children grow, the range of possible stances toward reality expands. By the time children are three and four they are faced with so many options—should they treat an object as if it is interesting or boring, enticing or repellant, pretend or real? Angeline Lillard and her colleagues invited mothers and toddlers into a playroom equipped with, among other things, a pretend tea party setup. The experimenter told the moms to play "tea party" with their child once they were alone together in the room. Lillard found that mothers give all kinds of subtle cues that they are pretending—not actually drinking tea, not actually eating cookies. Their gestures are slightly exaggerated, their eyebrows go up, their voices have a special lilt to them—in other words their behavior makes it clear that they do not think they are actually drinking tea, or swallowing cookie. Of course, it's altogether possible that adults behave that way simply because they are pretending. Perhaps they aren't cueing anything to the children, but just expressing their own reframing of familiar actions. However, the toddlers Lillard observed watched their parent's face and actions carefully. Lillard argues that children are learning when and how to take the pretend stance by watching the behavior of their parent (Lillard and Witherington 2004; Nishida and Lillard 2007).

Studies suggest that the same holds true when it comes to curiosity and exploration. Children are deeply influenced by their parents. Saxe and Stollak (1971) brought first-grade boys and their mothers into a playroom and rated their exploratory behavior. The boys were divided by play style (high curiosity–prosocial; low curiosity; aggressive; and neurotic). Mothers of high curiosity–prosocial boys were more positive, attentive, and permissive than mothers of low-curiosity boys.

Furthermore, mothers' expressions of interest and pleasure in their children's behavior were positively associated with their children's attentiveness, active manipulation, and information offering. The best predictor of the child's curiosity was the mother's curiosity, which showed a strong positive association. Clearly these data offer us little information about causes—do curious mothers have curious first graders, and if so, is it because of the behavior the mother has modeled for seven years, is it her responses to her child, or is it a disposition her child inherits from her? Saxe and Stollak argue that mothers and their children influence one another when it comes to exploration, but the data are silent on that question.

Endsley and colleagues (1979) observed nursery schoolchildren and their mothers interacting in a room filled with novel and familiar toys. They found a fairly strong correlation between the mothers' exploratory behavior, encouragement of their children's investigations and questions, with children's exploratory behavior and question asking. Conversely, maternal passivity correlated negatively, albeit weakly, with question asking. In other words, mothers who expressed curiosity and condoned their children's curiosity had children who investigated the novel toys more than the other children did. Hart and Risley (1992) found a strong correspondence between the frequency with which parents asked their children questions and the frequency with which they responded with interest and relevance to their children's comments—repeating, embellishing, or probing what their children said. In addition there was a negative relationship between the number of questions they asked and the number of commands and prohibitions they spoke.

But these studies only suggest an association. The data I've just described tell us little about whether parental encouragement leads to children's exploration. Fortunately, some researchers have attempted to experimentally manipulate the effect of a mother's curiosity on her child. In one such study, kindergarten-age children watched their mothers through a one-way glass, as the mothers sat at a table on which there were several novel toys. Some of the mothers were instructed to hold and manipulate three of the objects lying on the table (thereby modeling curiosity) while some mothers were instructed to simply gaze at a corner of the table. A third group of mothers were told to interact quietly with another adult who was in the room, paying no attention to the table or the objects on it. These last were considered the control condition. Children were then given time in the room with the objects. Those who had seen their mother handle the objects were much more likely not only to imitate their mother's manipulations but to engage in other investigatory manipulations with the objects on the table. In other words, aside from any genetic similarity, or stable association between some maternal behavior and a child's curiosity, children investigate more when they've seen their parent do so (Johns and Endsley 1977).

TEACHERS ENTER THE PICTURE

Nor is it just parents who influence the amount and kind of exploration school-age children engage in. Other adults do as well. In one study Bruce Henderson (1984) asked kindergarten and first-grade children to look at a series of pictures varying in complexity and choose which one they liked best. Then he offered them a chance to play with a toy that was in full view, or one that was partially hidden. Next they were given time to explore a box that had eighteen drawers in it containing small toys, a colorful box covered in various switches and latches, and a board that also contained items to be manipulated. Children's preference for complexity in the first task, attraction to the unknown in the second, and eagerness to try things out with the last three objects were used to tabulate a curiosity score, according to which each child was labeled as high, medium, or low curiosity. The children were then allowed to explore another room, supervised by an experimenter. Each child was assigned to one of three conditions. In the independent condition, the experimenter only reflected the child's questions back to him or her, or briefly answered them when the child asked a second time. In the active-interest condition, the adult experimenter was very attentive and encouraged the student's behavior with smiles, eye contact, and occasional interjections. In the focusing condition, the experimenter encouraged exploration by pointing out novel features of the stimulus, asking leading questions, and giving approving glances and comments when the child explored the materials in the room. When the adult encouraged the children's exploration, children expressed more curiosity with regard to the novel objects in the room. Interestingly, this effect was strongest for the children who had initially been designated as low exploratory. In other words, adult behavior does not have a uniform effect on all children.

Moore and Bulbulian (1976) found something similar. They asked nursery school children to arrange a miniature farm set in the presence of an adult female experimenter who was either friendly and approving or aloof and critical. After this phase, in which, in theory, children were getting a clear message about how free they were to try things out, play freely, and examine the toys, the children were asked to reach into a box and feel seven new, different toys and guess what each one was. Children in the friendly-approving condition took less time to begin exploring the objects while they were hidden from view, engaged in more blind manipulations, and were more likely to guess the identity of the hidden object at the end of the twenty-second trial. Children in the aloof-critical condition, by contrast, showed significantly less task-related curiosity and exploratory behavior.

Some of the signals children get about the value of a "curious stance" come from clues that are even more opaque than nods and smiles. For instance, researchers have shown that preschoolers ask significantly more questions when they receive informative answers (Endsley and Clarey 1975; Chouinard 2007; Harris 2012). One explanation for this finding is that children persist in getting more and more information when they can. In this view, their persistence is a sign of their interest. But it also suggests that when they get answers to their questions, they take it as a subtle signal that it's fine to ask questions. Zimmerman and Pike (1972) divided thirty-six disadvantaged second graders into four conditions based on teacher attitudes toward question asking: modeling plus praise, praise only, no model, and no praise. In the modeling-plus-praise condition, teachers demonstrated and encouraged brainstorming questions in response to stories read as a class. Students in this condition asked significantly more questions when prompted on a variety of follow-up tests. This response transfer provides some evidence that the effects of encouraging curiosity can be generalized to other teachers, settings, and tasks, though the effect was not strong. One might go further and say that while we have good evidence of the power of encouraging questions and exploration, we know very little about how long such an influence lasts, or under what conditions. If you encourage children at 10 A.M. to look in a box, are they likely to ask questions at 2 P.M.? If they are encouraged to explore objects in science class, are they also more likely to explore books during library? These questions remain to be answered.

Meanwhile, we have some evidence that illuminates why children are so responsive to environmental clues. It seems that as children get older, anxiety continues to be one of the levers that controls the expression of curiosity. In principle, there are a variety of explanations for why the presence or absence of encouraging smiles and words might affect how much a child explores her environment. It might simply be that most children are obedient, and wait for a sign that the adults around them condone their exploration. However, we have evidence that in fact there is a somewhat deeper mechanism at work. Recall that toddlers (and mice) are more likely to explore the environment when, for a variety of reasons, they are less anxious. The evidence suggests that early in life, this sense of security or insecurity emerges, in a large part, as a function of a baby's attachment to his or her mother. But as children get older, in addition to that underlying base of security or its opposite, they may also respond to situational triggers of anxiety. For instance, the anxiety of an angry teacher may have a strong effect on their behavior. Some evidence for this comes from a study done with subjects from the other end of the developmental spectrum, college students. Peters (1978) measured the curiosity level (considered as a trait) in college students. Then she surveyed the students to identify which teachers had a reputation for creating a threatening classroom atmosphere, and which did not. Then she compared the number of questions asked in the lectures of the two groups. In the low-threat condition, students with high trait curiosity asked five times as many questions as those with low trait curiosity. In the high-threat condition, however, this difference disappeared and counts of questions asked dwindled. Apparently, activating anxiety inhibited exploration more strongly than constitutional curiosity encouraged it. In other words, when students are in a learning situation that makes them nervous, their curiosity is depressed. Though the primary focus here is on preschool and school-age children, Peters's research suggests that anxiety is a powerful moderator of exploration and that teachers can be one source of such anxiety. Now back to the early years.

WHEN PEOPLE AND OBJECTS MIX

By the time children are five they appear in many ways to be fairly autonomous. They can dress themselves, help out with family chores, and seem to a great extent to already have a distinctive approach to the world. They are outgoing or shy, talkative or quiet, engaged or less so. They can use language for a wide range of purposes, and in our culture, at least, many are reading avidly by this age. They also, by five, have vast experience with the world of objects and events. They have interests, and often some expertise. Five-year-olds may know a lot about dinosaurs, tools, farm animals, books, and some of them about caring for younger siblings. And yet their interactions are still infused with the cognitive style and intellectual stance of adults. Moreover, the influence of adults seems to last. In one study researchers gave mothers a fully assembled Tinkertoy model and another full set of parts to make a copy of it (Laosa 1978). They then asked each mother to teach her child how to make a model like the one already assembled. Some mothers used questions and supportive comments to guide their children through the process, while other mothers simply demonstrated what to do and offered directive comments. Later these same children showed differences in the way they approached a subsequent task.

The influence adults have in shaping children's engagement with the world around them is not always simple or direct, either. A good example of this comes from research comparing the ways in which rural and urban children use their home environments. Perhaps unsurprisingly, children who live in rural areas feel greater freedom to explore their neighborhoods, and exert more autonomy within those environments. At first glance this seems both self-evident and unavoidable—a difference imposed by the physical characteristics of the two sorts of environments—cities present hazards that limit autonomy, while rural areas seem open, safe, and invite more kinds of exploration. However, when children are interviewed, it becomes clear that their eagerness to explore is shaped as much or more by what adults have told them as it is by the intrinsic characteristics of the environment. Girls, for instance, describe much less interest in the more natural places near their homes, and much more interest in stores and other gathering places. In his study of children's experience of place, Roger Hart asked the children to take him in narrated tours of their favorite places. It became clear that even the boys who were fascinated by the woods, and described it as one of their favorite places, rarely or never went into those woods. The cautionary things their parents had said seemed to offer a powerful constraint on their willingness to investigate.

To sum up so far, from infancy until at least the elementary school years, children look to adults for cues about how to respond to objects and events, how to interpret the things they witness and experience, and how to interact with the world. The cues children take from adults are powerful in the moment, but have long-term impact as well. Moreover, the influence extends beyond problem solving. Children also learn from the adults around them what kind of stance they can or should take toward the objects and events they encounter as the day unfolds. This is particularly important when it comes to inquiry. Because, as should be clear by now, inquiry does not bubble up simply because a child is intrinsically curious. Nor does it simply erupt when something in the environment is particularly intriguing. Whether a child has the impulse, day in and day out, to find out more, ebbs and flows as a result of the adults who surround her.

THE COMPLEXITY OF ADULT RESPONSES

All too often, in a political landscape where good teachers are stars and heroes, and bad teachers are villains (*Waiting for Superman* is one vivid example of the zeitgeist), we tend to think that nice teachers encourage curiosity, and the mean, derelict ones do not. However, the range of adult responses when a child is in the presence of intriguing or alluring objects cannot be boiled down to friendly or unfriendly. Tessa van Schijndel and her colleagues (2010) brought preschool children to an interactive science museum to participate in two different exhibits, one involving rolling cylinders down a ramp, and the other in which the child sits on a chair that spins, holding blocks of varying weights to find out what factors influence the speed of the spin. As children went through these two exhibits, a coach used one of three styles to interact with them: a minimal but encouraging response; a kind of scaffolding in which the coach elaborated what the child did or said; and an explanatory style in which the coach offered the child information about the inner workings of the experience (why the cylinders rolled at different rates, and why the weight of the block interacts with where the child held her arms while spinning). How actively each child explored the exhibit depended on what the coach said to her. Children explored the rolling cylinder exhibit much more thoroughly when the coach simply smiled and nodded, and said little. The children who heard explanations from the coaches were the least likely to try out different things with the cylinders. A somewhat different picture emerged when it came to the spinning-chair exhibit. Children investigated the blocks and their own gestures (holding their arms close to the torso, or spreading them out like wings) with more gusto when the coach scaffolded the child's behavior, making small suggestions for further experimentation or otherwise leading the child to slightly more complex interactions. Though the two exhibits seemed to call for slightly different behavior from the adults, explanation never seemed like the best way to get children to investigate.

Studies show that one adult can influence a single child's expression of curiosity. But a lot of the time children are not alone in a room with one adult. Often they are one of many children, and a lot is going on. Certainly this is the case in day care centers, where there may be one adult for every seven children, or schools, where there is often one adult for every twenty-three children. Are children influenced by an adult when things are noisier, messier, and more interpersonally diluted? Interested in finding out whether the adult's smiles or frowns would affect children's curiosity in a classroom setting, my student Hilary Hackmann and I built our own curiosity box based on the one used by Henderson and Moore (1980). The box had eighteen little drawers in it, and in each drawer was a small, novel object. We placed the box in kindergarten and third-grade classrooms and watched to see who came up to it, how many drawers each child opened, and how long the child spent examining the objects inside the drawers. Though we had shared the common assumption that children tended to be less inquisitive about the environment as they get older, our data provided a different picture. We found that, on the whole, the nine-year-old children were as curious as the five- and six-year-old children. Just as many third graders as kindergarteners came up to the box, opened the drawers, and examined the objects. However, not all classrooms invited the same levels of curiosity. In some rooms, many children approached the box, and did so quickly, taking their time to examine several objects. Upon walking into their classroom and seeing the odd box, children said things like, "What is that?" "Whoa, where did that come from?" "It says OK to touch, so I'm going to touch it" (in response to a small sign on it that said "OK to touch"). In other rooms, regardless of grade, few children investigated the box.

This suggests that the classroom environment is as important an ingredient in a child's curiosity as his or her age. But what is it in a classroom that serves to encourage or discourage investigation? We found that there was a direct link between how much the teacher smiled and talked in an encouraging manner and the level of curiosity the children in the room expressed. Teacher, rather than grade, explained the difference between the classrooms where children examined the box and classrooms where it was left relatively untouched. We found a clear link between the number of smiles and encouraging words the teacher said about the box, and the level of curiosity the children expressed. Teachers in classrooms where we saw lots of box examination said things like, "What do you have there? "Wow, I think you really like that thing. That's cool. Look at that." On the other hand, in the classrooms where we saw relatively little box exploration, teachers said things like, "Rachel, turn your body around and do your work" (when Rachel had turned to look at the box), or "I saw some of you up there by the box, and you owe me Friday's English."

Smiling and encouraging children to explore are two of the ways teachers influence children's curiosity. But as we know from a vast array of research, including some I have already described, adults influence children in other ways as well. Children watch adults react to objects and events, they listen to what adults say to other people, and they watch what adults do. Imagine a child who has two teachers. One asks questions, not only to the child, but to others as well, or even to herself. She looks things up in books. She looks out the window with interest; she watches as her students make things, or play with one another. Now imagine this child in the room just down the hall. This teacher rarely studies the children while they are playing. She knows a lot of answers but seems uninterested in things she doesn't know about. She is eager to steer the group away from topics she knows little about. She does not inquire about the children's experiences beyond school. She is warm, friendly, and energetic, eager for her students to learn what she has planned for them, but rarely shows an appetite for what she doesn't know. Would a child's own curiosity be influenced differently by these two teachers? Might not a teacher's expression of curiosity provide an invitation or a prohibition?

In order to answer that question, my student Madelyn Labella and I designed a study in which eight- and nine-year-olds were brought into a lab, one at a time, to do a science activity (Engel 2011). When the child came into the room, materials were set out on a table, and a worksheet lay nearby. Madelyn explained that she and the child were going to do a fun and interesting activity and then fill out the worksheet that went with it. Madelyn modeled her behavior on the prototype of a friendly, knowledgeable, and warm science teacher. As the child embarked on the activity, Madelyn explained various concepts, gave gentle guidance, and made friendly conversation. The activity, called "bouncing raisins," required the child to mix baking soda, vinegar, and water and then drop raisins into the mixture. In this mixture, little bubbles form on the raisin and the raisin eventually rises to the surface. As the activity unfolded, Madelyn directed the child's attention to the instructions on the worksheet and helped him or her fill out the questions at the bottom of the sheet, making the format of the session closely comparable to a common school science activity.

As they neared the end of the activity, Madelyn did one of two things. For half the children she said something like, "You know what? I wonder what would happen if we dropped one of these (picking up a Skittle from the table) in the liquid instead of a raisin?" With the other half of the children, instead of picking up a Skittle and dropping it in, she simply cleaned the work area up a little, commenting as she did it, "I'm just going to tidy up a bit. I'll put these materials over here." In other words, some of the children saw the adult/teacher show interest in exploring further and deviating from the script, while others did not. Then Madelyn left the room, claiming that she had to get some materials for the next activity and that she would be back in a few moments. As she left, she said, "Feel free to do whatever you want while you are waiting for me. You can use the materials more, or draw with these crayons, or just wait. Whatever you want to do is fine." Then she walked out. The camera, which had been on for the whole time, remained on so that we could watch to see what the children did when left alone.

Children who had seen Madelyn deviate from the task to satisfy her own curiosity were much more likely to play with the materials. They dropped raisins, Skittles, or one of the other items into the liquid. They stirred it, added other liquids, and peered into the beaker to see what was happening.

But children who had seen her tidy up instead tended do very little while they waited. They'd stand with their hands in their pockets, look up at the ceiling, or gaze away into space. Some of them fidgeted (one spent a fair amount of time fidgeting with the zipper on his jeans). But overall they showed little interest in the materials they had used with Madelyn, and little inclination to do more with those materials. Watching the tapes of all the children, one can see a pattern that fleshes out the statistical results. Children who had seen Madelyn do something unexpected and off-script, who had seen her display a little burst of curiosity (albeit a fairly tame "burst"), connected to the materials, and the activity, with more engagement and interest. In an experiment like this, even if someone other than Madelyn had interacted with the children, it would be impossible for the experimenter to be blind to the condition. One cannot intentionally express or suppress curiosity without knowing it. Worried that something about Madelyn's behavior other than the manipulation was signaling to the children whether they should or shouldn't focus on the materials in her absence, we asked outside coders to rate thin slices of the tapes. There were no differences between her behavior in the curiosity condition and the tidy-up condition, providing us with additional certainty that when an adult expresses curiosity, it affects children.

It seems clear that adults have a variety of ways of signaling to children that they can or can't, should or shouldn't explore objects. And those signals affect children. But it's not just what an adult expresses to children about their behavior that matters. After all, when children and adults are together, not everything the grown-ups do is in response to what the children are doing. Parents and teachers are not always gearing their behavior directly toward the children they are with. They are to a great degree just being themselves. They lift lids, tinker, look things up, watch things carefully, and ask questions. Or they don't. In fact, many adults do not express much curiosity in their everyday lives. There are plenty of adults who rarely want to find out about something new, or probe beneath the surface. Why wouldn't this have an impact on children?

Parents who read are more likely to have children who read; parents who yell or hit are more likely to have children who yell and hit; and adults who do things for others are more likely to have children who do things for others. Often people have attributed this influence to a genetic link between parent and child, or in some cases to a more complicated route of influence (children whose parents hit them, for instance, may internalize feelings of anger, which in turn causes them to be angry and aggressive when they get older). However, experiments have shown that there is, in addition, a very direct modeling effect. When children watch someone hitting an inflatable clown, they are much more likely to act aggressively within the next day or so (Bandura, Ross, and Ross 1963). Similarly, children watching an adult help someone else, by giving him money, candy, or sharing a toy, are more likely to be helpful and prosocial themselves both right afterward, and for several days. Children who see their parents reason out loud about the feelings of others are more likely to act empathically and eventually to reason about other people, as well. In other words, children watch and learn from adult behavior in the short run and in the long run. And now we have some evidence that the same is true when it comes to children's interest in finding out more. When parents give their children some freedom to wander, explore, and tinker, it makes a difference. When parents express fear or disapproval of inquiry, that too has an effect. But parents are just the beginning. When it comes to their urge to know more, children at least as old as nine continue to be extremely susceptible to the behavior of adults. And here it's worth remembering that children learn a lot at home from behaviors not directed toward them, and that at school the same is true.

Oddly, there has not been very much research examining how teachers' own habits and dispositions influence the children they teach. This is a surprising gap, given the amount of time children spend with their teachers, and the power those teachers would seem to have on the everyday experience of most children. The impact of an adult's behavior may not always be direct. In our study children didn't copy Madelyn, but they expressed more or less interest as a result of her behavior. But indirect influence may be just as formative. I have been trying to build a case that one of the things children learn from adults is what kind of intellectual stance to take—contemplative or not, interested or not, detached or not. It seems that adults mold the stance children take toward events around them, but also model a stance as well.

In everyday life, adult responses are probably usually fleeting, subtle, and buried in the flow of other activities. In order to think about how the experimental findings can illuminate what happens to real children in real homes and schools, one must imagine these influences cast against a noisy and busy backdrop. Consider the following two contrasting examples.

Kindergarteners are sitting on a rug, while their teacher leads them through various morning routines—an alphabet song, choosing children to serve snack that day, reading through a poem, and filling in the calendar. When they get to the calendar, the teacher points to one child and says, "Hank, why don't you go to the window and tell us what the weather is today, so we can put it on our calendar (here she points to several magnetic pieces that can be affixed on the board—one of a sun, one of a cloud, one of rain, and so on). Hank happily gets up and makes his way over to the window. He looks out and calls back, "It's sunny!" The teacher smiles approvingly and says, "Great. Now come on back and put the sun on today's box." But Hank hesitates. "Wait a minute! I see snow! Can it be sunny and snowy at the same time?" The teacher, who is extremely kind and gentle and never seems to get flustered or raise her voice, says, "C'mon Hank. We've got to keep going. Come put the sun on the calendar." The prohibition is quite subtle. But it is effective. Hank is discouraged from looking at the sky longer, or puzzling through the mystery of simultaneous sun and snow. He comes back and takes his place on the rug, and the group moves on to the next activity.

Compare that to the following exchange, also from a kindergarten classroom. Three girls are washing paintbrushes at the sink, while chatting happily. One of them suddenly says, "Hey, look. The paints are mixing! They're mixed!" One of the other girls says, "It should be purple. Is it purple?" At this point they are quite excited and they are letting out little shrieks of glee at the paint that is running off the brushes and blending in a stream. The teacher walks to the sink, peering over their heads. She is smiling, and then says, "Oh, look at that. That's amazing. Did they mix right away, or did it happen down at the bottom of the stream? I wonder what color it would be if you washed all the brushes at once?" This is just a passing moment in a day filled with lessons, schedules, and activities. But the difference between the responses of the two teachers will help shape the inquiry that will or won't unfold in the two classrooms.

Some of the studies I have described so far identify particular behaviors that influence a child's inquiry. In some cases adults subtly invite or discourage investigation, and in other cases their own expressions of inquiry set an important example. But of course in real life, these different avenues of influence converge and blend to create an overall environment that may be more or less conducive to children's curiosity. And in real life, whatever forces create an environment that invites or discourages exploration, that environment is likely to be fairly stable. There is likely to be something of a pattern to this influence. Consider the following example of a child from the now distant past, which illustrates the idea vividly.

By the time he was eight, Gas hated school, chafing at the dull and constant repetition of information and mundane tasks. He may have hated lessons, but he loved information. He was a dedicated and tireless collector of postage stamps, birds' eggs, and insects. From the time he was five, he was completely preoccupied with the outdoors, spending hours and hours in the woods near his house, collecting animal shells, interesting plants, and bugs. He was an inventor as well and spent hours creating secret codes. Delighted by any hint of mystery or surprise, he sometimes staged surprises to impress his family—once he hid some apples in a cupboard, and, hours later, pretended to discover them, as if the fruit had magically appeared in such an unlikely place. He got his nickname because of the laboratory he and his older brother set up in a shed next to their house. He spent hours there doing "experiments"— concocting potions, trying to make things bubble, smoke, and change consistency. He seemed to have an inexhaustible appetite for these investigations.

One day, when he was out in the woods near his house, collecting bugs, he found a beetle he hadn't seen before. He crouched down to examine it—as usual, looking closely and thoroughly at a creature that interested him. But, just then, another bug crawled into his line of vision, this one equally enthralling. Gas needed to inspect both—how could he grab the new bug without losing the one he already had? Quickly, he did the only possible thing to ensure that he could fully examine both new specimens—he popped the first beetle into his mouth, freeing his hands to capture the second bug. Unfortunately for him, the beetle, trapped and in danger, defensively released a noxious liquid onto his tongue. It was worth it, he recalled later. He got to study both bugs.

When the lives of famously curious people, like Charles Darwin, are examined, it's not unusual to find signs that they were more curious than others, even as young children. Darwin is no exception. He not only had an unusually large appetite for investigations; he also, early on, was drawn particularly to the natural world. Considering the lab where he and his brother did their "work," one might even argue that he had an inherent attraction to science and its methods. However, these powerful traits, which he seemed to possess along with his dark hair and his high intelligence, do not tell the whole story. Because a closer look suggests that those around him were issuing invitations at every turn. Darwin grew up in a permissive and lively household. As a young child he was encouraged to explore the land around his family's gracious rural home in England. It seems clear that his parents were not only tolerant of his investigations, but helped him pursue his interests. They provided him with space and equipment, and showed great amusement when he carried out his various tricks and surprises. He also enjoyed plenty of free time to pursue his interests, and lots of freedom to wander outside and investigate. In other words, just as Mozart's prodigious musical talents were fostered by the adults around him who were musical, and who took great lengths to nurture his talents, so too Darwin's appetite for novelty and information were encouraged at every turn. He is just one example, albeit an important one, of the idea that invitations or their opposite may provide a formative influence on the robustness of a child's determination to pursue questions, and stick with a line of inquiry.

5

Curiosity Goes to School

WHEN I WAS six I attended a red one-room schoolhouse, less than half a mile from my home. It was the same place my stepfather had gone to school in the 1930s, and thirty-odd years later it hadn't changed much. My desk was one of five, in the first-grade row, all the way to the teacher's left. Then came second grade, then third, and finally the very mature and accomplished fourth graders, all the way to the right. Our teacher, Mrs. Grubb, stood at the front of the classroom and told us what to do. She'd tell the first grade which page to read aloud, the second grade which page to read silently, the third grade which page of questions to fill in, and the fourth grade what section of the textbook to write a paragraph about.

My grade worked on the Dick and Jane readers, did addition and subtraction problems, colored in maps of the United States of America, and once a week we got to draw. I have a vivid memory of the day we were handed a sheet of shiny paper and four little plastic cups filled with brightly colored gelatinous matter, something like pudding, for finger painting. I mixed my colors until they were a muddy brown. But Donna Hildreth, suave and sophisticated, three rows over in the fourth grade, used yellow. I was sick with envy. Once when a child didn't keep her desk tidy, Mrs. Grubb made her stand in the garbage can during snack time. Mrs. Grubb's solid form was matched by her phlegmatic and dull manner. I was saucier than many of the children, more comfortable with adults. I once asked her whether her name meant food, or dirt. That was the closest I came to getting in trouble in first grade. But she wasn't interested enough in what I said to get mad. She shot me a dark look and directed my attention back to my *Fun with Dick and Jane* page. I cannot recall one interesting lesson or activity that whole year. But she was kind, and relaxed. One May day she announced that we would have no lessons, so that we could all go out and pick milkweed with her, in the fields beyond the school. And her indifference to learning had a silver lining—we had lots of freedom.

Here is what I learned a lot about that year. Worms, and penny candy. At lunch she let us walk the four minutes to the general store, which was also a post office. There was a penny candy case there, and I had a charge account. So each day at 11:30 I'd hurry over to the store to buy some candy. I knew every single kind of candy—not only how it tasted, but what it cost. Tootsie Rolls and Mary Janes, a penny. Heath Bars, ten cents. Red licorice rolls, five cents. The list was long and often shifting, and I took endless interest in thinking about the permutations.

I also learned a great deal about all my neighbors' business, since so much of it was transacted at the counter of the store. I knew who was sick, who was getting married, who had not paid a bill, and who was behind in his harvest. The other topic I mastered that year was worms.

At Sag School, everyone got a chance, about once a month, to present something at show-and-tell. This was pure ritual. Children were rarely interested in one another's show-and-tells, and Mrs. Grubb made no pretence of genuine interest in our demonstrations—it was just one of the regular features of our weekly schedule. One weekend, Saree Babinski and I found ourselves enthralled by a series of worm experiments we conducted in the field behind her house. We stretched them, we cut them, we buried them in mud, and we tried to feed them cookies. We couldn't get enough of the worms. And we brought our experiment to Sag school for our turn at show-and-tell. As I recall, the other students were transfixed, as much by our unexpected zeal for cruelty and guts as they were by the worms themselves. Mrs. Grubb sat at her desk, bored and tolerant, as always.

One might think that school is the place where curiosity blossoms. Before children enter kindergarten, learning is informal, and embedded in the context of everyday life. While at home, toddlers and preschoolers rarely do things solely in order to learn. Quite the opposite, young children do things they want to or must do (play baseball, clear the table, deliver newspapers, wait while their parents talk, argue with siblings, sit in the car, or pretend to be Batman). They acquire skills and knowledge as a by-product of those necessary or pleasurable activities. Adults don't often deliberately teach them, either. Mostly teaching, like learning, is a spandrel, the unintended effect of some more practical pursuit. Take, for example, learning to talk. Parents don't set out to give their children language lessons. Most adults, in most parts of the world, do not talk to their children in order to teach them how to speak. Catherine Snow has shown that parents talk to their infants and toddlers because they want conversational partners. Once their children are conversational partners, even rudimentarily so, somewhere between eighteen and twenty-eight months, their parents have added a new set of goals to their verbal exchanges—they talk to their children because they want to control them, tell them something, or share experience. Young children learn a great deal of other things, besides language, while they are at home. Whether helping out or having fun, they eagerly seek skills and knowledge about whatever interests them (bugs, manipulating adults, fairy tales, trucks, older siblings, or angry birds). When you think about it, a huge amount of knowledge and skill is acquired as a by-product of other pursuits. This kind of learning often seems accidental—no one sets out to teach children the ins and outs of laundry. They just want children to help them do the laundry. Rarely do parents think through all they want children to learn about family dynamics—parents explain, or children decipher. But no one sets out to deliver coherent, well-planned lessons on what makes the family explode, go mute, or happily coexist.

Most of us assume that when children go to school, they carry with them the tools for learning that they have already used to such good effect. We implicitly expect schools to build on the learning skills children have used in their homes. It's not unreasonable to expect that the voracious curiosity that is so apparent in toddlers and preschoolers, and which drives so much learning, would be a driving force once children get to kindergarten.

It's not unreasonable. But is it true? Do children bring their curiosity, and its tools, to school with them? Are students curious, albeit in a different way, when they are learning addition, phonics, geography, algebra, cell division, the writings of J. D. Salinger, and the history of World War II?

ARE CHILDREN CURIOUS AT SCHOOL?

It's not easy to get an accurate or reliable picture of children's curiosity at school. To begin with, the data are, almost by definition, descriptive. We can watch to see how many questions children ask, how often they tinker, open, take apart, or watch—but it's virtually impossible to track the thoughts of twenty-three children during a classroom activity. However, we can measure how much curiosity children *express* while they are in school.

When I started doing research in this area, the first thing I wanted to know was what kinds of curiosity were expressed in classrooms—I wanted to know whether some children seemed much more curious than others, whether certain activities or places in a classroom seemed to elicit more curiosity than others, and whether there were noticeable differences between individual classrooms. To answer these questions my students and I decided to compare the bookends of elementary school—kindergarten and fifth grade. We wanted to find out whether children expressed curiosity when they began grade school, and how different things looked by the time children were finished. We recorded ten hours in each of five kindergarten classrooms and five fifth-grade classrooms. Each time we visited, we recorded the children for two hours. Because we were interested in whether we'd find differences between various areas of the classrooms, we recorded samples of circle time, table time, and free play. In analyzing the data, we chose to count three types of behavior as episodes of curiosity: questions, intent and directed gazing, and manipulating objects. All behaviors that were in response to the same stimulus, and occurred contiguously, were considered part of one episode. However, in keeping with the notion that curiosity is almost always a convergence—someone's internal experience meeting up with some particular stimulus in the world—each of

these was context dependent. So, for instance, not all questions expressed curiosity—only those that sought new information about an
idea, an object, or a person. Not all staring expressed curiosity, only
when children seemed to be studying something out of interest. Not
all handling of objects involved exploration. Though these differences
are subtle, it turns out they are not that hard to detect. Three students
were trained to code the data, and achieved a high rate of inter-coder
reliability. It turned out it's not all that hard to spot curiosity in action. But what we found took us aback. Or rather what we didn't find.

On average, in any given kindergarten classroom, there were 2.36
episodes of curiosity in a two-hour stretch. Expressions of curiosity were
even scarcer in the older grades. The average number of episodes in a
fifth-grade classroom was 0.48. In other words, on average, classroom
activity over a two-hour stretch included less than one expression of
curiosity. In the schools we studied, the expression of curiosity was, at
best, infrequent. Nine of the ten classrooms had at least one two-hour
stretch where there were no expressions of curiosity. In other words, we
rarely saw children take things apart, ask questions about topics either
children or adults had raised, watch interesting phenomena unfold in
front of their eyes, or in any way show signs that there were things they
were eager to know more about it, much less actually follow up with any
visible sort of investigation, whether in words or actions. The easiest interpretation is that children are simply less curious by the time they are
in kindergarten and grow even less so by the end of grade school. However, the data don't support that conclusion. For one thing, we saw as
much variation between classrooms as we did between grade levels.

One kindergarten classroom had an average of 0.60 episodes of curiosity per two-hour stretch, while another had a high of 5.2. In two of
the fifth-grade classrooms we saw no expressions of curiosity during
the five visits, while in one classroom there was a total of seven episodes
on two occasions. The numerical differences between classrooms and
between grades may seem small, until you begin to visualize them in
real classrooms. Of the ten classrooms included in this study, nine had
more than one two-hour stretch without one expression of curiosity—and
that was in classrooms containing anywhere from sixteen to twenty-
four children. In the most concrete terms, imagine the difference between a classroom where children might spend the majority of their

time without engaging in, or hearing others engage in, any open in-quiry, and compare this to a classroom where such inquiry might be part of the mix once or twice in every two-hour stretch.

Our discovery, that there is little curiosity in grade school, is confirmed by the work others have done. Recall that Tizard and Hughes fitted preschoolers with tape recorders to get a picture of how many questions they asked at home with their parents (the answer, as described in Chapter 3, is that preschoolers ask a lot of questions). However, Tizard and Hughes also recorded those same children when they went to preschool (1984). Once inside a school building, the picture changes dramatically. While the preschoolers they studied asked, on average, twenty-six questions per hour at home, that rate dropped to two per hour when the children were in school. Even Judith Lindfor's somewhat rosier data are not that rosy. In her data, she reported that less than a third of the questions kindergartners asked were expressions of curiosity (Lindfors 1987).

When older children are asked about their enthusiasm for domains like science, many indicate a great interest in the topic itself, but say they have little interest for the way it is presented in school. In other words, observations as well as interviews and surveys suggest that though children are curious, students are not.

WHAT CURIOSITY LOOKS AND SOUNDS LIKE

Though curiosity was scarce in our data, it bubbled up now and then. And these occurrences offer intriguing clues to what it is children want to know about, and how they go about satisfying their curiosity, while at school.

There were, broadly speaking, two kinds of curiosity episodes—those that emerged in the context of a classroom activity, and those that erupted around the margins of the classroom.

It was not unusual for a child to ask a question about something the teacher had presented. For instance, in one of the kindergarten classes, a teacher was reading a story about plants.

> Little boy, pointing with his finger to an illustration: Are Venus flytraps really alive? Do they really catch?

Teacher: Yes, they can really catch flies. That's how they eat.

The children ask several more questions about Venus flytraps. After the third question, the teacher suggests that they finish the story and then they can go back and study the pages again.

In another more extended example of this, a fifth-grade group was learning how to bisect an angle using a compass and straightedge. A boy asked, "Is it possible to trisect an angle?" The teacher asked the rest of the children, "What do you think? Is it possible to trisect an angle?" Several of the children answered simultaneously, "Yes." The teacher replied, "Actually, it has proven to be impossible." Several of the children then proposed different ways you could trisect an angle. The teacher then responded, "I'm not surprised. It's natural to try to do something if you've been told it's impossible," at which point they move on with the lesson. Several things stand out about this interaction. The child's question follows directly from the material the teacher wants to focus on. In other words, the child's curiosity is topic relevant, from the teacher's point of view. Another teacher might easily have simply answered his question, but this teacher instead invited the other children into the exchange by repeating his question to them. Then, when they suggested yes, she suggested that they were wrong, that what they thought was possible was not. However, they persisted, offering several possible solutions. At this point the teacher did an interesting thing—she condoned their efforts, without actually developing or expanding those efforts. But even the limited way that the teacher and other children expanded on the child's original question was the exception in our data, not the rule.

Sometimes children expressed curiosity to one another about the lesson, or about one another's work on the lesson. For instance two girls in a kindergarten classroom were sitting at a worktable with a little boy who had colored over the words he had written on a piece of paper. They wanted to know what his words said, and were peering over his shoulder trying to read the words beneath the layer of crayon. The teacher came by and reminded them to return to their own work.

At other times the children's exchanges about curriculum-related activities develop more fully and often without any input from adults.

The following exchange occurred between two kindergarteners who were sitting at a table drawing dinosaurs:

BOY 1: So I would outrun him? (referring to the T. rex his friend had colored)
BOY 2: Yes, but you can't outrun a megaraptor."
BOY 1: Can a cheetah outrun a raptor?"
BOY 2: Probably not.
BOY 1: It could win, 'cause cheetahs weren't alive when dinosaurs were alive, so no one really knows, right?

Several important features are illustrated in this example. Children do seek new information in a classroom setting. Moreover, they are able to collaborate in building new knowledge—answering one another's questions, and extending the inquiry. In this case it seems that Boy 1 is the persistent one. He keeps posing the questions, and in the end insists that there is more to be learned. In fact, when he proposes that there are some things no one can know, he indicates his sense that curiosity can only be satisfied with authentic information. He implicitly indicates his sense that just because a response qualifies linguistically as an answer doesn't mean it adds to one's knowledge.

We encountered one unexpected and intriguing wrinkle when we closely examined the children's questions. Some of the time they expressed curiosity as a speculative statement. For instance, one kindergartener, while sitting in circle time, said, "I'll bet if we jump hard enough, we can make the floor shake." A fifth grader said, while sitting at a worktable, "I think if I counted all day long, I still won't get to googol." Just as scientists often cloak their questions in predictions, so too do young children. However, as far as we could tell, these speculations lived and died with the response of adults in the room. In our data, teachers rarely expanded upon children's speculations. It was not unusual to hear a child express interest in something, and for the teacher to ignore the interest or explain that it was off topic. For instance, the following exchange occurred during a science class in one of the fifth-grade groups.

CHILD: I've been a little curious this class. What is that? (points to some words on the board) I can't understand it.

TEACHER: Um, that was for another class. (returns attention to the topic she had been focusing on)

CURIOSITY IN THE MARGINS

While children did express curiosity about the lessons and material presented by their teachers, they also expressed curiosity, alone and with one another, about topics and events that were peripheral to the curriculum. Often these exchanges seemed to occur on the margins of the daily activities. For instance, one little boy in a kindergarten classroom was milling around during a free-play period. He stopped and looked at a globe, turning it a few times. Then he said out loud, to no one in particular, "Is it possible to survive on Antarctica"? No one answered this question, or in any way picked up on it, partly because though other people were around, he was not doing anything collaborative at that moment. A little girl in one of the kindergarten classes found that dried glue was all over her hands after an art activity. She tried pulling it, then picking it, and finally found that if she rubbed her hands together over the paper, the glue would come off. As she did this she noticed what was falling on the paper and exclaimed "I've made sprinkles!"

Sometimes these exchanges that occurred on the margins involved more than one child and lasted for more than one utterance or short sequence of gestures. Three little girls standing by their cubbies in a kindergarten classroom are talking—one of the girls is wearing a watch.

GIRL 1: (holding her watch up to her ear) I want to hear it.
GIRL 2: Me second.
GIRL 3: Me third.
Girl 1 eventually holds the watch up to one friend's ear, and then another's. Both listen intently. The girl only pulls the watch away when each of her friends makes it clear by her expression that she has heard the ticking. They each listen a second time.
GIRL 1: I think I know what time it is.
GIRL 2: You're supposed to look at the hands.
GIRL 1: I know that. I am.

This exchange illustrates two important aspects of our data. First, children often express curiosity in the context of social interaction. In this example, for instance, an observer would be hard put to say whether the two girls wanted to listen to the first girl's watch because of her interest in the sound of the ticking or their eagerness to bond with her. However, once having put her ear to the watch, the first little girl became visibly absorbed, first by the sound and then by the challenge of figuring out how to read the time. What may begin as purely social quickly becomes, in addition, a chance to find something out about the world. Second, by expressing curiosity with one another, children are able not only to satisfy their curiosity through their interactions with objects and information, but via one another. This finding is supported by the study I previously described, in which my student and I placed a curiosity box in the classrooms. We found that children in the third grade were much more likely to explore the box in groups than when alone.

Children seem to be curious about a wide range of phenomena—they inquire about things they are told, as well as about the objects they find around them. What we saw very little of, which surprised us, especially in the kindergarten, was any extended exploration of the physical world. For instance, in one kindergarten there was a shelf with two brightly colored microscopes on it. In the nearly fifteen hours of observation we conducted in that classroom, across an eight-week period, one child once went to the shelf, fiddled briefly with an eyepiece, and then put the microscope down. The exception to this general pattern occurred in every room where there was a terrarium or an aquarium. These two objects attracted steady attention—children watched and, in the case of the terrariums, touched, every time we observed. More typically, however, children explored conceptual domains (how did early man cross the earth, why do Band Aids say "moleskin," what is a snake likely to eat, do some people not believe in God, and so forth). In virtually every case where a physical object elicited inquiry, the inquiry quickly turned to a discussion of some more abstract aspect of the object, rather than a physical investigation of the object. There were several examples where a child or pair of children looked at an image (in a book, on the wall, or on a computer screen) and proceeded to discuss some interesting aspect of the image or, more typically, the meaning behind the image. For instance, one kindergarten student asked why there was an "A" next to the names of some of the children on an attendance sheet on the wall, which led to a discussion of what it means to be "absent." On another occasion a kindergarten girl asked a classmate why he put "bumps" on his drawing, leading him to explain why a dinosaur had bumps on his back.

Children were also curious about what they heard from others—particularly about the lives of their teachers. Of fifty-seven total episodes of curiosity, five concerned extended discussions that began when a teacher said something about his or her personal life. For instance, children wanted to know more when a teacher referred to something from her childhood, or mentioned a trip she had been on. In one fifth-grade classroom, the group had been in a meeting in which the teacher had mentioned riding her bike over the Thanksgiving break. After the meeting, while the children were getting ready for math, one boy said to another, "Did you know Miss Z rode a bike? Did she mean a bicycle or a motorcycle? You think she rides a motorcycle? She wears a leather jacket? She's a biker?" The other boy responded, "Yeah, you've got to wear those jackets on a motorbike, or you get windburn." The first boy returned to the key issue. "You think she rides all the time? You think she's a Hell Angel? You think they do bad stuff, or just ride around?"

One striking feature of these data was how curious children were about anything that seemed exotic to them. Topics that led to a series of eager questions included the Rocky Mountains, Pangaea, Venus flytraps, unusual geometric shapes, trips to Mexico, and the *Australopithecus* Lucy's descendants.

But their episodes of curiosity were brief, often fleeting. Some 78 percent of the curiosity episodes involved fewer than four conversational turns. We also timed these sequences, since we were interested in nonverbal inquiry. Not one episode lasted longer than six minutes, and all but three lasted less than three minutes. We never saw an episode of curiosity that led to a more structured classroom activity, or that redirected a classroom discussion for more than a few moments.

THE TEACHER'S ROLE

Though we found such a paucity of curiosity defined as episodes of inquiry, our transcripts were bursting with questions. To find out more about these questions we conducted a second analysis, in which we examined the frequency and kind of questions we heard. The most striking thing we learned is that most of the questions were asked by the teacher—in fact, overall, teachers asked almost twice as many questions as children did. We assigned each of the teachers' questions to one of six mutually exclusive categories:

Teacher Knows the Information: "When you divide twenty-four by eight, what do you get?"

Rhetorical Question: "Is that the way to enter this classroom?"

Open Ended: "If you were going to describe the way Cindy walked in this morning with a metaphor, what metaphor would you use?"

Seeks Child's Opinion/Preference: "Would you like to take the test before snack or after?"

Other: any of the teachers' questions that did not fall into the above four categories (there were very few of these, and they were not used in any further analyses).

By far the vast majority of the teachers' questions were either rhetorical, meant to guide children's behavior, or sought information that the teacher already possessed—reflecting what might be termed the "quiz model" of teaching, in which the teacher's question is an attempt to ascertain the child's knowledge of something. Most of the time these quiz questions were asked while the teacher was up at the board, or going over material the children were supposed to know.

Our impression was that most of the time teachers had very specific objectives for each stretch of time, and that a great deal of effort was put into keeping children on task and in reaching those objectives. (In the fifth grade this consisted of typical curricular goals such as mastering specific math skills, learning about particular events in history, or learning how to use various forms of grammar in writing.) Mastery rather than inquiry seemed to be the dominant goal for almost all the classrooms in which we observed. Often it seemed that finishing specific assignments (worksheets, writing assignments) was an even more salient goal than actually learning the material. In other words, the structure of the classroom made it clear that the educational activities we saw were not designed to encourage curiosity—nor were teachers using the children's curiosity as a guide to what and how to teach. However, as the numbers suggest, we did see small stretches of behavior, both linguistic and gestural, that revealed the children's interest in various topics, and gave some hints about how that interest manifests itself even in an environment not geared toward curiosity.

There were some examples of more lively hands-on activities in which teachers asked more open-ended questions. What was striking about many of these examples, however, is that while they reflected a different kind of question from the teacher, they didn't contain many questions from the children. We think we know why. In those situations it was still the teachers asking the questions—that is, there was little opportunity, given the volume of teacher questions, for children to pose their own questions. In other words, in the classrooms we visited, there was little or no evidence that an implicit or explicit goal of the curriculum was to help children pose questions. Either the teachers are posing questions to which they already know the answers, or they are posing genuine questions and hoping those questions will invite speculation and answers from the students.

For example, in one kindergarten a teacher walked into the room holding a clear plastic bag, which held water, algae, and a fish. Several children were immediately interested in the bag and its contents. One of the children quickly said, "I know what that is. That's an allergy in there." A little while later the teacher gathered the whole group to sit on a rug near the aquarium while she stood in front of them holding the clear bag.

TEACHER: What do you think is in here? What is this stuff?

CHILD 1: I know what it is. I know. It's a, it's a—it's a allergy.

TEACHER: It's an algae eater. Not an all*ergy* eater but an *algae* eater. Who knows what algae is?

CHILD 1: It's like stuff that get on there. (pointing to the glass walls of the aquarium)

TEACHER: Yup. Now is that dirt? What is it?

CHILD 1: Some people do have allergies.

TEACHER: That's true.

CHILD 1: Like allergies on a fish tank.

TEACHER: Some people do. That's true. What, what's in . . . what is this stuff? What actually is it?

CHILD 1: Allergies.

TEACHER: It's algae yes, but *is* . . . *it* . . . (drawn out as if to elicit a guess) dirt?

SIX CHILDREN TOGETHER: No!

TEACHER: Is . . . it . . . —what is it?

CHILD 1: It's like sand.

TEACHER: Same idea, but it's something else. Hm. Is it an animal?

CHILDREN: No!

TEACHER: No. Is it alive?

FOUR CHILDREN: No.

CHILDREN: Yeah!

TEACHER: Yup—it's plants. It's teeny teeny teeny tiny plants. And this kind of fish is a vegetarian. It's an herbivore. And it eats. . . . Now why haven't these (pointing to fish already in the fish tank), our two Oscars, the two big fish—why haven't they been eating it?

CHILD 1: Because they don't like it—

TEACHER: They're a different kind of eater. What kind are they?

CHILD 1: Meat eater.

TEACHER: Which is a—

CHILD 1: Plant eater! Carnivore!

TEACHER: Which is a carnivore. We have carnivores.

The group gets interrupted by a child's runny nose. When they return to the discussion they talk about some other fish in bags, which the teacher has brought in. One child says, "Are they called Oscarosaurs?"

The teacher continues with what she is saying. The child says, "But can there be a Oscarosaur? Can there by Algiosaurs?"

The teacher does not hear this or doesn't respond to it, and the group continues identifying the other fish she has brought in.

In this example the teacher brought in materials that immediately captured the children's interest and attention. She used what might be considered a kindergarten version of the Socratic method. She asks questions as a mechanism for getting the children to articulate or guess at information she wants them to know. In several places in this exchange, when the teacher's question didn't elicit the right answer, she asked a follow-up question that helped narrow the child's field of guesses. Such fine-tuning in the teacher's questions resembles scaffolding, in the sense that when the original question seems to be beyond the child's reach, the teacher provides a narrower question in order to make it more likely the child will guess the correct answer. In this passage the teacher asked ten questions (although four of them are variations aimed at eliciting the same target answer—that the algae is a plant). Up until the runny nose interruption, not one single question was posed by a child. Later, after the runny nose, a child did ask a question, wanting to know something about the connections between dinosaurs and the fish and algae they were viewing, but his questions remained unanswered.

This example illustrates an important but easily overlooked distinction between children's engagement and children's curiosity. A teacher can be talking about things that captivate the students, and the students can be deeply interested in a topic—quite engaged in a discussion or activity. But that in and of itself doesn't mean the children are asking questions, or that their questions reflect curiosity. In the example above, the children are clearly interested in the bag and its contents.

More typically, teachers deflected students' questions by reminding them to stay on task. For instance, two kindergarteners were sitting at a table tracing letters on a worksheet. At some point they paused in their tracing and began to look at some Popsicle sticks that were on the table, and on which were printed short simple riddles. The two girls began trying to decipher the words on the Popsicle sticks, at which point the teacher, who was also sitting at the table, helping another child, put the sticks in her pocket, saying "Let's put these away for now, so you can finish your letters." This example illustrates an interesting phenomenon that we saw several times—children expressing curiosity that was related in theme or skill to the teacher-led activity, but which was not directly part of the planned activity.

But what of older children? Once again, superficial appearances can be deceptive. Friendly teachers, hands-on activities, engaged children do not automatically mean curiosity is alive and well. Several years ago, I found myself sitting in the corner of one of the fifth-grade class-rooms where we were collecting data. A science class was unfolding. As I looked around, I saw many of the accoutrements of an apparently good classroom. There were posters on the walls showing reptiles and fish, a diagram of the periodic table, and a photograph of a scientist in a lab coat peering into a test tube. Along one counter were several microscopes, an empty terrarium, and some bins filled with droppers, measuring devices, and scoops. The desks formed a horseshoe, all facing the front, where the teacher's desk, a tall counter from which she could make demonstrations or set out materials, was placed. Behind the teacher's desk was a wall covered with a blackboard and a screen for showing movies or presentations.

Twenty-one boys and girls, all around ten years old, were sitting behind their desks. The teacher, Mrs. Parker, was explaining that the students were to form small groups and work on an activity to learn about how the ancient Egyptians had first invented wheels for transport in order to carry stones for their huge pyramids. She then organized the children into groups of three and invited each group to come up and get the materials they needed—a flat piece of wood with a metal eye at one end, some round wooden dowels, and a small measurement device that records newtons, the amount of force required to pull an object at a given speed for a given distance. The device had a string with a hook attached to it so that children could hitch it to the bar. She also gave each group a worksheet to fill out, which included step-by-step instructions about what to do with the materials, and a series of questions. Each group was to try pulling the wood piece along the floor, measuring how easily they could drag it both with and without dowels underneath it. By this time, it had become clear to me that the idea was for each group to "discover" that pulling the board was a lot easier with the dowels serving as wheels.

The children happily sorted into their assigned groups, materials in hand, and found a space on the floor to settle down and work. As they began completing the steps outlined on the worksheet, the noise level rose. Mrs. Parker wandered around, looking down on the groups from above, encouraging, giving tips, and reminding them to answer the questions on the worksheet. Several times she noted that they were "moving right along," "making good progress," or "getting there." I looked around the room to see who was pulling the wooden bar, who was recording the measurements, and who was watching quietly. Then I noticed one group that seemed to have forgotten the worksheet and was instead intrigued by the equipment. The children were trying to figure out different ways to use the bar with the spring scale attached—yanking, pulling, and even at one point holding the string up high so that the bar was simply swinging in the air, hanging from the device. Then they stood the dowels up like columns and tried to balance the bar on the dowels. Finally, they tried surfing the bar along the surface of the dowels, which they had laid down to create something like a conveyer belt. At this point, Mrs. Parker also noticed what they were doing. She called out to the group, over the heads of her students, in a loud, clear voice for all to hear, "OK, kids. Enough of that. I'll give you time to experiment at recess. This is time for science."

On the face of it, the teacher was doing just the kind of hands-on activity promoted by many educators. She was giving the students a chance to learn through active participation and to discover a principle for themselves rather than just memorize a rule or formula. And the children did indeed seem happy and engaged. But just when the children in one group began to make the activity their own by following their curiosity regarding the tools for the experiment—"What will happen if we pull it this way? What happens when we hang it that way?"—she stopped them. They had deviated from her plan. Ironically, this took place just as the children became interested in formulating and answering their own questions—when curiosity, the mechanism that underlies the best learning, kicked in.

And this brings us to a key finding of our research so far. Often the reason children ask few questions, and fail to examine objects or tinker with things, is that the teacher feels such exploration would get in the way of learning. I have even heard teachers say as much.

In one sophomore social studies class where I was observing, a fifteen-year-old boy raised his hand fifteen minutes into the teacher's presentation of the material (a lesson on the causes of the American Revolution). His teacher, a smart, lively woman, well liked by students in the suburban public school, said in her brisk voice, "I can't answer questions right now. Now it's time for learning."

We have experimental evidence to show that this is not an aberration. My student Kellie Randall and I decided to test my hunch that a hurried sense of obligation to requirements was getting in the way of curiosity in schools. We asked teachers to participate in a study of children's learning. The teachers who signed up to be subjects were brought to our lab and told that they would be guiding a third or four grader through the short, fun science activity called "bouncing raisins"—again, to see how little bubbles created by a mixture of baking soda, vinegar, and water adhered to raisins, making them rise to the top of the liquid. We told our subjects that we would be videotaping the whole activity. We set out the materials they would need, gave a brief explanation of the science underlying the activity, and handed them a worksheet that would guide them through the steps of the "experiment" and was to be filled out by the student with their supervision. The worksheet resembled the kinds of worksheets most children these days use when they are doing a learning activity at school (very similar, in fact, to the one the fifth graders had used when learning about the invention of wheels in Egypt).

Meanwhile, we trained four nine-year-olds to be our confederates. These children would act as if they were the subjects of the study. We showed them the materials and explained that each teacher they interacted with would believe he or she was helping the child learn about bouncing raisins for our experiment. Then we explained that halfway through the activity they were to drop something in the beaker that wasn't on the worksheet—a Skittle, instead of a raisin. We practiced what they should say if the teacher asked them what they were doing: "Oh I just wanted to see what would happen."

Our goal was to find out how teachers respond when children deviate from a task. This came from our sense that teachers are not intrinsically against exploration, but rather often seem to unwittingly discourage such exploration because they feel such pressure to finish tasks and stay on script. Because of this, we added one more wrinkle to the experimental situation. For half the teachers in the study, when we explained the activity, we said, "Here are the materials, so that you can help the student learn more about science." For those teachers, as the experimenter left the room, once everything was ready to go, the experimenter said, "OK, have fun learning about science." The other half heard something slightly different: "Here are the materials, so that you can help the student fill out the worksheet," and as she left the room the experimenter said to these teachers, "Have fun filling out the worksheet."

Our young confederates were excellent. None of them had to do it so many times that they got weary. And all of them kept to the plan. Halfway through the activity the children would drop a Skittle into the liquid mixture. Teachers had a range of reactions to the Skittle drop. Some gently steered the child back to the steps outlined on the worksheet. Some said things like, "Wait a minute. That's not part of the activity," or, "You can try that later. Now let's continue with the instructions," or simply, "No, no, don't do that." Others said things like, "Oh, that's cool. How'd you get that idea?" or "Hm, I wonder if that will be the same as the raisin."

When we analyzed the data, lo and behold, teachers who had been encouraged to help children learn about science were much more likely to respond well to the Skittle deviation, while those teachers who had been gently steered toward an emphasis on the worksheet were much more likely to discourage children from the unscripted deviation. Other characteristics, ones we might assume influence how a teacher would respond to a child's curiosity, did not seem to matter. It didn't matter whether the teacher was male or female, young or old, seasoned or novice. The study yielded one more fascinating and important insight. After each teacher had completed the activity with his or her assigned "student," the experimenter sat down and explained the real purpose of the study (remember that until that moment the teachers thought they were helping us collect data on the children). First of all, we gave each teacher the opportunity to keep his or her tape or ask us to throw it out, so that it wouldn't be included in the data (on the assumption that some teachers, once they knew we had been studying them, would choose not to be included in the data analysis). But as a part of the debriefing, the experimenter chatted with each teacher, to find out what it had been like to carry out the activity. When told that our real interest was in children's curiosity, most of the teachers, including the ones who had reacted negatively to the Skittle drop, said they championed curiosity in the classroom. One said, "Oh, I'm not very good at enforcing rules and following exact instructions like that. That is just not the way I am in my classroom. I hope it doesn't hurt your results at all." That teacher was one of the subjects who had responded restrictively and had even fished the Skittle out of the mixture right after the child dropped it in. In other words, many of the teachers had no idea what they had done just moments before.

We have another source of data about this last piece of the puzzle. A student and I sent out surveys to 114 teachers. In one part of the survey, they were asked to list the five skills or attributes they most wanted to instill or encourage in their students over the course of the school year. In the second part of the survey they were asked to circle five such desirable attributes from a list of ten. The list included words like "polite," "cooperative," "thoughtful," "knowledgeable," and also "curious." Some 77 percent of the teachers surveyed circled "curious" as one of their top five. However, when asked to come up with their own ideas, only twenty-three listed curiosity. In other words, when it's brought to their attention, teachers have some sense that curiosity is important; but without such prompting, it's not a top priority. This small finding supports my more general hunch that most parents and educators think they think curiosity is wonderful, important, valuable, and good. But most people do not have curiosity on the brain when they are teaching, planning curriculum, and evaluating teachers, schools, or classrooms. As is so often true, what people think they think is quite different from what they actually think.

For teachers, it's not simply that they aren't interested in, or focused on, curiosity. The impediments to curiosity in school consist of more than just the absence of enthusiasm for it. There are also powerful, somewhat invisible forces working against the expression and cultivation of curiosity in classrooms. Two primary impediments are the way in which plans and scripts govern what happens in most classrooms, and the pressure to get a lot of things "done" each day.

So, when we put these different strands together, what do we know about curiosity in the school-age child? Theoretically speaking, there is good reason to think that as children get older they get more discriminating in what they are curious about. Everyday life becomes familiar, so for much of the day quotidian events do not surprise or invite inquiry. On the other hand, the more one knows about something, whether it's the route to school, or a topic such as trucks, planets, or other girls, the more expectations there are to be violated. In other words, as they get older, children are curious about narrower strands of experience, and also curious at a more fine-grained level. Details in a script, rather than the script itself, call for attention. So we would expect that children between the ages of about five to ten appear curious less frequently, and also in more unexpected ways. One child turns his head to study a truck pulling into the driveway, because he actually knows a lot about trucks, and therefore notices the fact that this truck has more wheels than most. Another child studies an interaction between the teacher and another student, because she is keenly attentive to these interactions and therefore is curious why this child is talking to an adult in a way most children do not. In other words, curiosity becomes a narrower but perhaps brighter light, aimed with more intention. So, while some research has suggested a waning in curiosity with age, it's reasonable to interpret that as a sign that the activities presented in laboratory research don't elicit the same general level of inquiry from eight-year-olds that they do from five-year-olds.

At the same time, the role of adults seems to change as well. While parents of two-year-olds influence their children's fundamental curiosity via their basic relationship with the child and the patterns of question asking and inquiry encouraged or discouraged at home, older children are responsive to a wider variety of adults. These adults (experimenters, museum docents, and, more importantly, teachers) can lower or raise children's curiosity through smiles, questions, and comments. The less constitutionally curious a child is, the more susceptible he or she is to adult feedback. There is one more twist to the developmental part of this story. As children get older, their curiosity becomes more social. While the toddler's safe haven may be her mother, the nine-year-old's exploratory expedition may require a small team.

We can now place this noisy developmental picture into the larger mosaic of the classroom. Once children get to school, they exhibit a lot less curiosity. They ask fewer questions, examine objects less frequently and less thoroughly, and in general seem less inclined to persevere in sating their appetite for information. Even if we expected children to get less curious as they got older (and there is no basis for such a simplistic or general expectation), the drop shouldn't be nearly as precipitous as the school data suggest. Something about schools is decreasing the expression of curiosity, above and beyond inevitable, or intrinsic, developmental influences.

So what might explain the drop? When you look at children's sensitivity to social clues, and their increasing selectivity about what makes them curious, and you put this together with teachers' reluctance to deviate from a plan, the pressure they are under to meet certain goals (goals that are not consonant with sating one's curiosity), and the general neglect toward providing young learners with the materials that speak to their particular curiosity, one begins to see why children seem so incurious in schools.

This is not a new problem, or simply a result of high-stakes testing, or any other recent invention. In fact, tales of boring school go back at least to the eighteenth century. Denis Diderot compiled the famous French Encyclopedia of the Enlightenment, considered the "bible" of the Enlightenment. But not unlike other people of tremendous intellectual achievement, for him school was a prison, not a laboratory. As a little boy he got in trouble again and again at school for his unruliness. He found it so intolerable that he finally quit in order to learn cutlery at his father's side. But he found his father's workshop equally intolerable. He broke so many knives that he elected to go back to school, saying he preferred irritation to boredom. It's possible Diderot found many things to interest him in school, but little chance to pursue his interests, hence the irritation. In his father's workshop, there weren't even things to be interested in.

In a wonderful old study informally referred to as the Teddy Roosevelt study, Frank Barron (Barron and Harrington 1981) examined the lives of many of history's greatest achievers, in an attempt to identify the elements of their childhood that might explain their towering adult accomplishments. The only thing he could find that they had in common was unusually long periods of time out of school. It's just possible that what separated these motivated and highly able children from other equally talented children was the chance they had, outside of school, to pursue what interested them.

Schools are, to a great extent, a formalization of the learning children do in other settings. But now, in the second millennium, we expect more children to learn more than we ever have before. And we expect children to learn how to learn, to go on acquiring knowledge long after they finish their formal schooling. How odd, then, that we have somehow neglected to build on one of the most important elements of the learning process—the person's eagerness to find out. But it needn't be this way.

6

What Fuels Learning

WHEN I WAS seven years old I switched from the one-room schoolhouse in my farm village to a brand-new progressive independent school. It was there, on the second day of its existence, that I had my first formal science class. Along with all the other students who were ages six to eleven, I was brought to a long table, where we each took a seat. About six identical square white objects sat in a line, running down the middle of the table. The science teacher, Tony, asked us what those objects were. We looked at him expectantly. Most of us already knew that when a teacher asked a question, he or she undoubtedly knew the answer already. But he said nothing. So we looked again and, seeing almost instantly what the objects were, called out easily, "They're sugar cubes!" He then said, "How can you be sure?" At first we were baffled. He knew what they were. We were sure we knew what they were. But his question hung in the air, and since he refused to proceed, we had to figure out whether we were right. Maybe we were wrong. So we began to examine the cubes. Children picked them up, bringing them close to their faces so that they could inspect them. Several children sniffed the cubes, and a few turned them around to make sure they really did look the same on all sides. One little boy shook it next to his ear. Finally, I did the only sensible thing. I stuck my tongue out and tasted it. I was taking a risk. What if it wasn't what I thought it was? But that nice familiar zing of sweet greeted my tongue. Tony then said, "Yes, that's what scientists do. They observe. And you have five senses with which you can observe." I never, ever forgot that lesson.

Why didn't I? It's not because it was more fun than other activities. I did lots of fun things in school. And it's not because it was harder than other lessons. There was nothing hard about it. The reason was actually quite simple. I was taken in by the mystery. I wanted to know what would happen next.

The idea that you learn something better when you're curious about it seems so straightforward as to be obvious, and almost banal. However, since that insight seems so rarely used in educational practices, and since the idea is key to the argument of this book, it's worth considering the un-obviousness of it.

Most of the time children are expected to learn things for one of three reasons: they are afraid of what will happen when they don't learn it; they want the reward they will get if they do learn it; or they are convinced that learning it is essential to their future well-being (a sort of long-term, hypothetical reward). When children have trouble learning, we think we need to teach it in a different way, or impress upon them the importance or usefulness of what they are learning. We encourage them to try harder, or spend more time trying to learn, even though it's usually more effective to elicit their interest in the material.

THE POWER OF INTEREST

We've had experimental evidence for at least the past fifty years to support the idea that children's intrinsic interest is the most powerful ingredient for learning. Daniel Berlyne's experiments were premised on the idea that curiosity was a drive, much like hunger or sexual desire. And much like other kinds of arousal, it can be negative or positive. Either way, it motivates the person feeling it to reduce the arousal. The reduction of such arousal feels temporarily rewarding. The greater the arousal and its reduction, the greater the sense of reward. Berlyne posited four sources of such arousal—novelty, complexity, conflict, and surprise. In one of his most well-known tests of this construct, he read people a long list of facts. Some were more surprising or unexpected than others. Later, when asked to recall the information they had learned, subjects were far better at remembering those items about which they had expressed surprise. Some would argue that the work of researchers like Robert Bjork (Bjork and Linn 2006) and Nate Kornell (Kornell and Bjork 2008) demonstrates that difficulty is key to learning. In what is now a large series of studies, researchers have shown that when students struggle a bit with the material they are learning, they learn it better. For instance, in one example of this work, ten- and eleven-year-old children practiced four kinds of math problems that involved using formulas to find the total number of faces or corners on prisms. Half the children used a blocking technique (practice many examples of one type of solution at a time), and the other half used an interleaving technique (skip around practicing different kinds of problems, one after another). In general, people feel it's easier to use the blocking technique, and in fact, during the experiment, students struggled more with the problems when they used interleaving methods to practice. However, when the students took a test on the material, a day after the practice sessions, those who had used the interleaving technique did better (Taylor and Rohrer 2010). Alter has done a series of elegant experiments showing that when people encounter what he calls "disfluency"—small signals or roadblocks that momentarily trip the learner up—they process material at a deeper level (Alter 2013). Experiments like this suggest that though people are drawn toward methods that make learning seem easier, they actually learn more when they encounter some obstacles or a small amount of difficulty. However, there is another way to interpret these findings. The difficulties in experiments like this are usually small, and involve some kind of variability or unexpectedness. Perhaps difficulty is just another face of curiosity. Those things that "catch" your attention, or cause you to "think again," are things that trigger the kind of arousal Berlyne was talking about.

Decades of research have shown that attention is a central mechanism in the process of learning. In order to learn the material in a passage, one must pay attention to it. The more engaging the material, the easier it is to stop paying attention to other things, such as extraneous noises, other thoughts, and competing tasks. Having your attention "caught" by something is often the first step in learning about that thing. If a child is sitting in class watching the teacher explain long division, and suddenly the teacher begins to sing the procedure rather than speak it, students will pay attention, and they may well learn the sequence of calculations better (though it's always possible their attention may be so focused on the oddity of hearing their teacher sing that they remember nothing of how to borrow or carry over). However, in this example, the student's interest is not in the math itself, but rather in something external to the math. What about eliciting children's deeper interest in the material itself?

Dewey was perhaps the first and most eloquent spokesman for the idea that in order for children to learn, they need to feel that what they are learning has some meaning and significance beyond school. In his seminal work, *The Child and the Curriculum* (1911), he argued that children wanted to be part of their community, and that they would be eager to master topics and skills that connected them to the larger social world. Many teachers have taken this to mean that they should make school tasks more lifelike. But often this has been translated into a somewhat superficial and transitory concept. In one iteration, teachers and textbook writers thought that if they replaced dry mathematical word problems with stories about cool kids and cool activities (Marty and Sylvia wanted to race their skateboards. Marty skated at a rate of 3 miles per hour and Sylvia skated at a pace of 6 miles per hour. How far ahead of Marty would Sylvia be at 19 minutes?). As my former student Hannah Hausman once said, this represents an effort to engage students by presenting them with realistic problems rather than real problems. These "realistic" problems describe people, objects, and situations that might seem entertaining or relevant to children. Textbook writers are assuming that children will be interested in problems that contain certain child-oriented words, themes, or content. However, often such "realistic" window-dressing fails, because children don't feel any sustained connection to the actual problems or tasks they must complete. They feel little interest in the work itself.

This more sustained and internally generated kind of interest turns out to be just as important for children as it is for grown-ups. K. Ann Renninger (1992) has shown that infants and toddlers explore an object more thoroughly, and for a longer time, when it's an object in which they've shown prior interest. When eighteen-month-olds were given a chance to interact with an object they had shown prior interest in, they played with it longer, used more gestures to explore it, and employed a wider range of actions on it. In other words, even babies are more in-terested in some objects than they are in others, and once a baby is in-terested in an object, or a class of objects, she is likely to behave differ-ently with it than with other objects. Key to this is the idea of a kind of a distinctive personal repertoire: children's interests are not com-pletely transitory; they have some sustained life that is based on what the child finds compelling, regardless of how new or intriguing the ob-ject itself may seem to others. The object that interests one baby may be markedly different from the object that interests another, quite apart from which object has more "bells and whistles."

Moreover, some babies' interests border on the obsessive. In one of the more intriguing sets of data, Judy DeLoache and colleagues began exploring what they referred to as very young children's "extremely in-tense interests." In a series of case studies they described, one child was completely absorbed by balls, another by trucks, another by tooth-brushes, and so on. Such children develop something close to a fixa-tion on an object, or class of objects (DeLoache, Simcock, and Macari 2007). And as with Renninger's findings, the children in DeLoache and colleagues' work acquired much broader and deeper information about their extremely intense interests than other children who spent so much less time and commitment to exploring similar objects. Such data show that at a very early age, human beings are capable of feeling particular interest about particular things. Needless to say, this kind of interest is, to some extent, self-perpetuating. The more time DeLoache's sub-jects spent with their chosen objects or topics, the more interested they were. Juliet captures this perfectly when she tells Romeo, from her bal-cony, how her love grows from giving it to him:

> But to be frank and give it thee again,
> And yet I wish but for the thing I have.
> My bounty is as boundless as the sea,
> My love as deep, the more I give to thee,
> The more I have, for both are infinite.

(*Romeo and Juliet*, act 2, scene 2)

In other words, playing with an object doesn't sate a child; it leads to greater interest. If you think about it for a moment, this makes com-plete sense, and fits with the idea that though most children become more selective in what they are curious about, their curiosity for certain things often expands. We know that unexpected events, or surprising gaps in one's knowledge, trigger curiosity. As children get older, everyday life, on the surface, provides fewer surprises. However, as children acquire more knowledge about specific routines and domains, they also become attuned to subtler and more fine-grained types of surprise, inconsistencies, and gaps in their knowledge. The more one knows about an interesting topic, the more one wants to know. This loop connecting knowledge and curiosity is often what leads to expertise.

One need only conjure up the five-year-old who becomes obsessed with dinosaurs to see how true this is. Young children who gobble up books about dinosaurs, collect small dinosaur figures, and spend hours learning the names and features of all of them often seem insatiable, and amazingly knowledgeable. Years ago, Micheline Chi showed that such expertise made children seem far more advanced cognitively than they had appeared to be while performing experimental tasks using materials determined by the experimenter (1978). For instance, five-year-olds typically have trouble remembering the position of chess pieces on a chessboard, or long lists of words they have been read. However, when Chi and others asked five-year-old chess experts to solve memory tasks based on chess, their abilities were excellent. Similarly, young dinosaur aficionados employed memory strategies that ordinarily seemed impossible for children their age. At the time, these sorts of experiments were used to show that children's cognitive skills were more domain-specific than Piaget had argued—children don't simply think like a six-year-old, or a three-year-old. Even a six-year-old thinks in more sophisticated, powerful ways when he is thinking about something in which he has expertise. But in the context of curiosity, and its cousin interest, those findings take on another meaning as well. Perhaps the more a child interacts with an object or sets of objects, the more curious she is; and the more curious she is, the more thorough and far-reaching the knowledge she acquires. It suggests that interest leads to cognitive advances beyond specific knowledge in a given domain. This fits nicely with research showing that children learn more when they have greater interest in the material.

Bernstein had ninth graders score several passages of writing, in terms of how interesting they were (1955). A separate group of ninth

graders was then assigned to read either the passages rated as very interesting, or the ones rated as not so interesting by their age peers. The
subjects who read the very interesting passages understood what they
read better, offered more creative insights and responses to a series of
questions about the text, and even read the passages more quickly than
the subjects who had been given the less interesting passages. Shirey
and Reynolds (1988) found that college students, too, read interesting
sentences more quickly than uninteresting sentences. Several studies
confirm the commonsense idea that children remember text better, and
understand it more fully, when it has piqued their interest in one way
or another (Silvia 2006; Knobloch et al. 2004).

TWO KINDS OF INTEREST

The question then is not whether curiosity is important to the educational process, but rather what kinds of curiosity, under what conditions, enhance learning? Answering this question has proved trickier
than one might think. To begin with, we know that children's curiosity takes several different forms. Some children (and adults, for that
matter) have a general attitude of inquisitiveness. These people are easy
to spot. Everyone has noticed the friend or neighbor who always wants
to know more—who walks into a room and heads straight for the new
picture, piece of furniture, or trinket, or, upon hearing a story, asks a
stream of questions to get more information. These people have a high
degree of what has been called diversive curiosity. In the best case, the
person with a lot of diversive curiosity simply seems inquisitive and
interested. The child with an abundance of diversive curiosity can
also seem distractable. In some cases, children (and adults) use their
curiosity to distract others and prevent focus. But many children are
very curious about one or two things and very incurious about other
topics.

Two children might be equally curious, but not about the same
things. John Coie demonstrated this in the following way. He brought
first and third graders, one at a time, into four situations that invited
investigation. In the first situation, each child was left briefly in a room
containing a box with switches and a crank that, if manipulated correctly, would make lights flash or emit a buzzing noise. In the second

situation, the experimenter showed each child how combining certain chemicals caused them to change color; then each child was invited to "mess around" with the materials to see if she could figure out how the effect was achieved. In the third situation, each child was asked to wait outside for a few minutes until the experimenter was ready for a supposed "next activity"; meanwhile, two pigeon cages were set up so that they could not be seen clearly unless the child came up close to the cages. In the fourth situation, the experimenter pulled out an adjustable inclined plane, some rods, and some wheels. He demonstrated how the wheels could be made to roll differently when the plane was at a different slope and when the rods were attached to the wheel in different ways. The child was then invited to play with the materials to see if he or she could better understand the demonstration. In each situation, the researchers measured the time it took the child to approach the object, the length of time the child spent with the object, and the range of investigatory actions the child undertook. Coie found that few children were equally curious, or investigated with equal vigor, in all four situations (Coie 1974).

The fact that most children only seem curious about particular things presents something of an obstacle to researchers. If one child is interested in fish, and another in musical instruments, how is a researcher to choose experimental materials that will work similarly for all children? To some extent this problem is overcome when several studies, using differing materials, all point to the same findings.

But the problem of specific curiosity poses a different set of challenges for educators. For children to feel curiosity they have to have access to topics and objects in which they have some interest, or in which they might develop some interest, and no one set of objects or topics will be equally interesting to all children. Children's interests vary greatly, and can be quirky. Return to the textbook writer's "realistic," "lively," or "relevant" math problems. These might work for momentarily grabbing a child's attention. But in order for educators to encourage the kind of sustained exploration that leads to greater knowledge, children must want to hold, examine, manipulate, and talk about the topic, problem, or object. This is true of the child who seems curious in general, but may be especially true for the child whose curiosity is not a particularly salient or robust part of her usual response to things.

This means that teachers need to notice what interests their particular students. They cannot assume that the same topic or material, whether it's rocks, trucks, ballet, tornadoes, or revolutions, would interest all their students. There exists a class of objects that for whatever reason has captured the interest and attention of a given child. The more invested the child is in that class of objects, the more likely he or she is to learn about it. The investment itself seems to confer upon it qualities that lead to curiosity and learning. But interest isn't only in the eye of the beholder.

Though researchers and teachers must deal with the fact that there are significant individual differences in what stirs a child's interest or urge to know more, it is also possible to identify some general qualities that seem to make an object or a topic more or less intriguing to the majority of students.

Consider, for instance, the very important example of what children read. Is there any rhyme or reason to what makes a text more or less likely to pique interest? Earlier, I described research showing that children learned more from passages that had been rated as interesting. The studies I described used raters to determine which passages were interesting and which were not (both studies used raters who were the same age as the experimental subjects). The raters did not have difficulty coming to consensus about which passages were more interesting. This lends support to our everyday experience: while some of us love detective novels, some historical biographies, and some travel books, there is a surprising degree of consensus about interesting versus dull writing. Within genres, readers tend to flock to certain books, mesmerized by the way the writer writes. Yet children's sensitivity to style is all but ignored in classrooms, pushed aside in the interests of content.

Teachers often work hard to simplify material, in order to make it easy for students to attend to the main theme, information, or concept. Think back to the Dick and Jane reading series of the 1950s and '60s. The idea was to clear away all extraneous language and detail, so that young readers could attend only to variations in consonants and vowels. Or consider a set of scientific materials set out in order for children to "do" an experiment (actually not an experiment, since the outcome is usually known). But in these pseudo experiments, typically teachers set out just the materials the children will need, often with a very clear set of procedures or instructions, intended to guide the child through the activity. In these two examples, or hundreds more like them, the unspoken assumption is that simplifying material will help children learn it. But actually, children are as interested in complexity as adults are. Ruth Garner and Rachel Brown gave young teenagers passages to read. Some of the passages were straightforward and quite clear both in terms of the language they used and the structure of the prose—what some linguists have called "transparent" language. Other teenagers read passages containing more opaque language—language where a reader might be distracted by the sound or connotations of the word, or by the way words are put together—the prose. These more opaque passages also contained ambiguous information, phrases that weren't altogether clear, or details that didn't seem strictly relevant to the story or information being conveyed. The researchers then assessed how much the teenagers had learned from the passages (Garner et al. 1992). The teenagers remembered the complex, less straightforward passages better than the transparent ones. It's not hard to see why. Consider the following two descriptions, both from Charles Darwin's *The Origin of Species*.

> It is generally acknowledged that all organic beings have been formed on two great laws—Unity of Type and the Conditions of Existence. By unity of type is meant that fundamental agreement in structure, which we see in organic beings of the same class, and which is quite independent of their habits of life. On my theory, unity of type is explained by unity of descent. The expression of conditions of existence, so often insisted on by the illustrious Cuvier, is fully embraced by the principle of natural selection. For natural selection acts by either now adapting the varying parts of each being to its organic and inorganic conditions of life; or by having adapted them during past periods of time: the adaptations being aided in many cases by the increased use or disuse of parts, being affected by the direct action of the external conditions of life, and subjected in all cases to the several laws of growth and variation. Hence, in fact, the law of the Conditions of Existence is the higher law; as it included, through the in-

heritance of former variations and adaptations, that of the Unity of Type. (Darwin 1859/2003, 200)

That section, which ends chapter 6, provides a concise account of the core idea of natural selection. Contrast it with the last paragraph of the book, which conveys the same substance:

> It is interesting to contemplate a tangled bank, clothed with many plants of many kinds, with birds singing on the bushes, with various insects flitting about, and with worms crawling through the damp early, and to reflect that these elaborately constructed forms, so different from each other, and dependent upon each other in so complex a manner, have all been produced by laws acting around us. These laws, taken in the largest sense, being Growth with Reproduction; Inheritance, which is almost implied by reproductions; Variability from the indirect and direct actions of the conditions of life, and from use and disuse: a Ratio of Increase so high as to lead to a Struggle for Life, and as a consequence to Natural Selection, entailing Divergence of Character and the Extinction of less-improved forms. Thus, from the war of nature, from famine and death, the most exalted object, which we are capable of conceiving, namely, the production of the higher animals, directly follows. There is grandeur in this view of life, with its several powers, having been originally breathed by the Creator into a few forms or into one; and that, whilst this planet has gone cycling on according to the fixed law of gravity, from so simple a beginning endless forms most beautiful and most wonderful have been, and are being evolved. (507)

The first is important, and useful—providing a specific and detailed blueprint of the theory, for other scientists. The last, with its unexpected ebullience and integration of types of language, is breathtaking, and unforgettable. A second example will drive home the point, and ironically comes straight from the heart of psychology. In 1959 the great cognitive psychologist George Miller published a paper in a highly selective peer-reviewed journal, in which he argued that the human memory organizes things into chunks of seven, plus or minus two. Who, reading it, could ever forget his opening?

> My problem is that I have been persecuted by an integer. For seven years this number has followed me around, has intruded in my most

private data, and has assaulted me from the pages of our most public journals. This number assumes a variety of disguises, being sometimes a little larger and sometimes a little smaller than usual, but never changing so much as to be unrecognizable. The persistence with which this number plagues me is far more than a random accident. There is, to quote a famous senator, a design behind it, some pattern governing its appearances. Either there really is something unusual about the number or else I am suffering from delusions of persecution. (Miller 1956, 81)

Compare his description with the description psychology students encounter in one of the more highly regarded textbooks of recent years:

The capacity of working memory is sharply limited. Traditionally, this capacity has been measured by a *memory span* task in which the individual hears a series of items and must repeat them, in order, after just one presentation. If the items are randomly chosen letters or digits, adults can repeat seven items or so without errors. With longer series, errors are likely. In fact many tasks, not just memory span, show this limit of seven plus-or-minus two items, leading psychologists to refer it to as the *magic number*. (Gleitman, Reisberg, and Gross 2007, 236)

George Gleitman, an important and influential empirical psychologist in his own right, has presented Miller's idea with precision and clarity. But it has been vacuumed clean of all the connotations, flourish, and personal voice that made the idea so compelling to encounter. I doubt any college student remembers Gleitman's rendition. These passages from well-known texts show that seductive details matter to all of us.

Furthermore, books aren't the only place where a student can find subtlety and opacity. Physical environments can also be more or less dense and intricate. Walk around many school hallways and notice the posters and signs that hang on the walls. Most often these are quite straightforward. They offer little in the way of artistry, or dense aesthetics, and if they have a message, it's quite blunt (cool kids don't do drugs). Learning materials within classrooms are similarly cleansed of complexity. However, when we went into classrooms to find out where and when children were expressing curiosity, we noticed that the few places where kids lingered to observe were often the most dynamic places, the places where unexpected and irregular things could happen—the most common place was the aquarium, in classes where there was one. Children would often wander over to the aquarium (in one room it was a terrarium, with several spiders inside). They'd stand there gazing for up to six minutes (that's a long time for a school-child to quietly watch something, ignoring all the chaos and noise around her). They would track one fish (or spider) for a while. But then they would look around, behind the coral, or watch the seaweed float and change shape. We don't have the data that could tell us what it is exactly about the aquarium that so fascinated the students. It's possible that living things are always more interesting than inanimate objects. But it's also the case that these habitats offered much more irregular and changeable phenomena than elsewhere in the room.

Shulz and Bonawitz introduced young children to a box that contained two toy animals, which popped up from the middle when levers on the outside of the box were pressed. In one condition, adult and child simultaneously pressed down two different levers, so that two creatures popped out of the top at the same time, and it was impossible to tell which lever controlled which creature. In a second condition, adult and child took turns pressing their levers, so that it was easy to discern which lever caused which creature to pop up. After playing with the first box, a second, different-color box was placed on the table along with the first box, and the children were left to play on their own. When children were exposed to the ambiguous version of the first box (both people pressing their levers simultaneously), they preferred to continue playing with it, even after the experimenter left the table. However, if they had participated in the unambiguous version of the game, they preferred the new box (Schulz and Bonawitz 2007). The results suggest that children pay attention to novelty, but they are drawn in by complexity as well. When faced with ambiguous data about something appealing (like a colored box with levers and a pop-up creature), they are more eager to figure out what's going on than they are to encounter something new. In other words, when children are confronted with ambiguity and complexity, about objects that appeal to them, they are inclined to delve in.

The environmental psychologist Roger Hart (1979) has written about this with regard to playgrounds for children, arguing that children need

natural, complicated, and messy places to play—not the highly manufactured pristine equipment that often fills the most affluent playgrounds and recess areas. In fact, several studies have shown that when
children are exposed to natural environments in which there is a lot
of variety and detail, their subsequent learning (within a short time
period) is enhanced (Kuo and Taylor 2004; Taylor, Kuo, and Sullivan
2002). This is yet another example of the way in which a more complex and unruly environment elicits the kinds of curiosity that lead to
learning.

Another source of opacity comes from the way that topics themselves are framed. Lowry and Johnson (1981) asked small groups of
fourth-grade students to study a social studies topic by learning some
material together. Some of the groups were encouraged to use the materials to learn as much as they could about the topic. In a second condition, small groups of children were encouraged to zero in on a controversial theme within the topic. After several days of study
opportunity, the children's knowledge of the domain was assessed.
Children who had focused on a controversial aspect of the material remembered significantly more than those who had simply been encouraged to help one another learn it. Perhaps just as important, the children in the controversy condition were much more likely to forgo a
recess to watch a film on the topic, and they continued acquiring information. A wonderful demonstration of this principle can be found
in a paper by Stigler and Stevenson, called "How Asian Teachers Polish
Each Lesson to Perfection." The authors describe one example of a
lesson: The teacher walks in carrying a large paper bag full of clinking
glass. Entering the classroom with a large paper bag is highly unusual,
and by the time she has placed the bag on her desk, the students are
regarding her with rapt attention. What's in the bag? She begins to pull
items out of the bag, placing them, one by one, on her desk. She removes
a pitcher and a vase. A beer bottle evokes laughter and surprise. She
soon has six containers lined up on her desk. The children continue to
watch intently, glancing back and forth at each other as they seek to
understand the purpose of this display (Stigler and Stevenson 1991, 12).
The authors use this story to describe a pattern in their observations
of Japanese classrooms—the teachers' ability to use mystery and uncertainty to organize their lessons. Given a topic that may not have an

equal interest for all children, certain kinds of uncertainty can be built into the material in a way that incites curiosity and leads to better learning. In the observations of curiosity that my students and I have done in classrooms, we have noticed one more topic that consistently sparked children's curiosity—intellectual exotica.

In our observations, most of the questions schoolchildren ask in school have to do with procedures (Ms. Rumsey, should I put my test here on your desk? Can I stay out after lunch to play soccer? What should we do if we don't want to try out for volleyball?) or with social interactions (Did you go to the dance last night? Are you going to eat lunch or go to the playground? Did Miles punch Whitey in his gut?). But most of the questions they asked seeking new information about objects and events concerned things to which they had no direct access to in their daily lives—exotica. Take, for example, the following exchange between a teacher and two students, who were sitting in a circle with seventeen other students during a social studies lesson. The teacher had been reading to them about early humans crossing the Bering Strait.

The teacher has just put down the book she was reading aloud about early travels across wide distances.

CHILD 1: What, what was that thing? The strait? What did they do?
TEACHER: You mean the Bering Strait? That was a massive piece of land that connected Asia with North America.
CHILD 1: But how, what did, did it say that people walked across that?
CHILD 2: Yeah, it said that early man walked across that thing, Beringia, to get to America.
CHILD 1: But were they cold?
TEACHER: I don't know. Probably. What do you think?
CHILD 2: They were cold all right. Did you see that picture? They were practically naked.
CHILD 1: I wonder what they ate. Did they eat the same stuff we eat?

Often what ignited a line of questioning was a reference to something outside the children's zone of familiarity—unfamiliar places, historically distant times. This conversation, for instance, begins with a simple reference to an unknown piece of geography, the Bering Strait. But clearly, the little boy wants to know more than just what that label refers to. He wants to know what this previously unheard of place is like, and what it was like for the people who supposedly walked across it. In trying to sate his curiosity, he and the others must speculate, imagining not only what they've heard in the book, but imagining the answers to their own questions. Their use of the terms "think," "know," and "wonder" is evidence that their own mental activity will provide them with some sense of satiation.

In our study of dinner-table conversations, Laura Corona and I found similar evidence that children are often as curious about things they cannot see, touch, or directly experience as they are about what is going on right around them.

Take, for example, the following excerpt, in which a four-year-old boy is curious about the meaning of a word.

FATHER: On a whim, I bought ingredients for Rice Krispie treats.
CHILD: What's a whim?
MOTHER: A whim? *W-h-i-m.* It means, uh, it means without planning ahead, just because I felt like it in the moment.
FATHER: That's why I passed by a package of mini-marshmallows in the store and thought, "Hm, that might be a nice snow-day activity."

When I have interviewed adults, asking them to describe memories of intense curiosity or exploration in childhood, typical answers include: "The closet on the second floor that was locked." "Going up to the attic, which we were told not to do." "There was a large tree outside our house, and my father told me the branches were too high, and too thin to climb on." In other words, the mysterious and forbidden lured children, enticing them to find out more about the forbidden place. When people recall curious episodes from their teens, they mention wanting to know more about whatever story was most shrouded in secrecy (a grandfather's wayward youth, a secret marriage, a mental illness) or whatever topic adults (teachers or parents) wanted to avoid— politics, money (Ron Lieber, who writes about finance for the *New York Times*, says that as a boy he longed to get into the file drawer and see his parents' old tax reports), or the greatest curiosity spark of all times, sex. In other words, the more unknown and unfamiliar a topic, and the denser with details its presentation, the more it may invite learning.

There is one more form of intellectual complexity that sparks curiosity, and it already abounds in the lives of schoolchildren: stories.

The first book my mother allowed me to stay up late into the night so I could finish it, was a story of Joan of Arc. I just couldn't put the book down. Perhaps I became a historian that evening. I was in the 3rd grade, and we lived on an American Air Force base in Japan, my teacher's name was Ms. Swedzinksi, a striking redhead who wore her hair in a French twist. I don't remember if she pointed the book out to me or if I picked it out during our trip to the library, but that began my love of books. (Wong 2013)

Almost as soon as children can talk, they begin to attend to stories—listening to those that others tell, and trying to tell their own. Research has shown how universal the narrative impulse is. Part of this seemingly innate capacity is a sense of sequence, which soon becomes a sense of plot. When toddlers and their parents co-construct past experiences, it is common for the toddler to watch a parent with eager and careful scrutiny, anticipating the next contribution to the shared story, dismayed if the adult doesn't put events in the right sequence, or if the story doesn't resolve in the way it should (Engel 1995). If you watch young preschool children listen to stories being read aloud you can see them lean forward attentively, eager to hear what happens next. When children tell stories to or with one another, they are equally sensitive to the primacy of plot. Jerome Bruner has argued that, early and easily, children come to appreciate the essential components of story (1966). Chief among these components is the idea of a problem (the story's high point) and its resolution. By three, children are already attuned to the power of uncertainty in a story. During the early years, whether they are telling stories about their lives, with the help of parents, or telling stories to other children, they naturally build in suspense. Often when their stories fail to attract attention from others, they go back and revise, heightening the drama and uncertainty. This provides evidence that they are not only curious about what will happen in the stories they hear, but aware that they can incite curiosity by making others want to know what will happen.

Cliffhangers in a narrative are the most accessible and surefire form of uncertainty. It's hard to find a child who, halfway through a good story, doesn't feel that she *must* hear how the story ends. Teachers regularly report that story time is the one time of the day when all children easily pay steady, rapt attention to what the teachers are saying.

One might argue, as Kieran Egan has, that stories are the central tool of education, for just this reason. The impact of a story rests, in good part, on the reader's uncertainty. That uncertainty is what makes us turn the page. Finishing a book or story, most readers long for a sense, however temporary, that their uncertainty has been resolved.

But science has its own narrative form. Every experiment, by definition, asks a question, to which the answer, one hopes, is unknown. The scientific cliffhanger, in its most vivid form, is the moment before the scientist looks at the data. Long before a student engages in formally structured experiments, children have opportunities to observe or participate in informal versions of the scientific cliffhanger.

As a young father, Sigmund Freud loved to plan small surprises for his family. Once, while looking for mushrooms in the meadows around his home, he tossed his hat over a particularly wonderful specimen, so that the children could be surprised when they unearthed it. He knew a basic truth about learning—we all want to discover what's in the box, hidden from sight, or behind the curtain. Fortunately, one doesn't need to be a genius, or a trained scholar, to build small experimental cliffhangers into a child's daily experience. To some, it comes naturally.

Take the following exchange between a four-year-old boy and his grandmother, as they walked along a path in the woods, near their home. The little boy had picked up a leaf and examined it. Then he noticed a small bug hurrying along the path. He asked his grandmother if the bug would eat the leaf. She could have just answered. She is a knowledgeable naturalist, and was in familiar terrain. But she didn't. Instead she said, "Let's find out. Why don't you put the leaf down next to the bug. Let's just wait here and see what happens." That phrase, "Let's see what happens if/when . . ." is the cliffhanger embedded in every scientific experiment. Some children live in homes where they hear a lot of words, a lot of description, many questions, and long exchanges. Others live in homes where there is little of any one or all of those linguistic features. Similarly, some children live in homes where the scientific cliffhanger is casually built into many experiences, and others do not.

When we began coding the observations we had done of children in schools, my students and I expected to count and code all the questions children asked. But early on we stumbled upon an unexpected wrinkle. In a fair number of episodes children seemed to be expressing curiosity out loud, but without actually forming a question. We quickly realized that almost all these utterances were speculations of one kind or another.

"I'll bet the clock would stop working if I pushed that button in."

"I wonder whether the moon is colder at nighttime."

"I think if we put two Band Aids on, it will stick together."

In these examples, children seem to be testing a hypothesis, but only hypothetically. None of them can act on these speculations, or seem to expect an answer from someone right away. Instead, they are mental versions of the "what will happen if/when" implicit in the investigations conducted by children and scientists.

There is one more potential source of curiosity fuel in every single classroom—peers. Given our earlier finding, that eight- and nine-year-old children were more likely to approach a "curiosity box" in groups, it seemed likely to me that peers play an increasingly important role in children's curiosity as they develop. This shouldn't surprise any developmental psychologist. Research has shown again and again that thinking occurs between children as much as it does within children. Beginning with the work of Lev Vygotsky, we've seen that one child can have a profound impact on another child's level of problem solving. In his classic formulation, Vygotsky argued that the help of a more competent or highly developed peer not only lifted the performance of a child in that specific activity, but also predicted the child's cognitive level, unaided, at a future date (Vygotsky 1978). His studies focused on the way in which a more competent peer could subtly lead a younger child to use more advanced cognitive strategies to solve problems. Subsequent research has shown that children often act as informal teachers, scaffolding one another's strategies, skills, and ways of thinking across a wide range of activities and settings. Peers affect one another in all kinds of ways. We know that the presence of peers can lead young teens to act more impulsively than they would on their own, to change their judgments about objects and people, and to help other children when they are in need. Recent evidence also shows that knowledge spreads horizontally through peer groups. In a wonderful experiment, Whiten and Flynn taught a preschooler one of two techniques for using a tool to manipulate levers that would cause a small toy to drop out of a box, into a chute and the child's hand. Having taught one child how to do it, the experimenters placed the box in a playgroup classroom with twenty-two other children for five days. They then tracked how many of the children learned the technique by either watching the target child or receiving instruction from the target child. They also watched each child transmit what he or she had learned to others in the group. The results show that children readily and effectively share knowledge with one another (Whiten and Flynn 2010).

In sum, children exert a powerful influence on one another along a whole range of cognitive and social dimensions. So there is good reason to believe that when it comes to inquiry, peers matter. But how?

To learn more about the role of peers, my student Daniel Silver and I conducted what we like to refer to as the "Curious George in the classroom" study. Our basic question was whether curiosity is contagious between children. We developed our experiment using a paradigm developed by Jamie Jirout and David Klahr called "the fish task" (2012). In this activity, children play a computer game in which they are told they will be in a submarine, looking through a window where they will see fish. They are then asked to choose a set of fish from which one fish will swim by. Each child can choose a very small set of fish, limiting how surprised they are likely to be by the actual fish that swims by, or a very large set, increasing their uncertainty (potential for surprise), or they can choose to see no set at all—in other words, total uncertainty. This measure rests on Klahr and Jirout's claim that the amount of uncertainty with which a person is comfortable is the most precise and content-free way to assess a person's level of curiosity.

But for us, the measure was just a means to an end. Our real purpose was to find out whether children could influence one another's appetite for uncertainty. Once every fourth grader had participated in the game, we had a baseline measure of each child's level of curiosity. Children who had consistently chosen small sets of fish from which the fish swimming by the window might come were considered "low curiosity," while those who had consistently chosen very large sets of fish were considered "high curiosity." Weeks later we returned to the school for the second phase of the study, at which time we paired each low-curiosity child with a high-curiosity child. We then brought each pair into a room to do some new activities. One activity was to watch a segment of David Attenborough's *Planet Earth* film, about the ocean. We encouraged them to chat about the film and generate questions. We then gave the children some time with a few complicated and unfamiliar gadgets, while they "waited" for the next segment of activity. Our goal was to give the high-curiosity child a chance to be contagious to the low-curiosity child, and we reasoned that such contagion, if it were to happen, would have to take place in the context of activities that invited exploration. After this short series of joint activity, each child was assessed for a second time using the fish task. Our hunch, that more-curious children would "infect" less-curious children, turned out to be only partly correct. Those children who got a low score the first time around did in fact become more curious after interacting with a very curious child. But so did the incurious children who were partnered with another incurious child (something we had done to disentangle the effect of any peer from the effect of a curious peer). Interestingly, this was not the case for children who were originally assessed as being moderately curious. Those children's scores did not go up after interacting with another child. Our interpretation is that children do affect one another's curiosity. But the very curious child is not infecting the incurious child with an appetite for uncertainty. Instead, social engagement, and the external embodiment of curiosity (asking one another questions, goading one another on to test out a toy or tinker with an object), trigger curiosity in children whose curiosity seems somewhat dormant. The lower a child's individual level of curiosity, the more likely it is to be lifted by interacting with other children.

To sum up, from an early age, some children are more curious than others. But there is also great fluctuation from one setting to another. A child who is usually timid about opening things or asking questions can be beckoned into inquiry. Children who are ordinarily inquisitive can be hushed into a kind of intellectual listlessness. The characteristics that fuel curiosity are not mysterious. Adults who use words and facial expressions to encourage children to explore; access to unexpected, opaque, and complex materials and topics; a chance to inquire with others; and plenty of suspense . . . these turn out to be the potent ingredients.

7

The Gossip

I OFTEN SPENT my weekends in my grandmother Helen's kitchen. I usually slipped through her kitchen door feeling bored and hungry. I'd eat Hostess cupcakes, or she'd fix me sherbet with Fresca poured over it. When I was especially hungry, she'd heat up some Spaghettios for me. But my favorite part of those long listless afternoons was listening to Helen talk on the phone with her best friend, whom we called Aunt Louise, though she was no relation to either of us. The phone would ring and Helen would pull a vinyl chair right up to the wall where the phone was mounted. She'd pick up the receiver and say, with something close to a southern drawl, "Heeellllooo?" Then she'd mouth to me who it was, settle back into the chair, and begin discussing everyone near and far, familiar and un, with Aunt Louise. Sometimes Louise rattled on for so long that Helen would leave the phone receiver hanging on its long curlicue cord, amble over to her fridge for some soda, or a cookie, and slowly make her way back to the vinyl-covered chair, where she'd pick up the receiver and say, "Mmm hmmm," as if she had been listening the whole time. Obviously whatever information Louise was imparting didn't lose much with those periodic lapses. After maybe an hour of chat, Helen would say good-bye to Aunt Louise, hang up, and tell me the highlights. Those long afternoons of eavesdropping opened the window onto an essential source of information: gossip.

THE MOST COMMON CURIOSITY

When my students and I observed children in kindergarten and fifth-grade classrooms, in addition to counting the number of "episodes of curiosity" we also made an inventory of the questions children asked. We heard questions about planets, foreign countries, weather patterns, bloody wars, bugs, and earthquakes. But children also asked many questions about one another. They wanted to know who was going to buy milk at lunchtime, who was going to try out for band, who had thrown up the night before, and who got invited to the middle-school dance. In some classrooms, children asked more questions about one another than they did about anything else. In any given two-hour stretch, kindergarteners asked 6.68 questions about their friends, and fifth-grade students asked just under 2 questions about one another. But once again there were large differences between the classes—in one class kindergarteners asked nearly 11 social questions in any two-hour stretch, while another group of kindergarteners asked a mere 2.4 social questions during any given session. Similarly, one group of fifth graders asked virtually no questions about one another, while another asked nearly four per session. We interpret these particular data with caution, since it seems clear that children can only express as much of this interest as a teacher allows. In other words, kids are only allowed to gossip if the setting permits. But we did come away from those nearly one hundred hours of observation very certain that it would be a mistake to overlook children's curiosity about one another's lives.

Almost everyone—even those who show little curiosity about plant life, who don't want to know much about their government, and seem completely uninterested in the lives of people from far away—wants to know what's happening in the house next door. Most of us are extremely curious about our neighbors. This seems to be the one kind of curiosity that transcends educational level, intellect, or social milieu. In a fascinating essay on the uses of gossip to gain information, Maryann Ayim compares what she called "investigative gossip" (talking to find out what your neighbor is up to) to Charles Sanders Peirce's depiction of science, "the pursuit of those who are devoured by a desire to find things out" (Ayim 1994, 87). Research has suggested that people spend between 65 and 90 percent of their conversational time gossiping (Dunbar, Marriott, and Duncan 1997; Emler 1994). One group of authors put it perfectly: "People gossip with an appetite that rivals their interest in food and sex" (Wilson et al. 2000, 347).

Though it's more common than a cold, most people don't like to acknowledge that they do it—it's everybody's guilty pleasure. For a long time, psychologists and sociologists have also demonized it—assuming that people tell bad things about another only in order to lower that person's value in the eyes of peers, and thereby gain something.

And yet there is ample though indirect evidence that sharing information about third parties is essential to communal life. In F. C. Bartlett's classic studies of memory, he showed that when people pass on stories within a community, the stories get revised, ever so slightly, in each retelling. By the time a story has been passed around a group of friends, it has morphed in ways that reflect the community's biases, codes of conduct, and worldviews (Bartlett 2003). His main point was that remembering is a social process. But his data and theory rest on an equally fundamental idea—that passing on stories about one another is central to community life. Everyone does it, all of the time, at the bus stop, the water cooler, the grocery line, the little league game, and of course, on the Internet. Gossiping, as a form of social glue, is one of our oldest accomplishments. Robyn Dunbar argues that once humans evolved language, gossip replaced grooming as a way for us to bond together (Baumeister, Zhang, and Vohs 2004; Dunbar and Dunbar 1998).

And though psychologists have so often taken a dim view of our motivations for gossiping, the truth is our gossip serves several purposes. Bianca Beersma and Gerben Van Kleef (2012) asked people why they engage in various kinds of gossip. Their answers revealed four motivations: to exert negative influence on someone else, to regulate social norms, for social enjoyment, and to provide group protection. But their four categories leave an important question, which is why hearing stories about other people, even when the stories are completely benign, feels so good. Some of the pleasure comes, no doubt, from schadenfreude, just as many novels provide one with a happy comparison to one's own situation, and a chance to practice bad feelings without facing any consequences (Bruner 1986, 1990; Engel 1995). But passing on stories about the people you know also satisfies a more general (and productive) need to sustain and flesh out an understanding of others. In their paper "Gossip as Cultural Learning" (2004), Roy Baumeister and his colleagues make a case for this, showing how people use gossip to learn the rules of their culture. Baumeister (2006) points out that people's tendency to tell bad things about one another supports this view. In other words, contrary to the argument that people's preference for passing on negative stories is evidence that gossip is mostly a tool of aggression, Baumeister says that people tell negative stories about one another in order to provide friends with warnings about what they shouldn't do. This view offers an intriguing hint about the connection of gossip to curiosity. In Baumeister's account, negative anecdotes (the child who runs out in the street and gets hurt, the elderly man who unwittingly trusts a telemarketer, the neighbor who foolishly tries to deceive her husband) help communicate social rules. But, he argues, these rest on the fact that people pay more attention to bad than good, and to violations of the norm. Just as curiosity is elicited when someone encounters something unexpected, gossip may provide "unexpected" information—those norm violations may offer cultural lessons, but they do so by piquing people's curiosity. And conversely, gossip satisfies more than prurience. It can advance people's knowledge in the most unexpected ways.

When the great earthquake hit San Francisco on April 18, 1906, it was just after 5 A.M. People were sleeping, making coffee, pulling out their vegetable wagons, and preparing for work. Some were thrown out of bed, others were knocked to the ground, and some were caught on bridges. Many were living in flimsy homes, completely vulnerable to the devastation that was unfolding, though the quake itself lasted mere seconds. Williams James, who was teaching for the year at Stanford University, woke and felt "the bed waggle." He later recalled a powerful thrill, a sense of wild joy that he was in the midst of something catastrophic, huge, and uncontrollable. After checking on his wife, Alice, he quickly set out to be part of things, soon making his way into the center of San Francisco, to watch and find out what people were going through. At the end of the next day, his complete journal entry read, "Talked Earthquake all day" (Richardson 2007). Given his stature as the philosopher who practically single-handedly created the study of mental experience, and forecast almost every important domain of modern psychological inquiry, it shouldn't be surprising to find that his way of understanding an earthquake, that most nonhuman and nature-based event, was through talking to others. He knew, better than most, that what people said about the event, and one another, would be fascinating and informative. He satisfied his endless curiosity through one kind of gossip.

EARLY GLIMMERS OF GOSSIP

Gossip stems from our fundamental curiosity about other people's lives. When does that kind of curiosity begin? My lazy hours of overheard gossip between my grandmother and Aunt Louise happened from the time I was about five until I left home for college. But the truth is, like children everywhere, I began to learn about gossip long before that. A child's first encounters with talking about others occur in the high chair.

As a graduate student in New York City, I spent two years recording toddlers and their mothers having breakfast. I was conducting a study to find out how children learned first words in the context of everyday conversations with their mothers. I expected to hear lots of talk about the Cheerios, the family dog, the juice cup, and whatever else was going on in the kitchen. What took me by surprise was all the talk about things that had already happened—the "there and then." At about the same time, other scholars were zeroing in on the emergence of what Jacqueline Sachs called "Talking about the There and Then" (Sachs 1983). Researchers began to realize that toddlers were learning to use language not only to name and narrate what was happening in the moment, but what had *already happened.*

The breakfast conversations I recorded showed that some parents tell lots of stories about other people (*who* did *what, where* and *when*), while other parents rarely did, sticking instead to what was going on at the moment, or telling stories about the past that did not emphasize other people. The mothers who did tell stories about other people usually offered fairly simple vivid descriptions, instinctively crafted to capture a young child's attention: Remember last week when we went to the park with Rosie, and she ate five brownies? Subsequent research showed that children whose mothers reminisced developed in a way that was slightly different from children whose mothers did not. They told more personal stories themselves, and the stories were richer in detail (Engel 1995; Miller et al. 1990; Dunn 1988).

Most of that research examined two interwoven lines of development: how children learn to tell stories, and how they learn to remember their own lives—part of what Ulric Neisser called "the extended self" (Neisser 1988). The focus of most of that research was on what children learned about storytelling, and what they learned about themselves. But a return to those data shows something else as well. While most of the stories toddlers participate in are about their own experiences, both ordinary and special (trips to the park, bruised knees, a visit from a relative, spilled orange juice, a fire alarm, as well as breakfast time, bath time, and bedtime), along the way they also overhear a great many stories being told. Some of these they might actively participate in, and some they may quietly listen to. Many of the stories they overhear adults tell are about other people.

Sprawled on a chair in my grandmother's kitchen, I learned a lot about what was worth passing on about a neighbor—misdemeanors, strife, wealth and poverty, grief, sex, and what women say to one another in confidence. Nor am I the only child to have benefited from all that eavesdropping. For her classic study of the way people talk in two southern communities, Roadville and Trackton, the anthropologist Shirley Brice-Heath interviewed mothers, fathers, children, and storekeepers. She hung out in their homes and recorded their daily conversations with one another. A careful look at those conversations showed that children overheard and absorbed a lot of what adults were saying, even when the children were not directly involved in the conversations. The children in Trackton, a black working-class community, learned that stories are supposed to enthrall, while the children in Roadville, a nearby white working-class community, learned that stories should be used to impart moral principles. Each community not only handed down a different idea about why stories are told, but imparted to its youngest members an implicit set of guidelines about how to tell those stories (Brice-Heath 1983).

During the first four years, when it comes to gossip proper, children are mere bystanders to their parents' exchanges with one another. We know, from the work of Brice-Heath and others, that in many communities children are frequently privy to language not directed at them. The conversations adults have with one another influence how children talk and think. For instance, adults in Madagascar think young children are not ready to know about ghosts and spirits. They discuss these matters while the children are supposed to be playing separately. However, research shows that the children do hear those conversations and are influenced by what they hear—their own beliefs about the afterlife reflect those overheard discussions (Astuti 2011). Certainly here in the United States, most children hear a great deal of talk that is not directed at them. Children hear their parents talking, they hear older siblings talking with one another and with friends, they hear teachers talking to one another, and they hear neighbors exchanging information. Given the ubiquity of gossip, it is reasonable to assume that many children are exposed to lots of stories—what child is in trouble, what parents are divorcing, who lost their job, who eloped, and who just got inexplicably richer.

THE VALUE OF SECONDHAND KNOWLEDGE

Recently researchers have begun to document the ways in which children learn about the unseen and unseeable by listening to what adults tell them (Harris 2012). That body of research has, for the most part, emphasized the way in which preschoolers learn about things such as germs, God, the tooth fairy, and death by overhearing what adults say. But when you put that together with Baumeister's argument, it is no leap at all to see that children also learn about the somewhat unseeable, unknown world of social codes and personal mores through the stories they hear. Some of those stories may be told directly to the children, but some may not. Many years ago my student Luke Hyde and I asked four-year-old and seven-year-old children to tell us stories about members of their family. Among other topics, we asked them to tell us stories about how their parents met, and stories about their grandparents. In particular, we were trying to find out if they knew stories about things they couldn't possibly have witnessed—secondhand information. Virtually all the children we interviewed knew at least one story that happened to their parents (or in a few cases a much older sibling) before they were born. In other words, they had heard, paid attention to, and remembered stories about loved ones that gave them vital information. It was clear from those data that children do indeed pay attention to and remember secondhand information about other people's lives.

By the time children are four or so, they not only listen to their parents talk about other people—they also begin, in fledgling form, to gossip themselves. The sociologist Gary Fine has shown that children as young as four talk about one another, and do so for a wide range of purposes—to evaluate other children, to tease them, and to learn about the ways of the world (1977). He found that unlike adults, children are quite matter-of-fact and brazen about their gossip, often talking to one friend about another right in front of the child. He describes children practicing gossiping, repeating stories several times to different friends in an effort, he claims, to tell the story in the right way. In her book *The Beginnings of Social Understanding*, Judy Dunn documents the narratives of preschoolers (1988). She argues that by the time children are three years old, they tell more stories about other people than they did when they were toddlers, and she argues that this reflects preschool children's increasing interest in other people.

In a wonderful study of gossip, Daniela O'Neill and her colleagues tape-recorded the snack-time conversations of twenty-five preschoolers over a period of twenty-five weeks. Over 77 percent of the conversations children initiated with one another referenced other people, and nearly 30 percent mentioned people's mental states. In other words, the children were strongly inclined to talk about people, and to talk about their thoughts and feelings—clear signs of budding gossipers (O'Neill, Main, and Ziemski 2009). Peggy Miller's work (Miller et al. 1992) shows that by the time children are five, more of their stories include information not just about themselves, but about themselves in relation to other people. In one of the most inventive studies of children's narratives with one another, Alison Preece tape-recorded three young children in a car as they drove to and from school each day, for a period of eighteen months (1987). She identified sixteen different narrative forms, including two that emphasized other people: "vicarious experience" and "tattle telling." These two forms accounted for 25 percent of the total number of narratives. Anecdotes of vicarious experience tended to depict out-of-the-ordinary events, transgressions, and misadventures.

As the three children got older they told more and more of these anecdotes.

In 2001 my student Alice Li and I wanted to find out what kinds of things children know about one another. Alice simply asked children to tell her stories about a good friend. The children knew quite a bit about their friends. They seemed to carry around three kinds of such knowledge: timeless information (her friend has three brothers); routines (she always gets on the bus at the corner of Elm and School Streets); and unusual experiences (when he went camping with his dad, he got a bloody nose). The older children told longer stories, included more descriptions, more evaluation, and more focus on the internal landscape of their friends. While the younger children mostly told stories of things they had participated in, older children told more stories that they had heard from their friends and, increasingly, heard about their friends. In other words, gossip became a more important tool for learning about others. Looking at the actual reports shows that children are keenly interested in one another's habits, experiences, and quirks. For instance, one ten-year-old boy said this about his friend D: "D likes to read so we call him the bookworm. And so, like he would sharpen his pencil when Ms. G's speaking so he's not supposed to and he sharpens it on his desk. And sometimes when he's not supposed to read, he just keeps it on his lap and just looks down every time. And at snacks, he just gets a Clementine and starts to eat it. He doesn't even care, and reads at the same time. Gets a Clementine and gets up on his desk and holds down on his book and starts to read it" (Engel and Li 2004).

GOSSIP BECOMES A SOCIAL WEAPON

By the time children are six, stories about the lives of others take on a whole new relevance and power. Moving beyond their family circle, they become caught up in a world of friends, allies, and enemies their own age. And they discover that information about all those peers is as valuable as money. As the politics of friendship take center stage, getting and giving information about others becomes a potent new tool.

Even in preschool, children already show an awareness of whom they prefer to play with and whom they do not. What may begin as an evaluation of who is "fun to play with" or "nice to me" begins to include an awareness of other children in terms of one another. By the time they are six they know who is popular, who is not, who gets invited to play regularly, and who tends to be left out. By asking children questions like "Whom would you most/least like to spend time with?" or "Who is the most/least popular person in the class?" psychologists can map the social alliances of schoolchildren. We even have some clues about why this fuller awareness of the social world emerges when it does. Sometime during their fifth year, all typically developing children show evidence that they now have a "theory of mind"—an awareness that other people's thoughts are different from their own, and that those thoughts and intentions are based on the particular experiences each person has had. In the most famous version of this, Josef Perner told children a story in which a little boy named Max placed a chocolate bar into a drawer in the kitchen before going out to play. While he was out, his mother moved the chocolate bar to a cabinet above the counter. Perner asked preschoolers where they thought Max would look for the candy when he came back inside. Before the age of five, children think that Max will look in the correct place, the cabinet—they show no understanding that Max doesn't know that the chocolate has been moved. But almost all children seem to answer correctly by the time they are six—they know that Max will look in the drawer because he had no way of knowing what the listener knows, that Max's mom has moved the chocolate. In other words, sometime during the fifth year, almost all children seem to develop an understanding that people's beliefs are based on what they have encountered, and that those encounters (and the beliefs they lead to) might be different from one's own (Perner 1992). Psychologists take this, and the legion of studies that followed it, to show that at around age five children develop a psychological theory in which people's experiences and thoughts are not necessarily alike, or like one's own.

Once children are able to think about the thoughts of other children, they may begin to use this newfound ability to think about how peers think of one another. In some sense their representation of the world of peers moves from two-dimensional to three-dimensional. This more layered understanding of the social world manifests itself in several ways. Robin Banerjee (2002) told children between the ages of six and nine a story in which the protagonist was either moving to a new school and would meet some unfamiliar children, or was moving to a new neighborhood and would meet some new adults. Subjects were then asked to choose which of two phrases the protagonist should use to describe him or herself to these new acquaintances; they could choose between "I always work hard at school" or "I run very fast." In another trial, the choice was between "I always work hard at school" or "I share things with friends." In the first trial Banerjee found that only the oldest children made their choice based on their sense of the audience (children or adults). But in a second trial, when the subjects were told a little about what kind of child the adults in the neighborhood or children in the school might favor (clever children or sporty children, for instance), even the younger children based their advice on what they had been told the imagined audience would prefer. In other words, children begin to learn about self-presentation and the role it plays in what other people might think about you. In another demonstration of this emerging awareness, Peter Blake and Katherine McAuliffe provided children between the ages of four and nine with an opportunity to divide candy with an unfamiliar peer. In one condition, the child could press a lever that dumped one candy on her side of the table, and dumped four candies on the other child's side. In a second condition, the child could press a lever that gave herself four candies, and the other child just one. During these sessions, parents and experimenters were watching. Children of all ages rejected the disadvantageous option (none of them one wanted the other child to get more than they did). But only the eldest children also rejected the option of giving the other child fewer than themselves (all children got several chances to pull a lever that allowed each of them to get one candy). Blake interpreted this as showing that the oldest children were uncomfortable with the unfairness of getting four candies and giving only one to a partner—their choices were governed by a sense of equity (Blake and McAuliffe 2011).

But it turns out the situation is not that straightforward. In a subsequent study, Blake manipulated whether the audience (parents and experimenters) could see what was happening or not (by virtue of a screen) and whether the partner could see which option the subject had chosen. Only the older children were more likely in this version of the game to choose the advantageous option (getting more candies than the partner) if they knew no one could see. In other words, by the time children are eight, their sense of reputation can guide their behavior (Blake 2012). Sociometric data have shown that by the time children are nine years old they make a distinction between which children they'd actually like to play with and which children they think are popular (Parkhurst and Hopmeyer 1998). At this point, children's representations of the social world take on yet another layer. Not only do they have some awareness of other children's reputations—they know that those reputations are based in part on the things people say about one another. The psychologist Valerie Hill (2007) told six- and ten-year-olds gossip about hypothetical children, and asked them to reflect on what they had heard. She found that children as young as six understand that unpleasant gossip about a person will make that person less popular, and that telling a nice story about someone unpopular will help that person make friends. In other words they already know, by six, that gossip can have an impact on one's reputation.

Taken together, these studies suggest that during elementary school, children become keenly aware of their own and other children's social standing and reputation. By the time they are in third grade they carry around mental representations of dynamic social matrices. They almost always picture themselves within a matrix, whether it is the social world at school, on the block where they live, or among cousins or a baseball team. These reputations are built, in part, on what children do (who is good at baseball, who is funny, who is pretty, and so forth). This is particularly true of younger children. So, for instance, when my students asked schoolchildren to talk about their closest friends, one four-year-old said, "J hurts me a lot, because she pushed me off the beam outside on the playground and she threw sand in my eye." But as they get older these direct observations become laced with more reputational concerns. A ten-year-old said, "She just acts really weird sometimes. She's mean sometimes. But we're still nice to her because we don't want her to know that we don't like her." Now, instead of a narrative based only on the speaker's direct experience with her friend, her description conveys information about what has transpired with others, in relation to the friend. As these representations become more multidimensional, they also begin to incorporate more secondhand information. One seven-year-old said about his friend, "He got hit by a golf club once around his eye. I think it was W's sister who did it." In other words, the speaker's knowledge of his friend now incorporates the rumor that the sister hit his friend in the eye. Children during this period also begin to be interested in what their friends do, see, and experience when they are not together. A ten-year-old said about her friend, "She visits her dad every other week on the weekend. She takes the bus. Not a school bus or anything, but like a regular bus. She said it's like really freaky 'cause everybody reeks or smokes."

A fly on the wall of any elementary or middle school hallway would hear a steady stream of children's commentary about who is part of the group, who is not, who is mean, and who is cool. Children are monitoring the lives of other children, just as adults monitor one another's lives. But that is not all they are doing. Just as adults learn about their community, discuss norm violations, and enrich their picture of others' lives, children also gossip in part just to get more information. They collect information about other people the way they do about machines, bugs, and dragons—to satisfy a fundamental interest in other people.

There are wonderful data that demonstrate this. Kristina McDonald and her colleagues invited sixty pairs of fourth-grade friends into the lab to have a snack and "talk like you normally would on the playground, at lunch, or at one of your houses" (McDonald et al. 2007, 398). Fifteen minutes of each of these sessions were analyzed for the amount and kind of gossip the girls engaged in. Gossip made up nearly half of the girls' dialogue. Though the couples varied a lot, on average, each dyad engaged in about thirty-six "gossips," discussing twenty-five different people. Most of the gossip was about friends, and most of it was neutral (not mean, or even particularly evaluative). Most of that gossip concerned other people's behavior, rather than their physical or personal characteristics. And contrary to our stereotypes about gender, girls are not the only ones gossiping.

Michael Bamberg followed a group of ten- to fifteen-year-old boys longitudinally, collecting the stories they wrote, told one another, shared during group conversations, and told to an experimenter. During the time the boys were together with a moderator, talking about various matters of interest, they engaged in a fair amount of storytelling, including what Bamberg refers to as "small stories"—snippets of conversation that put ideas and experiences into narrative form but are fleeting, incomplete, and often seemingly inconsequential. Some of these small stories are clear examples of gossip. For instance, when the moderator asks the ten-year-old boys what they like about girls, after a lot of hemming and hawing, one little boy whispers a story about a friend, who supposedly no longer lives in the neighborhood, to another of the boys at the table, who then shares it with the larger group: "There's this cute girl that lives on his street and his friend said that said that um look he looked at her legs and she was wearing a dress and he said WHOAA" (Bamberg and Georgakopoulou 2008, 384). This is a perfect example of children sharing personal information about an acquaintance, as well as relevant information about how one should or should not behave around girls. In other words, children not only learn through gossip they overhear from adults; they also learn through gossip they exchange with one another. When four-year-olds are asked to talk about their friends, most of what they say describes the friend's physical characteristics (she has a bicycle; he has darkish hair) or shared experience (S is funny; we were on the bus and S was being really funny; we were like making silly things). But by the time children are ten, much more of their knowledge about their friends conveys information about a friend's internal landscape (she likes to read; she likes books and she likes Harry Potter; she just read *The BFG* for our book report but she hated it 'cause the teacher told us that the author doesn't like children so he makes bad stuff happen to them) and biological information (her parents got divorced when she was little). It seems clear that as children's intellectual worlds expand and deepen, so too do the style and the focus of their gossip.

In addition, our data provide intriguing evidence that children's ideas about the social dynamics involved in sharing gossip are fairly subtle. We were interested in whether children noticed who was soliciting gossip from them. So two different young women conducted the interviews. Children were far more forthcoming, and provided more information and details about the information, when talking to one of the women than they were when talking to the other. Pellegrini and Galda (1990) argue that children commonly shift what they say, and how they say it, in response to their conversational partner. The fact that children are so sensitive to specific characteristics of their interlocutor presents a methodological challenge to researchers, but this sensitivity is also illuminating. Children's responsiveness to audience suggests that at an early age they are interested not only in the content of the story, but also in the dynamics between the teller and listener of the story. Not only will they gossip differently with different persons (who doesn't?), but they interpret gossip differently, depending on who is passing on information to them. By the time children are ten, they have a fairly developed idea about the motives of gossip, and the way it reflects on the gossiper, as well as the target of the gossip (Hill 2007; Ben Ze'ev 1994). In this sense, when children gossip, they acquire three kinds of information—knowledge about the target of their gossip (who pushed whom, who lives in a big house, who kissed a classmate, and who got punished), knowledge about what is condoned and frowned upon in their social group, and knowledge about the person with whom they are gossiping. Though perhaps only a biologist would leap at the chance to look through a microscope, and only a historian would give anything for access to original documents, every Tom, Dick, or Harry is eager for the vast knowledge available just by leaning over the fence to talk.

NOT EVERYONE'S A BUDDING TROLLOPE

And yet, not all children are equally interested in other people. It is self-evident that children, like adults, vary in their eagerness to hear the doings of a classmate or a child who lives next door. Some children, from a very early age, seem especially alert for clues and stories about other people—how they live, what they do and say, and what has happened to them in the past. In a set of interviews I conducted with parents of kindergarteners, while almost all the parents spontaneously described their children as curious, only some mentioned their children's zeal for watching people interact and eavesdropping on other people's conversations. One mother told me that when she and her husband or friends were talking in the kitchen, her five-year-old daughter would leave the area where the children were playing and whisper to her mother, "Tell them to talk louder." There is some empirical support for the idea that this is a stable and important individual difference.

Simon Baron-Cohen and colleagues have argued that children tend to be either empathizers or systematizers. Empathizers experience the world in terms of other people and their feelings, while systematizers are more attuned to objects and the patterns they create (Baron-Cohen, Knickmeyer, and Belmonte 2005). This echoes a distinction Dennie Wolf made over thirty years ago between two kinds of play in childhood—that of patterners and that of dramatists (Shotwell, Wolf, and Gardner 1979). In her model, patterners were interested in blocks and other toys that lent themselves to organizing, categorizing, and creating interesting structures. Dramatists were drawn to toys that allowed them to enact scenarios. While patterners might take a group of action figures and organize them by color, or type, dramatists might take a group of colored blocks and turn them into characters. Similarly, there is evidence that some children are particularly interested in finding out about other people.

Kristina McDonald et al. (2007) asked 139 fourth-grade girls to choose a friend to participate with them in a study. Each pair of friends was then recorded for thirty minutes while eating snacks and making crafts, having been encouraged by the experimenters to "talk like you usually do." The girls gossiped a lot—more than half their dialogue was gossip. Some of the time, they used gossip to evaluate others.

M: Tyson is ugly.
H: What's so bad about Tyson?
M: Nothing's wrong with Tyson, it's just that. . . .
H: He got monkey ears. (403)

A good deal of the time, however, the gossip was fairly neutral in tone. Instead, the girls seemed to simply be exchanging information with one another about other children. For example, one girl told the other about a gift she got for another friend. "J: Lisa, I got one for her. She was wanting a real Tamagachi, but I got her a Pet Vet. It's about the same thing, except four buttons and three buttons. It's kinda different. And, um, she plays with that a whole lot, and she taught me how to play" (402–403).

The authors noted interesting individual differences as well. In their sample, pairs composed of African American girls gossiped more, and about a greater number of other children, than the Caucasian girls. In addition, McDonald et al. found that popular girls gossiped more than

rejected girls. Obviously these data do not allow us to see if girls become popular, in part, because they are such skillful gossips, or whether
gossiping constitutes the spoils of war.

In her ethnography of black children in Philadelphia in the 1980s,
Marjorie Harness Goodwin showed how boys and girls talked to one
another in order to construct a social world. Gossip was chief among
their conversational tools. Often they exchanged hearsay as a way of
solving disputes. For instance, the girls in her study engaged in what
they called "he said, she said," in which one girl accused another of
talking about her behind her back. Both Goodwin's analyses and the
examples themselves show how much intricate information the girls
provided to one another through their "he said, she said" exchanges.
Using somewhat different conversational rituals and rules, the boys also
used gossip to resolve disputes. In one lively example, a group of twelve-
to-fourteen-year-old boys are in the backyard of one of the boys, Tony,
playing a familiar game involving slingshots. Tony is trying to make
Chopper, one of the other boys, leave. Chopper doesn't want to and is
trying to gain the upper hand. He begins telling a story about Tony to
the other boys, as a way of discrediting him. "Lemme tell ya. Guess
what. We was comin' home from practice, and three boys came up there
and ask us for money and Tony did like this [raising hands up], 'I ain't
got no money.'" (See Goodwin for detailed linguistic comments on this
quote.) Though gossip was a powerful currency for almost all the children Goodwin studied, she also found that some children used gossip
more often and more skillfully than others, and that there were important differences between the ways in which the boys and girls
gossiped.

It seems likely that just as some children become fascinated by the
animal kingdom, and others by machines, some children's curiosity
zeroes in on the way people behave, think, and feel. It may well be that
by adulthood there are more people who are curious about their neighbors than there are people who are curious about the stars, entomology,
or history. Gender, personality, social milieu, social standing, and cir-
cumstance probably all play a role in determining just how avid a person
is for information about the lives of others.

As a child I lived in a bath of gossip. My mother did it, and so did
my older sister. My grandmother did it all the time, in one form or

another—often after she and Louise got off the phone, we'd watch soap operas together, simply a more passive and distant form of gossip. When I went to college, though she was barely literate, she'd send me letters about what had happened to our favorite characters. But these relatives were not my only mentors in gossiping.

When I was a little girl, Truman Capote floated in and out of my house. He was my mother's close friend and lived just down the road from us in Sagaponack. He would sashay into our house, calling out my mother's unlikely name, Tinka, in his high lisping singsong, "Oh, Tiinnnkkka." Often he'd walk straight past us children, with his nose in the air, irritated by our very presence, straight into her bedroom, to sit down on her chaise longue so that he could spend a good long session gossiping with her. If he came at lunchtime he'd bring Beluga caviar for the two of them to eat at our kitchen table. My stepfather, whose family had been farming potatoes for over two hundred years, and who came into the house from the fields for lunch every single day, hated caviar. He'd have a peanut butter sandwich and listen tolerantly as my mother and Truman gleefully exchanged stories and bits of information about neighbors and friends—what husband had been unfaithful to his wife with another man, what famous friendship was cracking at the seams, and the writer who hadn't written a word in seven years. From the time I was four until I was a teenager, I'd linger on a couch nearby, not hungry for food, but ravenous for every morsel of information and story Truman and my mother were sharing over lunch. One blustery winter night he dropped by to say hello, and because we were in the living room, where the fireplace was, he stayed awhile to chat with all of us. That night, instead of dishing on high society, he gossiped about a long ago Thanksgiving meal, in the house where he'd lived as a child, in Alabama. I listened in a sleepy way. I was six or so, and often aggravated by his voice, his outlandish behavior, and his claim on my mother's attention. But I loved hearing every detail about his cousin Sook Faulk, and the other strange relatives he lived with. I couldn't get enough of hearing about such a different kind of home and all that went on inside it. It was only years later that I realized he was telling the story that would become "The Thanksgiving Visitor," a sequel of sorts to his classic book *A Christmas Memory.* Truman drifted in and out of my childhood home, and in and out of my thinking. And in Truman, I had a shimmering example of what a person could do with gossip. As a young author living in New York, Truman befriended all kinds of people, but particularly women in high society. He was charming and sharp-tongued—eager to vacuum up every detail about who slept with whom, who had lost their money, and who had betrayed their best friend. He knew that through them he could unearth a treasure trove of material for his work. Drawing people out about their hidden stories became the golden path to the knowledge he wanted.

Truman would tell my mother that the best way to get someone to talk was to tell your companion something about yourself. He would confide in someone—a stranger, a friend, or a housemaid, just to prime the pump. And he wouldn't just offer some bland or innocuous bait, either. He'd go to interview someone and begin by confiding some sad private detail about himself that made his listener feel she were privy to something special. Next thing you knew, that person would be telling him all about her darkest secrets. His rapt attention, his sympathy, his thorough interest in what the other person was recounting elicited far more potent material than the most well-designed interview ever could.

When he lounged in my mother's bedroom trading stories, it seemed like quintessentially idle gossip—salacious, slightly mean, and funny. But his gossip was not idle. It was fodder for his examination of human frailty. He took every story, every piece of retold conversation and tidbit of information and transformed it into narratives that illuminate the way people live and what motivates them to cheat, murder, hoard, lie, brag, and betray. All his books contain gossip of one sort or another, but his final work, *Answered Prayers,* was so transparent in its use of gossip drawn from his own social life that it cost him many friends.

Recently, some forty-five years after my childish eavesdropping, I dreamed that I was sitting at an outdoor café, in a city quite a bit like Nice, France. People in my family were there too—both of my sisters, some of my nieces and nephews, my mom, and maybe a few of my kids, a group that might be on vacation together. Then out of nowhere, as people do in a dream, Truman walked up with the two bulldogs, Maggie and Charlie, he had owned and loved for many years before his death, on leashes. When he saw us, he wandered straight over to talk. After a few minutes of friendly conversation I stood up and began to stroll away with him and his dogs, down the small cobbled streets into the heart of the city. As we walked, I said to him, "You and I are just alike. You love to read and write. And I love to read and write." And he said to me, in his lilting whine, "Yes Susie darling, and we both love to gossip."

What did my dreamed Truman think we had in common? Just that psychologists and novelists share an appetite for the inner workings of the social world. We want to know what people are saying and doing, especially the things that happen behind bedroom and kitchen walls, the things we are not meant to know—the things that tell the real story. For those of us who are curious about the inner lives of others, gossip is key.

Some of us turn our love of gossip into a life's work. But we're not the only ones who want to know what's going on behind closed doors. While a significant minority of adults pursue an intense interest in subjects like volcanoes, World War II, or stamps, nearly all of us are at least a little curious about our neighbors, our coworkers, and the lives of our favorite movie stars. Most people spend time at the water cooler, leaning over a backyard fence, or whispering on the checkout line at the grocery store. And call that what you want—prurience, nosiness, or schadenfreude—our interest in other people's business is what binds communities, creates good fiction, leads to the insights that help us navigate the social world, and turns some of us into psychologists. It follows, then, that its roots can be found in early childhood.

Though adults in our society often discourage children from asking too many questions about subjects like history, geology, and numbers, we aren't able to kill their curiosity about others, particularly other children. It may be one of the most resilient forms of curiosity.

8

The Uses of Time and Solitude

WHEN I WAS ten my teacher's name was Kelly Patton. She was from South Carolina, and her primary love in life was the theater. I have no idea how or when she realized I was an avid and fast reader, or what we were studying that made her offer me a copy of *Gone with the Wind*, but that's what she did. All I can recall of the assignment, if you can call it that, was Kelly saying, "Here, I think this will be a good book for you to read." She handed it to me in October. From the first I was completely hooked. I read obsessively, finishing in February. I must have spent over two thousand hours, nearly eighty-six days, reading it.

Though the Civil War battle scenes bogged me down (and during the five months it took me to get through it, I vaguely recall taking breaks to read mysteries written for teens), my inner life became suffused with Scarlett O'Hara, Rhett Butler, and all the objects, scenes, and elements of their saga. I was completely oblivious to its terrible politics, the shameful and diminishing way Mitchell portrayed black people, and its repulsive view of the KKK. All I could see or feel was the life of a southern belle, the absorbing details of wartime, the blood, velvet, iced tea, horse-drawn carriages, and sweeping lawns of the white American South in the 1860s.

When I finally finished it, I was devastated—partly because Rhett left Scarlett, and partly because the book was over. I couldn't accept either finale, and solved both problems with one solution. I kept re-

reading it, going back to the parts where they kissed, where they were in love, where she said charming things to him, where he ravished her (the implied rape in one crucial scene completely eluded me), and where they were happy together. I reread those parts so many times I could recite them, easily, from memory any time of the day or night.

My obsession did not end there. My mother gave me a green leather copy for my twelfth birthday, with my name embossed in gold on the spine. When I was thirteen, my grandmother's dressmaker made me a green velvet gown, like the one Scarlett had made from the drapes, in an attempt to save Tara after the war and climb her way out of destitution.

I also learned a great deal about the Civil War. For several years, I knew far more about that period of history than any other (at some point in my early teens, I gained similar familiarity with the Russian and French revolutions and the English Reformation because of *Dr. Zhivago*, a historical novel about Marie Antoinette, and a biography of Queen Elizabeth I).

At dinnertime I'd finish before the others and go lie on the couch nearby where I could read my current novel, and periodically eavesdrop on the dinner conversation that continued in my absence. We lived very close to the ocean, and in the summer I'd soon tire of the beach, leaving after thirty minutes or so, long before anyone else, to come home and lie in the cool shady living room so that I could read my book. I was a fiction lover, and the closer a book came to the melodrama and rich depiction of life in the past contained in books like *Gone with the Wind,* the better. I read every Regency romance written by Georgette Heyer, and every historical romance by Victoria Holt. By the time I was thirteen I had discovered the pleasure of reading good writing. Charlotte Brontë, Jane Austen, and Emily Brontë had replaced the cheaper thrills of my preteens.

When I was young, I had a nearly insatiable appetite for reading and for the information I could absorb through novels. I learned far more that way than I did almost any other way. I learned about wars, about city and country life in the 1800 and 1900s, I learned about farming methods, rape, aristocracy, slavery, medicine, and childbirth, to name just a few of the topics imbedded within those novels. One year, when I was about thirteen, all I wanted were books about movie stars. There was a dusty crowded bookstore in nearby Southampton, with an irritable owner named Bob Keene. But he liked me because I liked books, and because the bookstore was the only place, besides the penny-candy counter, where I had a charge account. Each time Mr. Keene got in a new volume on one of the old Hollywood stars (Greta Garbo, Clark Gable, Ava Gardner, Charlie Chaplin), he'd call me up and tell me, and I'd beg a ride into town to get the book, which I would then study backward and forward until I knew every piece of information contained within. What makes some children turn to books to satisfy their curiosity? My interest was superficial, somewhat prurient, and escapist. But I absorbed a great deal of knowledge, perusing all those books.

Not everyone satisfies her curiosity by tinkering or gossiping. Some turn to a book. The habit of turning to a book, an article, or a page of Wikipedia begins, for most, at an early age. And like many habits, it begins not with what a child does, but with what she sees others doing. We've long known that children understand language before they can produce it, and their level of comprehension continues to be a step ahead of their production at least into the middle of elementary school, if not beyond (Snow 1983; Brown 1973; Bloom 1973). Once they can understand even some of what others say, they begin to attend to the stories those around them are telling. I described this process in some detail in Chapter 7, on gossip. But it is not only the information they hear about neighbors and relatives that sinks in. From what they hear, children also learn a great deal about the process of telling stories. And in many families and communities the art of making up a story is just as important as the art of gossip (Miller et al. 1990; Mullen and Yi 1995; Engel 1995).

The urge to hear and tell stories is universal—people in every community construct narratives for one another (Bruner 1990; Chafe 1980). In many communities people also tell each other what could have happened, and even what couldn't have ever possibly happened. As Jerome Bruner famously argued, a narrative is indifferent to facts (Bruner 1986). For something to be a story, it needn't tell the truth, be accurate, or contain facts about real life. It just needs to depict an action, or a series of actions, a sense of sequence that conveys meaning, a protagonist, and a perspective—a narrative voice. And yet, as Russell and Lucariello (1992) argued, not everything is a narrative. If I tell you I had coffee with hot milk for breakfast, I have not offered you a narrative, just a detail from my day. If I complain on and on about my stepmother, I have not constructed a narrative, though a friend or therapist might construct one based on my various complaints. A narrative is a story told in writing or talking, or implied through actions (depicted through gesture, in a ballet, or drawing, in a comic strip).

We know that some families tell more stories than others. And we know that the number and quality of those stories seem to have an impact on a child's tendency to tell stories as he grows up. Children who hear more stories, and just as important, tell more stories collaboratively, *with* their parents (Engel 1995), tell more stories, for a wider range of purposes, as they get older. Children who reminisce, when they are toddlers, with their parents, are more likely to depict events in a rich, detailed, and clear way when they are telling stories on their own, as preschoolers and beyond. Studies suggest that children who rarely reminisce with their parents are much less likely to tell elaborate or informative stories as they get older, and less likely to use personal stories as a way of thinking about their lives (Spence 1983; Schafer 1992).

Here, the human mind and human habits collude. We seem to be born with an urge and ability to understand the world as a series of stories (hence the primacy of scripts in early cognitive development). Anthropologists and cross-cultural psychologists have found that though every culture uses stories, cultures vary greatly in how frequently they tell stories, how they form their narratives, and why they tell stories. But one thing everyone everywhere seems to have in common is the ability to follow a plot. And therein lies the first reason reading satisfies curiosity. As I argued in Chapter 6, everyone wants to know what will happen next.

But in addition to the ways in which narrative structure (the plot) and content (gossip) may feed curiosity, early narratives play one other crucial role in the growth of curiosity. There is a clear and sturdy path leading from storytelling at home to literacy at school. Children who hear and tell more stories as toddlers and preschoolers have an easier time learning to read. Again, this is no surprise. Though decoding and grasping the sound-letter correspondence is an essential component of learning to read, having some sense of narrative is equally important

(Wells 1986; Smith 1998). There is also some evidence that children who lean toward using words to describe things (as opposed to using words to *do* things) have an easier time learning to read. All of this seems to converge on a connection—children who are surrounded by stories are more likely to become readers. But only if they have access to reading materials, and see others read. One of the most unambiguous findings in the past fifty years of developmental research is that children who grow up with parents who read are much more likely to become readers themselves. But what does this actually mean? Though studies have shown that having parents who read is the best predictor of the likelihood a child will read, researchers still aren't completely sure why. It could be because parents who read more tend to be more educated, which leads them to encourage their children to engage in educational activities (like naming things, talking, and ultimately reading itself). It could be because parents who read more are smarter and have smarter children. It could be that parents who read simply provide a powerful role model. Most likely, the strength of the relationship comes from a convergence of all three causes—if your parents are privileged and educated and read regularly, you are very likely to read. Even if only one of those factors is true, it increases the chances a given child will read with ease. However, the ability to read is not altogether the same as the disposition to read.

What strand of behaviors and characteristics leads children to use books in order to satisfy their curiosity? It begins, in part, with the discovery that books offer them information about things to which they have no direct access—it might be big trucks, exotic birds, farm animals, monsters, fairies, or just details about those who live far away, or lived long ago.

For some, getting information from such an indirect and authoritative source (prose) is unappealing or even incomprehensible. A rural neighbor of mine has vast knowledge about the physical world around her. Growing up she became highly skilled in hiking, mountain biking, kayaking, rafting, and camping. Moreover, she knew a great deal about certain aspects of nature—how to identify birds, mark a trail in the woods, or navigate a river. But by the time her first child was three years old it was clear that he far preferred a book to a hike, complaining loudly to us on one such hike, "Mom, I don't like the nature. I'm tired of the nature." However, hand him a Tintin comic book, an encyclopedia of superheroes, or even just a copy of *National Geographic,* and he would settle in, absorbed for hours, oblivious of the people and activity around him. The grown-ups in his family became quite upset that he was such a bookworm. They couldn't understand why he would rather read than wander, touch, and look. For them, the word does not hold more satisfying information than the thing. Concerned, his parents sought advice from a child psychologist, worried that he "buried his head in books all day" and often became "lost in a book." To them, his reading indicated that he was withdrawing from the engaging world around him. But he may well have felt that he was withdrawing from a concrete and limited world, into one that was vast and open. He wouldn't be the first child to feel that way.

Of course, there are obvious explanations for why a given child might prefer a book to the people and things around him—distressing family life, a reluctance to interact with people, a strong need for quiet, to name three common ones. But it's just as plausible that books offer a nearly endless supply of food for the hungry mind. It may be that children like my young neighbor want to know more information, or different kinds of information from what they can get walking in the woods.

Even among avid young readers, however, there are important differences. Imagine taking a group of fifth graders to the library to choose any book they like. To begin with, of course, some will have such disinterest in or difficulty with reading that they'll figure out how to not find a book. But of the readers, some will head straight for the fiction, and some will instead have eyes only for encyclopedias, how-tos, and other nonfiction sources of information. These two categories of books sate the reader's curiosity for different reasons.

COLLECTORS

The one who rushes over to find a book on mushrooms or submarines wants information—the more of it, the more detailed and encyclopedic, the better. Not all children leave this nearly bottomless appetite for information behind them as they grow up. There are, lurking among us in the adult world, plenty of people who collect the information that they find in books—sometimes they begin collecting the books themselves.

A wonderfully recursive example of this centers on the author Simon Winchester. His most famous and successful book was the best-selling *The Professor and the Madman*—an account of the strange collaboration between Dr. W. C. Minor, a Civil War veteran, and Professor James Murray, the British scholar responsible for overseeing the creation of original Oxford English Dictionary. Minor was incarcerated for violently stabbing someone to death, for apparently no reason. Murray depended on a number of outside amateur philologists to send him material for the dictionary. When he discovered that one man (Minor) had sent him more than ten thousand entries, the committee wanted to honor this important contributor. That's when they learned that he was in prison for murder. Winchester's best seller dramatizes the unfolding of Murray and Minor's strange connection, but its real story is a tale of word collecting. Winchester went on to write a book called *The Meaning of Everything: The Story of the Oxford English Dictionary* (2003). A perusal of Winchester's work shows that while he is both a historian and a best-selling author of nonfiction, he is actually, at heart, a collector. What he collects most passionately is information about books, collectors, and collectors of books. His works include a book about Joseph Needham, the Asian scholar who studied the history of Chinese science, accumulating a vast collection of Chinese works of science and reference; a book about the photograph Lewis Carroll owned of Alice Liddell, the little girl for whom he wrote *Alice in Wonderland*; and a book about Alan Dudley, a collector of bones and skulls. In one vivid example of this absorption with other word collectors, he wrote a review for the *New York Review of Books* about Jonathon Green's *Dictionary of Slang* (2012). He begins that review by describing an apartment on Perry Street in Greenwich Village, in New York City, and its inhabitant, Madeline Kripke, a women who, he says, for decades has been collecting books, manuscripts, and other related materials that have to do with dictionaries, with a particular interest in dictionaries of slang. In other words, Winchester is a collector of collectors of words. When asked, in 2012, why he thought people collected, Winchester responded without hesitation, "It's a need to dominate." It's an illuminating answer, coming from a collector who studies other collectors. How does this relate to curiosity? Because it may be that for collectors, the urge to acquire information is linked in some way to a sense of authority and, with it, a sense of power. But that's mere speculation. I only would go so far as to argue that collecting represents one form of inquiry—a strong impulse to gain a kind of exhaustive expertise over a domain. In Winchester's case, this urge to collect is completely intertwined with his obsession with books as a source of knowledge. In fact he describes more than one incident in which he unexpectedly and serendipitously discovered some volume that kept him up all night reading and led him to a whole new line of inquiry and, in some cases, a new idea for a book.

Sean Pidgeon, an editor of reference books at John Wiley, writes, "You may pity me, if you wish, but my compulsion is relatively mild. As a longtime publisher of scholarly and scientific reference works, I am addicted to looking things up" (2013). For him, like many of us, the process of looking things up is in and of itself somewhat addictive. We read a piece (as I first read his) and then find something in the piece we must know more about—a word, a name, a time in history, a topic—and before we know it, days have been swallowed up, as we follow each new intriguing thread to something that feels like a natural stopping place. He describes "research rapture" like this: "A state of enthusiasm or exaltation arising from the exhaustive study of a topic or period of history; the delightful but dangerous condition of becoming repeatedly sidetracked in following intriguing threads of information, or constantly searching for one more elusive fact."

Google has only made this addiction easier to feed and may actually encourage a certain kind of curiosity among many more people. I say "a certain kind" because, as I described earlier in the book, research has shown that there are, broadly speaking, two kinds of curiosity among adults at least—diversive and specific. Specific refers to a need to find ever more information on a particular topic. The person who has insatiable curiosity about, say, volcanoes, may in fact show very little curiosity about people's private lives, or even something more closely related, like, say, other explosive natural events (earthquakes, for instance). But some people seem to have what's called diversive curiosity—a somewhat less penetrating or sustained curiosity about many things—a general sense of interest. Imagine the difference between

Denis Diderot, whose vast and far-ranging interest led him eventually to create an encyclopedia, and, say, Jane Austen, who kept her unwavering laser eye on the nexus between the inner and outer lives of those who lived around her. Diderot would no doubt have been more tempted to spend hours and hours tracking things down on Google, while Austen would only have been tempted by certain sites that helped her delve into the lives of other people.

In the past ten years there has been a surge of empirical work examining the patterns of people who look things up online. An enormous volume of data is available through sources such as Wikipedia, and web designers have carried out a great deal of this research, interested in finding out how people search for information. This behavior even has its own wonderful name: foraging. This metaphor is particularly apt, since it suggests that information, like food, feeds an appetite. It turns out people tend to employ one of two strategies—one when they are after some particular kind of information, or trying to learn about a very specific topic, and another when they are simply browsing. These two patterns mirror the two kinds of curiosity that researchers have identified—diversive and specific.

There is every reason to believe that among children who read, a taste for nonfiction may emerge early. But they are not the only readers.

FICTIONAL WORLDS

The one who heads for novels wants to know about the worlds conveyed through fiction. Often, readers of novels are curious, perhaps without knowing it, about the thoughts and intentions of others. In a series of experiments, David Kidd and Emanuele Castano gave adult subjects well-written passages to read. Some subjects read fiction (for instance Louise Erdrich and Alice Munro), and some read nonfiction (from publications such as *Smithsonian* magazine). Then all the subjects were asked to do a variety of tasks measuring their ability to think about other people's thoughts, intentions, and feelings. For instance, in one task subjects were asked to interpret the emotions portrayed in photographs of pairs of eyes. In others they were asked to solve a complex false-belief task. Subjects who had read fiction that was, in the words of the authors, polyphonic and writerly, scored better on tests of empathy and theory of mind than those who had read well-written non-fiction (2013). People who read a lot of fiction may be very similar to William James, eager to know what other people are feeling and thinking. Novels provide an endless source of information about the characters, whose lives may differ so widely from one's own, but also about the author, who is thinking out loud for the reader, showing at least one version of how they think and feel about the world (hence the notion of polyphony, described by Mikhail Bakhtin).

Reading, then, provides an important and vast source of satisfaction for many kinds of curiosity. But it is not only what is in books that makes reading a valuable resource for the curious mind. When I spent all hours at home on the couch in the shady living room, it was not only the worlds created by Mitchell, Austen, and the Brontës that drew me in—it was also the fact that when I read, I was by myself.

SOLITUDE

Solitude plays an important and often underrecognized role in a child's chance to pursue her questions and interests. In recent years there has been such focus on the importance of peer relations, and on the value of good instruction and good schooling, we may have lost track of an equally vital strand of childhood experience—free time and time alone. The bulk of contemporary developmental research has emphasized the perils of time alone, which tends to be cast as loneliness rather than solitude. Research has focused on children who have trouble making friends, or who are alone because of adverse life circumstances (weak family structure, poverty, and so on). It's no wonder then that a relationship emerges between solitude and various kinds of problems—depression, and difficulty in social situations, to name two. The link, once established, leads to research that frames solitude in its most extreme or persistent forms—children who unwillingly spend time alone, or spend copious amounts of time alone.

This is reflected in society at large, were sociability is valued so highly. When children report on how they feel when they are by themselves, they may unconsciously see such time as the absence of companionship, rather than the opportunity to think, garner one's personal resources, or experience things without the noise or dilution of others.

The bias toward sociability overlooks the importance of unstructured solitude when it comes to developing one's interest and feeding one's curiosity in specific domains. A look at the lives of many of our greatest minds suggests that time spent daydreaming and exploring while alone, free of responsibilities, is crucial to the acquisition of knowledge—in other words, crucial for the curious mind. First-person accounts and biographies of writers, painters, and scientists, for instance, abound with descriptions of time spent alone in childhood—E. O. Wilson, Barbara McClintock, Charlotte Brontë, and Andrew Wyeth are just a few examples. Free time and solitude are, no doubt, just as powerful for the young child in contemporary life. In a widely viewed TED talk, the filmmaker J. J. Abrams described a sealed cardboard box containing the materials for a series of tricks, which he bought at a magic store when he was just a boy. Now in his forties, Abrams has never opened the box, preferring the persistent allure of the unknown. In a series of interviews with me, Abrams linked this to his obsession for making films:

> The idea of creating illusion and magic . . . I always loved movies and TV, and I always loved magic. I remember magic as early as I loved TV—I loved Adam West on *Batman*. And getting little magic tricks at Fiddlesticks on Northern Boulevard in LA. I liked that little eggcup trick thing. I loved knowing the secrets of how to do something and being able to fool the audience, being able to know what the illusion was and seeing the illusion—the power of making someone believe what I was doing.
>
> I loved Batman. I loved the show. I loved the idea of people in costume—it didn't occur to me at first that it was funny for grown-ups to be dressed up in costumes. I just thought it was cool. I remember very clearly that the amazing thing about the world was the infinite possibility.
>
> I brought my Batman costume to school. I shared my love of movies at school. My fifth-grade teacher let me film a movie in class. The whole class was very excited because we didn't have to work that day. "The Ghost and I." The teacher was in the movie. Mr. Karlin. He wore a costume and everything. . . .
>
> I was not very athletic. When you are successful at the norm, that's the path you follow. When you're not, you don't. You could shut down, you could be stagnant, you could be an outsider. You look outside the

school. Or in my case, I discovered making movies. I was the last picked in baseball. It was horrible. It's a recipe for other. It was a result of not being a great or interested student. Making a movie, thinking about a movie, writing a movie. (2012; excerpted from a series of interviews I conducted with J. J. Abrams)

Nor is this only true of those who grow up to be artists. Consider a passage from the memoir of the cognitive psychologist George Miller, recalling a key moment from his childhood:

> One day when I was seven or eight years old, I was walking home from Kanawha School, down the long 1500 block in Virginia Street in Charleston, West Virginia.
>
> In the dirt between the sidewalk and the curb I found a small wheel that had come off some other child's toy. I cleaned it enough to see that it was an unusually nice wheel: red, with a small rubber tire. As I walked along slowly, alone, examining the wheel, it occurred to me that if I had another just like it, all I would need would be an axle and it could roll along. And if I had another pair, I could make something. I could mount them under a block of wood and make a car. To make it better I could carve the block of wood in the shape of a car. When I reached my front walk at home, I was trying to remember where I had seen a small can of paint.
>
> As I started up the walk, I looked in my hand and saw nothing there but the single wheel. Surprise etched the experience into memory.
>
> In the 60 years since, that boy, staring dumbly at his toy wheel, has revisited me many times. Soaring imagination mocked by hard reality—who has not experienced the discrepancy? I, being insufficiently critical, have experienced it more than most.
>
> The tendency to see what something could be more clearly than what is has sustained me as a teacher, but I have heard it said that scientists should avoid it like poison. I wonder. Is the goal of science nothing more than the objective description of reality? I could not have remained a psychologist if I were less addicted to counterfactuals.
>
> Reality is vastly overrated. It is merely the point of origin from which everything interesting departs. (Miller 1977)

These two accounts are separated by almost a century, one describing a young Christian southern boy who would grow up to an illustrious scientific career and the singular accomplishment of shifting the course of American psychology, the other a young Jewish boy, living in Los Angeles in the 1970s, who would grow up to make huge blockbuster films. They are linked by virtue of the sense of curiosity that drives their professional lives. But they also share memories of a childhood that included plenty of time on their hands, and solitude. In fact Abrams singles out the experience of feeling that he wasn't part of the "in" group, and insists that that is what pushed him toward a more solitary pursuit—one based on thinking rather than simply doing.

Though we actually know fairly little about how children spend their time, the data support the idea that it's good for children to have free time. Sandra Hofferth and John Sandberg (2001) drew subjects from the 1997 Child Health Development Supplement to the Panel Study of Income Dynamics, a thirty-year longitudinal survey of a representative sample of families. The families were asked to keep diaries of their children's activities as a way to get a picture of how contemporary U.S. children spend their time. The data are revealing. While three-to-five-year-olds spent approximately seventeen hours a week in free play, most of them spent less than one hour a week outside, and less than two hours a week reading. By the time children were nine years old, they spent no more time outside, and far less time in free play (just under nine hours a week). They spent even less time reading (one and a quarter hours per week). The authors suggest that pleasure reading in particular seems to decline as children get older, even though it is associated with good school performance. In another enlightening picture of how children spend their time, Reed Larson, using the event sampling method, has shown that children between the ages of nine and twelve report being alone about 17 percent of the time (Larson 1990). His data suggest that adolescents don't like to be alone, but that those who spend more time alone appear to be better adjusted. He attributes this to the role solitude might play in facilitating the developmental task of identity formation. But he ultimately concludes that solitude becomes more valuable (and appreciated) as people get older.

Meanwhile, developmental research has consistently shown that free play and solitude are both extremely valuable to intellectual development. Piaget's whole theory of intellectual development centered on the discoveries children made while interacting with the physical world around them. In fact, the theory is premised on the idea that un-expected events push the child to change the way she thinks about things—a ball that doesn't roll the way other balls have rolled, a toy that floats in water where others have sunk, or a box out of which something pops spurs the child to study, experiment, reconsider, and ultimately expand her way of thinking, or replace an old scheme with one that better fits the new data. As children get older, the kinds of things that spark this intellectual sequence change. In one of his simplest yet most powerful examples, Piaget describes himself as a young child, dis-covering that no matter how he laid out the pebbles (circle, straight line, scattered), they equaled the same number—leading to the essential dis-covery that quantity remains constant no matter what the pattern or shape of the objects. Again and again, in both his observations and his experiments, Piaget emphasized the intellectual mileage children get from following their own hunches, questions, and urges, when it comes to interacting with objects (Piaget 1964b). His core assumption was that when children interact with objects (by putting them in their mouth, dropping, shaking, or banging them, by trying a series of actions on them) they do so not in an idle way, nor, it should be said, to create, but rather to answer a question, no matter how implicit or unconscious that question might be. Though Piaget rarely offered advice to teachers or parents, and had little interest in the practical implications of his model, the fact remains that the logical conclusion of his theory is that children benefit from the opportunity to interact in their own way with objects around them, and that left to their own devices they will en-gage in gestures, actions, and sequences of behavior that lead to intel-lectual progress. John Dewey shared some of Piaget's views. Though Piaget was a scientist, basically unconcerned with actual children, much less their education, and Dewey a philosopher, uninterested in research but very interested in children and education, their work overlapped.

Dewey argued that children have four basic impulses: to create, to communicate, to inquire, and to construct. Unlike Piaget, Dewey was interested in the role teachers might play in building on these four impulses. But he shared Piaget's conviction that when children are allowed to act freely, their need to investigate and acquire new information will guide much of their behavior (Dewey 1911; Cuffaro 1995).

Though Piaget was not interested in education, per se, some of his heirs were. In her essay *"The Having of Wonderful Ideas,"* Eleanor Duckworth, Piaget's student, translator, and eventual collaborator, described how a classroom could build on Piaget's theory of intellectual development (1972). As her title suggests, an education based on Piaget should make it possible for children to develop ideas through their own activity—these ideas would incorporate new experiences, and change in response to information that challenged the old ideas.

THE ROLE OF TIME

In a classroom based on the ideas of Piaget, Cuffaro, Dewey, and Duckworth, children would get much more time to experiment with the world around them—to try things out, to follow false leads, to make and test predictions, to investigate, to muck around—to explore. Much has been said over the years about the open-ended nature of such a classroom, most famously perhaps in the work of John Holt, Herb Kohl, Barbara Biber, and Deborah Meier, to name just a few. But these writers have typically focused on the benefits of removing concrete and/or rigid learning goals from the classroom, giving up scripted lessons, and instead following up on children's own interests and initiatives. Less has been said about another powerful yet nearly invisible component of this kind of learning time. In order to try things out, learn from one's own experiments with objects, and answer one's own questions, children need plenty of time, and the time has to be free of an adult's script (first you do *a*, then you do *b*, follow these instructions until you accomplish *c*). In the story I told about the teacher saying "I'll give you time to experiment at recess. This is time for science," it was clear that she felt she had to be very careful with the children's time, to make sure the learning objective was achieved. There are two problems with her response. First of all, she assumes that the important questions to answer are the ones she has supplied, rather than the ones the children might come up with; and second, she assumes that she can regulate the time it will take for any question to be answered. Genuine learning takes time, and to the extent that real learning rests on real questions, first a child has to have enough time with some domain or material in order to become familiar with it. Once familiar with something (a pile of mud, a gadget, the fish in an aquarium, planets), a child has a chance to detect anomalies, or figure out the parts that merit further inquiry. Then she has to actually have time to fiddle around. These fiddlings might be very subtle—imagine a six-year-old interested in whether black crayons obliterate all other colors, trying to see if she can draw over a black area with red or yellow or blue; such an experiment might take twenty minutes and might look remarkably unproductive to a teacher who has test scores on her mind. Or imagine the child who becomes interested in magic, and wants to spend hours reading books about magicians. Some of the time she will simply be looking at pictures, taking in biographical information about famous magicians, or reading how to do magic tricks. At some point she may become interested in the very idea of illusion—but it may take her awhile to get there. The process of inquiry is filled with false starts, consideration of new data, and new possibilities for inquiry.

Support for the value of free time comes from an intriguing, and fairly new line of work—research on the use of the Internet to gain information. In an examination of how adults use the Internet to pursue a recreational interest in genealogy, Crystal Fulton (2009) found a link between amount of pleasure and effective persistent information-foraging strategies. The key to her argument is the role of time—she points out that when students feel pressured to complete an assignment, they experience less pleasure, and also engage in less thorough search behavior. That finding is replicated in a wide range of studies of online foraging.

One of the reasons teachers often balk at giving their students plenty of time to explore, follow false leads, and browse is that they feel such pressure to help children achieve learning goals that are obvious, explicit, and measurable. Along with these goals is a somewhat new emphasis on the value of ensuring that children understand just what it is they are supposed to learn or, as the case may be, have already learned. This is embodied by the widespread use in U.S. schools of something called "SWIBAT," which stands for "students will be able to. . . ." Teachers are encouraged to put a SWIBAT on the board at the beginning of each day or lesson, so that everyone is aware of the specific learning objective for that day. It is a common practice for teachers to ask children what they have learned as a way of making sure they understand the material. While studies show that when children make their knowledge explicit it adds valuable depth to their understanding (Vygotsky 1978; Bruner 1966; Brown 1997), researchers have also shown that a fair amount of learning, especially during childhood, occurs at an implicit level. For instance, Robert Siegler has shown this with his experiments looking at how children solve computation problems. He and his collaborators asked children to solve three-part addition problems that could be figured through straightforward computation $(3 + 5 - 3 = ?)$ or be done, more quickly, using a heuristic (in this case, that when the same number is added and subtracted, the third number remains unchanged). They found that children were solving the problems more quickly (indicating that they were using the time-saving heuristic) before they could articulate the "rule" (2000). In other words, their discovery was, at first, implicit. Clearly, some of the most important learning happens at an implicit level, and is discovered by children on their own, rather than taught to them by someone else. Deanna Kuhn has demonstrated something similar in the realm of science education. Starting with the premise that in order to become scientifically skilled and/or knowledgeable, children must learn the fundamental concept of controlling variables in an experiment, Kuhn challenges the claim made by Klahr and Nigam (2004) that the best way to teach this concept is through direct instruction. Instead Kuhn gave children a chance to experiment, virtually, with the conditions that lead to tornadoes. In one condition children were instructed explicitly on the importance of manipulating only one variable at a time, and in another condition they were given the opportunity to experiment on their own, though an adult was there to answer questions and make suggestions when asked. Weeks later, when children were asked to either critique someone else's science experiment or conduct a new kind of experiment, children who had been given more freedom and less direct instruction showed a much stronger and clearer understanding of the concept of controlling variables. These findings underscore the valuable role time and autonomy play in the learning process (Kuhn and Ho 1980; Kuhn et al. 2008).

Many studies looking at children's free play have revealed the crucial kinds of higher-order thinking that emerge during such play. Take, for example, the acquisition of counterfactual thinking—a linchpin of the educated mind. Scientists, historians, and business analysts all engage in it when they consider alternative outcomes based on alternative facts. For example, a political analyst might think about what U.S. Middle East relations would now be if Colin Powell had not believed there were weapons of mass destruction in Iraq. A historian might consider what would have happened to modern Christianity if King Henry VIII had married Mary Boleyn instead of her sister, Anne. In a particularly famous example, Galileo would not have made his essential scientific contribution if he hadn't carefully imagined what would happen if one could remove all physical forces except for gravity from the environment, and drop an object in such an environment.

Joseph Lister, a British physician during the nineteenth century, stumbled upon a paper by Louis Pasteur, showing that fermentation and rotting occurred in various organic material when bacteria were present. Lister began to think about the high rate of infection that regularly occurred during and after surgery. He realized that contrary to the conventional wisdom of the time (that something in the air caused infections), the culprits were probably microorganisms contained on the hands of the doctor and on the surface of the surgical tools. In the paper, Pasteur had recommended heating and then separating the bacterial matter from tissue, or using chemicals that might kill the microorganisms. Lister began to speculate about what would happen if he used the chemical carbolic acid to clean surgical equipment prior to an operation. By connecting facts not ordinarily viewed together, he imagined a sequence that had never actually unfolded, which led in turn to a revolution in medicine.

We are not born with the ability to think counterfactually. Nor is it taught formally in school, though it is essential for most complex forms of academic thought. Recent studies show that the capacity to think this way emerges spontaneously, during pretend play (Harris 2000). Specifically, when children act out scenarios, enact dramatic roles using small figures, or create narratives to accompany building with blocks, they regularly consider alternative sequences ("Let's say Superman didn't have his cape—then he'd fall down, and Supergirl would have to save him"). In other words, their play leads them to consider how things might be, if certain facts were different. This is just one, albeit robust, example of the valuable kinds of intellectual development that can occur when children are given time to pursue their own interests. But this book is not about play per se. It's about curiosity—a disposition that is nurtured when children are given time to play. The argument is not that play is necessary for children to feel curiosity, or pursue their curiosity, but rather that curiosity benefits from the same conditions that seem to nurture play, a critical activity for the development of other key intellectual accomplishments.

In recent years, there has been a palpable shift in focus—away from the value of free time and self-guided activity toward an emphasis on the importance of teaching children to control themselves and work toward explicit academic goals. This recent emphasis has roots in behaviorism. The work of Skinner and others suggested to researchers and educators that through the use of reward and punishment children could be taught to stay in their seats, raise their hand when they wanted to be called on, stick with a task for a long time, and try hard on challenging work. During the past ten years or so, this model has resurfaced in a slightly different guise, encompassed by a focus on children's "executive control." The core idea is that there is a cluster of abilities that govern children's capacity to avoid distractions, stay focused on a task, control their impulses, and persevere in the face of challenge. Key to most models of executive control is the notion of self-discipline.

When children have trouble keeping their feet to themselves, withstanding a small temptation, focusing on the task at hand, they are much less likely to do well in school as they get older. Cybele Raver and colleagues have argued that when children are trained to exert more self-discipline, they get better at it, and so does their school performance (2011). Angela Duckworth and colleagues, too, have put a lot of energy into identifying methods for training children to increase their self-control and improve their academic prospects (Duckworth, Tsukayama, and May 2010). Ironically, the implication of that line of work is that self-control comes by way of the input of others. But a study by Wendy Grolnick and Richard Ryan, which predates the work of Raver and Duckworth, underscores the role of autonomy in such executive control (Grolnick and Ryan 1987). They asked fifth graders to study a passage from a social studies book about the history of farming methods. In one condition, children were told they'd be tested on the information, and were urged to work as hard as they could, because they'd be graded on their performance. In a second condition, they were told they'd be asked questions about the material, but that it wouldn't be a test, and that they should read the material in whatever way they felt was best. In a third condition, they were simply given the material and told they'd be asked some questions afterward. Children in the second (directed/noncontrolling) and third (nondirected) conditions showed far greater interest in the activity and the material, and showed greater conceptual understanding of the material as well. Grolnick and Ryan argue that a sense of autonomy and freedom enhances learning. So, it seems, if you want children to develop self-control, you need to give them some autonomy.

When Diane Sawyer was interviewed in 2013 about what drove her as a journalist, she said, "We live in a simultaneous world of the stories that we're reporting for six months, and the stories that come across the wire where you have to jump, so you're living in three dimensions, and it doesn't stop—which is also the most wonderful part of the day. It's adrenalizing, and adrenaline is addicting, and that's why we're there—we like it, we need it, we want to know." Then the interviewer asked her what other career she might have chosen if she hadn't become a journalist. "I think I would probably still be wandering the world and looking for answers. I wouldn't be harnessed to anything the way I am now, but I would be out there asking questions. . . . I also loved getting lost as a kid . . . go out there and just see what happens" (Wilson 2013, 272).

Giving children a chance to direct their own learning also appears to help them absorb, understand, and retain various kinds of information and skills. Elizabeth Bonawitz and her colleagues gave preschoolers a chance to explore a complex and intriguing contraption. When an adult offered information about the contraption that explained how it worked, the children were less likely to explore the contraption fully on their own. The authors describe this as the "double edged sword of pedagogy," suggesting that instruction can limit exploration (2011). In another study demonstrating the value of autonomous exploration, Marylyn Arnone and Barbara Grabowski gave first-grade children a chance to pay a virtual visit to an art museum (1992). But the researchers varied the amount of freedom and adult advice the children received. When they subsequently tested the children for their knowledge about the art they had seen, children who had some autonomy had learned more about art in general, and about the particular things they had seen, than children whose visit had been completely controlled. Moreover, the children with more autonomy showed greater curiosity, measured by their interest in looking at a new piece of art, the time they spent on it, and the number of questions they asked. Needless to say, pursuing one's curiosity requires persistence. The children who will get the most out of opportunities to work on their own (deciding what to tackle, and what to concentrate on) are the ones who can stay focused, stick with a question, and plan how to solve whatever problem intrigues them. In other words, at their best, autonomy and self-regulation go hand in hand. But in the world of real classrooms, every teacher must figure out how to balance the two. If a child doesn't seem to have a great deal of perseverance, focus, or self-control, the teacher must decide whether to give him more autonomy so that he has a chance develop self-regulation, or whether to make autonomy the prize for self-control. In her book on the psychology underlying the Montessori method, Angeline Lillard points out that many of the features of a Montessori classroom are designed to help children slowly but surely acquire the dispositions and skills to figure things out on their own (Lillard 2008). As children get older, the need for time to direct their own intellectual pursuits only increases.

In their research on adolescents living in Chicago, Mihaly Csikszentmihalyi and Reed Larson gave teenagers beepers and diaries in which to record their actions, their companions, their whereabouts, and their thoughts and feelings, during random points in the day when the beeper went off (1984). The study dramatically illuminated the inner lives of teens and showed how moods and thoughts related to where the kids were, what they were doing, and with whom. Two of the most important insights the data led to were that teens feel dull and disengaged most of the time they are in school. The one exception to this general sense of enervated ennui emerges during times of the day when they feel they have some choice and autonomy over what they are studying. And though many reported not liking to be alone, in fact those who spent significant periods of time alone were often the ones who also thrived—had passion for various pursuits, felt engaged with others, and felt accomplished. Unfortunately, we don't have similar data about younger children. However, if you put the above findings together with the research showing the kinds of thinking afforded by free play, it becomes quite clear that time alone, and autonomy or freedom, can be extremely valuable to the development of inquiry and the interest that motivates such inquiry.

Many years ago I taught second grade full time. Watching the children in my own classroom, as well as those slightly younger and slightly older in the nearby classrooms, I began to see that children had very different styles of using the materials and spaces in school. I wondered if there were styles of use, and further whether certain styles lead to greater intellectual engagement or more distinctive work (writing, art, math projects, etc.). I chose three girls and three boys whose grades fell in middle of the group. I kept a running record of each child's activity for three hours at a time, for three days in a row, at five different time periods during the year. Four of the children were similar to one another—methodical, following the teacher's rules and plans, finishing one thing before beginning another, and generally conforming to expectations and norms. Two of the children, however, had quirkier ways of moving through their days, often beginning things and then putting them down, drifting through the room periodically just to gaze out the window, or watch what other children were doing. During group activities, these two children were slightly more fitful in their contributions, often waiting a while before helping at all, and then helping in an intense, short burst of activity. I subsequently created portfolios of their work for the year, and went back to look at similar collections of their work a year later. The two who had followed a more idiosyncratic rhythm in the classroom were also the two who did the more distinctive work—writing that was more complex, vivid, and personal, and artwork of a similar character. A year later the same was still true, as judged not only by me but also by their current teachers. At the time, I was interested in how children use their classroom environment. But now, looking back, it seems to me that what I then saw as idiosyncrasy might just reflect a greater need for autonomy. Those two kids either felt more need for freedom and solitude while they worked within the classroom, or they simply asserted that need more than the other children.

Curiosity is an internal phenomenon—a feeling like a tickle, or an itch. But it's a feeling that leads to action (including the act of thinking). This book for the most part has not focused on fleeting moments of curiosity, but the kind of curiosity that persists, unfolding over time and leading to sustained action (inquiry, discovery, tinkering, question asking, observation, research, reflection). Such sustained inquiry may be more likely to blossom when children have free time, and some time alone. This chapter began with a book—because reading is one of the most accessible and richest ways for people to satisfy all kinds of intellectual appetites. But books require time alone, and the kind of reading that satisfies curiosity depends on freedom to read what you want. Those hours and hours I spent lost in *Gone with the Wind* were, for better or worse, pivotal to my intellectual development.

9

Cultivating Curiosity

WHEN I WAS fourteen I moved from the funky school my mother and others had started to the local public high school. The big hurdle for me, the grown-ups said, would be math, since the math I had done at the Hampton Day School was so unconventional and haphazard. It was decided that I would take ninth-grade algebra with the dragon lady of math, but tenth-grade classes for everything else. I was warned I'd have trouble with Mrs. McMahon because she was so demanding, so rigorous, and so ferocious. Everything else, they said, would be easy: tenth-grade biology, social studies, English, and French. Math, it turned out, was easy—all I had to do was follow the rules meticulously. My real education came in biology. The teacher, Mr. McDonald, owned the liquor store in town and seemed genial enough, if somewhat smug and plodding.

On the first day of class he told us that we'd begin the year by studying cells. He handed out the textbook, explaining that we should turn to chapter 1 and go through it together, page by page. He pointed to a diagram, naming each part as he went along: this is the nucleus, this is the cell membrane, this is a mitochondria. Somewhere during those first two weeks we got to look at cells under a microscope. That was my favorite part. I remember how intrigued I was by what I saw through the scope. I liked finding out how cells were structured, and some of the cool things about what they did: divide, absorb one another, and wiggle. Then it came time for the test, which he had mentioned frequently and which I had barely registered, anticipating it with an easy mind. I had enjoyed the subject matter, loved the labs, and asked a lot of questions. What was there to worry about? I failed the test. I was completely baffled by my F. I went up to Mr. McDonald to ask what I had done wrong. I explained that I had been really interested in cells, had read all the additional material he had offered, and enjoyed the hands-on activities we had done. "Yes, but did you memorize that section of the textbook?" "I read it," I said. His mouth screwed up and moved over to the side of his face, "Ah, but did you memorize it? The test is based on memorizing the facts in the textbook. Don't worry so much about the labs, and you don't really need to bother reading all the extra material I handed out in class. All you need to know is what it says in the textbook. If you get those terms and definitions down, you should be set." During that brief exchange, which took no more than five minutes, I could feel my eagerness for science drain right out of me, like water in the bottom of a bathtub. I also remember my disappointment. The bad grade was nothing compared to the dismay his advice triggered. Don't bother with the labs? My interest didn't matter? Just memorize some stupid lines in a boring textbook? I remember thinking, "He doesn't really like this stuff. He wants to help a good student like me get the grade I want. But he doesn't care if I like biology. And he sure doesn't care if I understand anything." I got an A+ on all the remaining tests in that course, but for me, that was the end of biology. While in school, I never regained my original interest. Luckily, I got a second chance, many years later, through my youngest child, Sam.

By the time Sam got to college, nature was already a huge part of his life. As a child, he had spent hundreds of hours in the woods and ponds near our house. His babysitter knew a great deal about the natural world. Almost every day they went outside to watch, collect, and explore. A day didn't go by without her pointing out an interesting leaf, or bringing a stick bug inside to see what it would do if placed on the table. She lived on a farm nearby, and more than once I came home from work to find a sheep's bladder, or some other animal organ, in a bowl on our kitchen table. "We're going to dissect it," my son would happily announce, when I protested some dish of bloody tissue lying near the mail and the groceries. Nor did they simply gaze at these fascinating objects. Sam and his babysitter liked to try things out, poking, deconstructing, and testing. His babysitter's favorite phrase was, "Let's see what happens if we . . ."

In eighth grade, having finished all the regular courses, and trying to think of how to spend his time, Sam got the idea of doing a year-long study of the pond by our house. From September until August he went out there once or twice a week to document everything he could see—changes in the plants, the habits of fish, birds, and insects, and patterns in the light and weather. After each session he'd come back inside and begin looking things up on the Internet and in his books, so that he could not only write what he had seen, but what others could tell him. In high school he got a grant to study caddisfly larvae; he set up a lab in our basement and wrote a paper about the way in which the larvae influenced one another's "house-building" techniques. When it came time to apply to college, he chose one known for its good reputation in the biological sciences. He seemed set on his path.

But as he became more knowledgeable and skilled, he also became a little less dazzled by the daily stuff of scientific work, and all that surrounded it. At the end of his second year of college he arranged to spend the summer at a different university, doing an experiment on the evolution of altruism in single-cell organisms. The data would allow him to write a thesis. But it wasn't an easy setup for him. He would be living alone, in an unfurnished one-bedroom apartment, in a city where he knew not one single person. The city was ranked the second most dangerous in the United States. He was told there were neighborhoods where he shouldn't pass through by car because there was so much gang violence erupting in the streets. Many days the temperature reached 102. He often worked fourteen hours a day, making slides and handling tiny tools on tiny organisms, the same procedure again and again, on specimen after specimen. Then he'd return to his drab apartment in a drab part of town, and heat up black beans for dinner. I could hear in his voice a growing sense of doubt about a life in science. The graduate students he met seemed nerdy and odd to him—not the kind of person he was, or wanted to be. Sometime that summer he read an article in *Scientific American*, by a young computer scientist at Harvard. In it she explained how to organize your life during the pre-tenure years.

He told me, distaste dripping from his voice, how much he hated the article, how it made academic life sound horrible. I could hear his love of science ebbing away, while his doubts about the architecture of an academic career grew. Meanwhile, in the third week of the project, a whole batch of amoebas representing what he told me were "the ancestor line" perished. He might have to start over. Three weeks of nonstop work, erased. He seemed to be turning away from biology.

Then one day, four weeks after he had begun the project, he called to tell me that he was headed into the lab—he was going to count up amoebas to find out what the results of his experiment were. His voice held an expectant energy that I hadn't heard for a very long time. He said, "I'm psyched. I'm gonna find out what's been going on. I can't wait to see what happened."

That kind of counting (hundreds of amoebas on hundreds of slides, prepared in three different ways) required tedious, meticulous, relentless work. Boring work. Hours of work. As E. O. Wilson puts it, "To be a scientist you have to think like a poet, work like a bookkeeper."

Five hours later my phone rang. "Great data! It's so cool. The noncheaters resisted the cheaters." Notes of clarity and relief hummed in his voice. And something else. A renewed sense of energy and investment. He launched into a long, detailed explanation of the different kinds of amoebas and what they could have done, what they did do, what they might do in his next experiment. Curiosity sated, curiosity stirred. That experience—the sustained, demanding work, the bona fide question that actually mattered, and the genuine uncertainty of the answer he might get—those were the essential components that sparked Sam's regained enthusiasm for science.

EMBRACING AMBIGUITY

The research described in this book shows that curiosity is nearly universal in babies, and, in our culture at least, continues to propel children, intellectually, through early childhood. Beyond early childhood, however, its fate rests in great part on the people and experiences that surround and shape a child's daily life. While there are some situations where it would not be good to ask too many questions, or investigate too persistently, there is a clear empirical link between the hungry mind and the educated mind. Cultures in which young children's questions and exploration are encouraged also tend to emphasize formal education. Even within the United States, inquiry is more likely to be fostered in educated families. In other words, fostering curiosity goes hand in hand with the kind of education our society values and depends upon. Moreover, studies show that curiosity is a potent ingredient in learning—children learn better when their curiosity is piqued. This is true in short periods of learning, and over time as well. Thus any school where the goal is to help children understand a complex world of ideas and information would benefit from harnessing its enormous power.

Unfortunately, schools do not always, or even often, foster curiosity, despite the fact that it transforms the process of education, makes learning come alive for most children, and increases the chance that any given child will become a curious adult. Though research has helped us identify the psychological underpinnings of curiosity, making use of those findings in real classrooms is easier said than done. Skilled, kind teachers, eager to make learning more active and engaging, often miss the key moment when a student's curiosity is piqued.

In 2008 I spent several months observing a high school biology teacher named Ms. Horn. In January, Ms. Horn announced to her college-bound biology class that, having learned the requisite content, the class was now ready to conduct one of the key labs for the course—an experiment to measure whether or not plants use up CO_2. The students were delighted to embark on a lab project. And they understood the basic concept—that in the presence of plant material, CO_2 should disappear from the air. Working in small teams, each group carefully put a small piece of living plant into one test tube, but left a second and third test tube without any plant. Then each team dropped a prescribed quantity of liquid dye into the three test tubes. The dye would turn yellow in the presence of CO_2 but if deprived of CO_2 would turn blue. In order to have a baseline, the class created one set of tubes that were unsealed, and for good measure, a student on each team blew bubbles into those, ensuring that the dye in those test tubes would be exposed to plenty of CO_2. They sealed the second set of tubes that contained only the liquid with dye, as well as the set of tubes containing the liquid with dye and some plant material. Then they carefully placed the test tubes in racks and left the classroom for the day. As they walked out, the teacher promised them that when they returned, they'd be able to see for themselves that plants absorb CO_2.

The next day, when they returned to the science lab to see the results, they found, as expected, that the unsealed test tube into which they had blown bubbles had turned yellow. The human breath contained plenty of CO_2, and the dye had done what it was supposed to. The sealed test tube without the plant material was also yellowish green, because small amounts of CO_2 had been trapped in there. Next the teacher and her students turned their attention to the experimental tubes, the sealed tubes containing plant material. In theory the plants should have used up any CO_2 caught in there, and the liquid should have turned blue. But instead, the liquid in the tubes was the same yellowish green liquid as the rest. No difference. Ms. Horn turned to the kids. "So everyone. What does this tell us? Why did the third set of test tubes not turn blue as we expected?" One of the better students in the class raised her hand. "I guess we made a mistake." Ms. Horn smiled approvingly. "That's exactly right. Something must have gone wrong when we were preparing the mixture, or sealing the test tubes." But another student raised his hand. "But what if we didn't make a mistake? What if our prediction was wrong?" Ms. Horn looked a little surprised. This was her top student. "No, Stephen. That couldn't be. As you read in the textbook, plants use CO_2 to make oxygen. By putting a plant in the liquid, we should have deprived the mixture of CO_2. It should've turned blue." But Stephen was tenacious. "Sure. We might have done something wrong. But maybe not. Because another possible conclusion is that plants don't actually use up CO_2. Maybe our experiment is evidence in favor of that conclusion. It's possible, right? Isn't that why people do experiments? Because you might get results that make you change your theory?" "No," said Ms. Horn, firmly. "We know plants use up CO_2. It's in the textbook. We just made an error preparing the slides."

In one efficient exchange, Ms. Horn showed just how a teacher can make a lesson challenging, active, and engaging, and still steer clear of the feelings and thoughts that are key to deep learning. Those kinds of feelings and thoughts involve uncertainty. And most students are not taught to love that feeling, or to use it as a springboard. For the most part, teachers tend to avoid uncertainty, at least in the classroom. Even college teachers who may welcome it in their scholarly work are wary of it in the company of their students.

One day, years ago, when I was struggling to make sense of some data I had collected, my college psychology professor said to me, "Embrace ambiguity, avoid chaos." That idea instantly tattooed itself in my brain. I felt I understood exactly what she was saying—that reality was rarely neat, simple, or clear-cut, and that the richest interpretations came from acknowledging the messiness of human behavior, and the uncertainty of the scientific process. Years later, in my first year teaching at Williams College, a few of my colleagues were standing in the hallway chatting. We were discussing what we could do to help our psychology majors see that the most interesting topics didn't have easy answers or firm answers, that data could be contradictory, that sometimes facts were elusive. Those long-ago words of wisdom from my college professor blinked in my head like a small neon sign. I said, "Yeah, we want them to embrace ambiguity, but avoid chaos." My senior colleague's face stiffened in surprise and distaste. She looked furtively up and down the hallway. "Oh my goodness, don't let any of the students hear you say that. You'll only confuse them." Many teachers share my colleague's sentiment, and do what Ms. Horn did that day in the lab. They discourage uncertainty, emphasizing instead what they know, or feel the students should know. They are more comfortable encouraging students to learn trustworthy information than to explore questions to which they themselves do not know the answer. Instead of using school as a place to formalize and extend the power of a young child's zest for tackling the unknown or uncertain, teachers tend to squelch curiosity. They don't do this out of meanness, or small-mindedness. They do it in the interests of making sure children master certain skills and established facts. While an emphasis on acquiring knowledge is reasonable, discouraging the disposition that leads to gaining new knowledge squanders a child's most formidable learning tool.

While no teacher wants her students to be permanently confused (and no scholar should feel complacent not knowing), the first step in putting curiosity at the center of the classroom would be to help students see that not knowing things, at least temporarily, feels good. The pleasure of not knowing something is similar to the pleasure of feeling hungry. Hunger feels best when you know you will eat good food soon. Not knowing, like hunger, feels bad when you don't anticipate satiation. The food analogy is worth extending, because it also offers illumination for teachers. Imagine you were worried because your child didn't eat, or didn't eat the foods you thought best for her. You could try, as many parents do, to reward her for eating broccoli by giving her a cookie, or warn her that if she eats the chocolate you've forbidden she cannot watch television that night. You can tell her she can't leave the table until she's eaten three bites of each food on her plate. Those are similar to many of the techniques that are used every day in classrooms. Learning gets rewarded, failure to learn gets punished, and perseverance seems to be the operative technique. But actually, when adults offer children healthy food that they like (sweet watermelon, not mushy apples, and raw carrots rather than overcooked peas), children develop a taste for it. Research shows that a child who is given fresh, tasty food is more likely to develop good eating habits than one who is simply disciplined to finish her spinach. Because curiosity is, in many ways, an appetite, the analogy is fruitful. Rather than disciplining children to learn, why not create the conditions in which children actually are hungry for knowledge?

Though learning and pleasure are rarely viewed as partners, in fact they co-occur. In an important paper, "The Wick in the Candle of Learning" (Kang et al. 2009), researchers showed that when subjects encountered answers to questions about which they had been curious, there was increased activity in the caudate regions of the brain, which typically are activated when people anticipate a reward. In other words, we now have evidence that when people's curiosity is satisfied, they feel pleasure. Moreover, in the same study the researchers showed that the memory regions of subjects' brains were activated when they were offered correct answers to questions about which they had felt some uncertainty. The authors conclude that when people's interest in information is piqued, their memory for that information is enhanced. In other words, learning feels good when the material satisfies curiosity, and such learning tends to last.

The sense of uncertainty and surprise that my son Sam relished the day he headed to the lab to count his amoebas was not random, or frivolous. It was the grown-up, somewhat formalized version of a younger, more unfettered and diffuse curiosity. But children don't simply leap from a youthful appetite for experience to the deliberate form, embodied, for instance, in a good biological experiment. That journey takes time, and it can be nurtured at school.

CURRICULA BUILT ON CLIFFHANGERS

Mrs. Seeger's fourth-grade classroom was a beehive of mostly polite activity. When I first met her she had already been teaching for twenty-four years in a rural school where 40 percent of the children lived below the poverty line, and only 20 percent of the parents had graduated from college. As with many wonderful teachers, it's not altogether clear why, how, and where she acquired the disparate skills that accounted for her excellence. Even more elusive, it was not easy to figure out how she connected those skills so seamlessly, so that in the more than two hundred unexpected encounters she had each day with her students, somewhat contradictory behaviors flowed together so powerfully and effectively. She was unfailingly warm and patient, never raising her voice. Yet she was quite firm, and hers was one of the classrooms with the fewest outbursts from out-of-control or rude children. She tended to attract the brightest and most high-achieving students, but children with great difficulties also seemed to thrive in her care. She formed intense and personal connections with each of her students each year, but it was a room where an observer would find it impossible to tell who her favorites were.

The subject Mrs. Seeger loved the most and had the greatest success with was literature. Year after year, parents, children, administrators, and other teachers commented on her uncanny ability to get so many children to love reading and to become habitual writers. In my many conversations with her and observations of her teaching, it was easy to see that a lot of this came from her own great love of books and of great writing. She was comfortable with the written word, and wanted her students to be as well. She brought in a wide range of texts (Langston Hughes, Isaac Singer, Willa Cather, to name just a few) and read aloud nearly every day, making sure that all the children, at all times, had a book they were interested in, and allotting a large amount of time to the process of writing and rewriting.

But when No Child Left Behind took hold in her district, she found her vibrant approach to writing being whittled away. Day after day, from her perspective, she felt compelled to cover specific skills in an increasingly dull and somewhat robotic way—a worksheet on identifying nouns, practice at topic sentences, endless vocabulary exercises. She began to feel that while the children were learning some valuable information and becoming more practiced with a few specific writing devices, they had slid backward when it came to the heart of the matter—the acts of reading and writing.

She had always asked children to write every day. But in recent years, the pressure she felt to "cover" certain material had bogged her down. Her assignments, she said, were getting more didactic and directive. And the kids seemed to dislike writing more and more. In more ways than one, writing had lost its drama.

One afternoon, she sat talking to a colleague about her frustration that writing had become such a chore. The colleague laughed and said, "You want kids to like writing? You'll need a magic trick." But Mrs. Seeger knew good teaching is not magic. And that's when a funny image popped into her head. She saw herself coming into the classroom each morning, holding a black top hat. She imagined inviting a different child each morning to pull an assignment out of the hat. In her mind's eye, she could see their excitement, wondering what might emerge. That's when she began replacing the alluring image with a teaching plan. She realized that if the children were no longer engaged with writing, she had to reengage them, by putting drama back into the day. What if she did begin each day pulling an assignment out of a hat? Wouldn't the kids be curious to find out what their task was? What if she asked the children to come up with a whole hatful of writing prompts and then each morning invited one child to pull one of those prompts out of the hat? She combed the local thrift stores until she found a top hat. And her Cliffhanger writing program was under way.

When I observed in her classroom in the weeks after she began using the black top hat, I noticed that the children's sense of surprise and uncertainty about what assignment would appear each morning seemed to give them a jump start. What had been predictable had become mysterious. I doubt that would have been enough, however, if the prompts themselves hadn't been so varied and lively. Because twenty-four children were responsible for them, they were inconsistent, and many seemed perfectly designed for the mind of a ten-year-old (one was "Write an essay convincing Mrs. Seeger why we should have a party every Friday," and another, "The most horrible dream I ever had").

Researchers have known for quite some time that introducing a sense of drama and surprise into a classroom can transform a learning activity (Stevenson et al. 1990). In their effort to explain why Asian children seem to do so much better than similar U.S. students on a wide range of academic tasks, Stigler and Stevenson provided a detailed description of how Japanese teachers craft a learning experience. In their paper, "How Asian Teachers Polish Each Lesson to Perfection" (1991), they describe one particular lesson in which a Japanese elementary school teacher walks into class holding a brown paper bag. She begins the lesson by silently lifting out of the bag various containers. The lesson goes on to be about the measurement of volume. But key to its success, the authors argue, is the way she begins—with drama and mystery. She makes sure the children are eager to find out. First they want to find out what's in the bag. Then they want to find out the answer to the question she poses: how to measure the volume of various containers. There is nothing direct or self-evident about the sequence of the lesson—surprise and detours are built into it. The authors link this use of drama to the success Asian teachers have, even with seemingly prosaic topics, such as measurement.

Mrs. Seeger reported to me at the end of that year that she seemed to have gotten her writing program back on track. Children came in each day eager to write, with a sense of uncertainty not only about what the assignment would be, but what they each would come up with. The story is a helpful reminder that tapping into children's natural curiosity need not be confined to the science corner. Children's need to know can be fostered during writing, reading, the study of people in other times and places, and in mathematics. Creating lessons that emphasize the unexpected is only one of the ways teachers can nurture curiosity. By the time children are in school, what began as a ubiquitous urge can become a disposition—an orientation toward knowledge and a set of habits for sating the hungry mind. How do teachers help children build such a disposition?

HOW TEACHERS CULTIVATE CURIOSITY

At first, they do it by encouraging discussion. As I showed in Chapter 3, children are natural conversationalists—and asking questions is one of their best tools for finding things out. Granted, adults do not always want to encourage inquiry, and there is plenty of cultural variation regarding the utility, politeness, and value of asking questions. But as I have tried to show throughout this book, there is a great deal of evidence that in a culture such as ours, where formal education, scientific knowledge, literacy, invention, and the exchange of ideas are valued, questions are a key ingredient in the educational process (Harris 2012; Gauvain, Munroe, and Beebe 2013; Snow 2010). Needless to say, however, it's a lot easier to answer a child's many questions, and encourage her to pursue a line of questioning until she's satisfied, when you are at home with one or two children. It's a whole other challenge to encourage such talk when you are in charge of twenty-four children in a classroom. That said, it can be done.

Some years ago, I spent time observing a teacher, Ms. B, who worked in a school where the groups included wide age spans. Her fourteen students ranged from six to eleven years old. She herself was a big talker, and an avid reader. And the whole faculty where she worked believed that conversations were a core component of any good classroom. Some of the conversations that happened in her room were planned (a daily debate about a newspaper article, regular roundtable discussions about books the students were reading). But Ms. B also had a sharp ear for the stray comment by a child that could be developed into something more. One morning when I was watching, one of the eight-year-old boys in her class leaned over and said to another little boy, "When you die, you're going to hell. We all are." The other little boy's eyes widened for a second. Then he said, quietly but furiously, "I'm not. You are. I go to church." Ms. B must have heard this, though she was seated with a different group of children at another table. "Maury. Did you just tell Zeke he was going to go to hell?" Maury looked a bit abashed. His comment had been for Zeke alone. But Ms. B saw it as a golden opportunity. "That's so interesting. Remember last week I read some of Milton's *Paradise Lost* to you. When you say that, Maury, what do you think hell will be like?" Maury seemed captivated, Zeke more so. Everyone leaned in to hear what Maury would say. "It's probably dark. And cold." "No," said Zeke, "It's burning hot." "How do you know, though?" said Ms. B. The children in her classroom knew that wasn't a challenge, but a genuine question. Lydia answered, "Because I saw it in a picture. There were flames." The conversation lasted twenty-eight turns, and contained five children's questions. That's substantially more than the frequency of questions documented in most classrooms.

Creating an environment that is friendly to conversation begins with noticing the conversations that children have. Examples of this kind of unobtrusive attunement abound in the work of Vivian Paley (1984/2013). All teachers can notice these exchanges, and use them as clues to build on. The following set of exchanges occurred in the span of one day in a classroom for five-year-olds.

Three girls, Ellie, Miriam, and Tuware, are playing in the sandbox. They are playing a game where they take turns "burying" each other with sand, and later progress to burying various toys lying around. Ellie is undoubtedly the leader of this game, and seems to enjoy giving instruction. The two other girls playfully follow her directions.

ELLIE: You need to . . . to . . . to . . . unbury it!
MIRIAM: Tuware, it's time for you to unbury it!
ELLIE: Can you guys help unbury me?
(Ellie buries a small truck and leaves the sandbox area.)
TUWARE: Ellie, you have to unbury it before you leave!
ELLIE: Why?
TUWARE: Because if you leave it buried, it will stay buried, and then you can only get it back in the spring!
ELLIE: Why not earlier?
TUWARE: Because it will all freeze with the snow in the winter, so you can only get it back in the spring when everything melts again.

This conversation leads to a discussion about favorite seasons:

TUWARE: I like winter and summer.
ELLIE: Why do you like winter? We can't play outside in the winter!
TUWARE: 'Cause I can eat snow in the winter!
MIRIAM: Do you pee the snow out later?
TUWARE: I guess.

During these exchanges the three girls show a great deal of interest in how to use the word "unbury," and in the various possibilities for unburying things. Their interest also leads them to a set of questions about winter, which leads in turn to a question about what happens to snow once you eat it. The girls are quite good at asking for, and receiving, information. The skilled teacher, listening to this conversation, could learn quite a bit about the specific curiosities of these three girls. Noticing the questions children ask, and the things that stir their interest, need not lead to specific curricula. Rather, by noticing what particular children are particularly interested in, and how they express their curiosity, teachers are likely to encourage it without any deliberate changes in the activities they introduce to the classroom.

When the author Stephen King's three children were young, he'd put them to bed with bedtime stories. But not in the usual way. The novelist and his wife, Tabitha (also a novelist), would require that the children tell the grown-ups the stories. Two of Stephen's three children are now published authors. We'll never know whether story time was key to the young Kings' emergence as authors. But that habit does illustrate an idea that is all but lost in many educational settings: it's not what adults do to children (the questions they ask, the activities they present, the tests they give, or the knowledge they transmit) that shapes a child's unfolding intellectual abilities—it's what the child does him or herself. Jerome Bruner and Ann Brown refer to this as agency—the child's ability to act upon the world, guide and monitor her own learning, and make decisions about what and how to learn. Often this gets misinterpreted. Educators think that as long as children are getting up, moving around, manipulating objects, making things, and doing "projects," they are engaged in "active learning" and that this provides them with a sense of agency. But that is not what Bruner or Brown meant. Agency is a psychological state having to do with thinking about your own learning.

The purest example of such intellectual agency is the child who wants to know something, knows she wants to know it, and thinks about how to sate that curiosity. Agency also involves an awareness of when your question has been answered. All of which begins with the child, rather than the adult, asking the question. Just as King's children told the stories, in the best classrooms the children are asking the questions.

But it's also true that teachers can more deliberately and concretely encourage and expand their students' speculations and questions. For instance, consider the following exchange between a five-year-old girl, Lindy, and her teacher, David. Lindy has just finished playing in the sandbox and is wiping sand off herself so that she can head inside and have lunch. Suddenly, while wiping down her legs, she stops and looks closely. Then, she calls over to the teacher.

LINDY: David! Look, David, my legs are shiny like on TV!
DAVID: That's true. They're all sparkly! Why do you think they're shiny?
LINDY: Because of the sun!
DAVID: Really? I think it may have something to do with what you were playing with.
LINDY: Because of the sand!
DAVID: Well, let's see. Is the sand shiny?
LINDY (EXAMINING SAND): Well, only the top parts where we didn't dig holes are shiny.
DAVID: Really? Why do you think that is, lady?
LINDY: Don't call me lady.
DAVID: All right. Why do you think that is, Lindy?
LINDY: I don't know! I'll tell you when I find out!

In this exchange, the teacher skillfully takes the child's cue (my legs are shiny) and expands it into a line of inquiry (Why do you think they're shiny?). Note that when she makes the wrong guess (the sun), he nudges her toward the right answer, but even then, rather than just confirming it (you're right), he encourages her to test her speculation against some data (is the sand shiny?). He tries to push it further, but at that point she is ready to move on.

Spontaneous and casual exchanges are only the first step. By the time children are ten or so, the ability to craft a question in the absence of a guiding adult and pursue its answer, outside of the cushioning effect of conversation, becomes invaluable. What's the educational path between those two points?

Mr. C was a young teacher, just two years out of graduate school. He was tall, athletic, and full of vitality. The children flocked to him, and as is often the case, his slightly jockish air gave him an immediate authority with his first-grade students, which is more valuable than a trunk of gold, and about as hard to come by, if you don't have it natu-rally. Early in his second year in his suburban public school, he got per-mission to keep a boa constrictor in the classroom. On the second day he explained to the kids that they would have to feed the snake small rodents every week or so. One little girl named Beth said with a slightly anxious look on her face, "What happens to the mouse once it's in him?" "Good question," said Mr. C. "How could we find out?" "We could feed him a mouse, and then cut him open and look," offered one of the other students. "We could, but then what would happen?" said Mr. C. "Rufus [the name they had given the snake] would die." "Yes, so what else could we do?" Mr. C. put the children into groups of four and invited them to spend some time figuring out how to learn what happens to a mouse once it's inside a boa constrictor. They then considered the possible re-sults each method might yield. The project ended up requiring thirty-five minutes on several successive days. They didn't follow through on any of the plans. After several days of debating the various proposed methods of inquiry, they looked the answer up online. But the children had a memorable and extended lesson in planning how to get an an-swer to a difficult question. One of the things this story illustrates is the pedestrian but important point that developing mature forms of curi-osity takes time. As earlier chapters have demonstrated, curiosity takes time to unfold, and even more time to bear fruit. In order to help chil-dren build on their curiosity, teachers have to be willing to spend time doing so. Nurturing curiosity takes time, but also saturation. It cannot be confined to science class.

Good questioning can happen in classrooms other than the chem-istry lab. Ms. Erickson teaches high school math in a suburban town in western Massachusetts. In 2012 she was given the Presidential Award for Excellence in Mathematics and Science Teaching. I asked her to tell me about a class she had taught recently that went well.

> We were exploring unit circle for the first time. This is usually studied in geometry or trigonometry, courses they had not taken yet, so the ideas were new to them. It strikes me that introducing new topics is the easiest place to tap into student curiosity. Once something looks familiar, there is a tendency to connect it to what is already known. Of course, those connections can be wonderful, but sometimes the students think they are supposed to find a certain connection or for-

mula, and lose the sense of investigation. They fall into trying to find the right answer. Ugh!

Many topics in trigonometry can be modeled by studying a point traveling along the circumference of a unit circle. A unit circle has a radius of one unit and is centered on the origin. The point begins at the coordinates (1, 0)—the three o'clock position on a clock face—and travels counterclockwise. Without telling my students they were investigating trigonometry ideas, I gave them a copy of a unit circle on a set of axes and the information about the point traveling along the circumference. I then asked them to collect and graph data about the x coordinate of the point as it traveled. My hope was that they would see the repeating pattern and relate it to previous data they had seen about average temperature.

They did make those observations, but also asked questions such as: Do I have to keep measuring if I know what will happen? (My answer to her was, "Convince someone else that you are correct and you can use your new method.") Some values are positive and some are negative, and they always stay between –1 and 1, so how do we change the setup to get the temperature data values? What happens if you look at the y coordinate? What if the point travels around an ellipse instead of a circle? This last one is particularly exciting because it is similar to a question often studied in college-level math courses.

In this example, a mathematical problem is complex enough to provoke questions among young high school students. Very often math is taught as a set of procedures that lead to correct answers. And yet most mathematicians will say that math is not a set of procedures, but a way of thinking. Mrs. Erickson's own knowledge of mathematics is deep enough so that she is willing to set her students loose with a complex problem, and feel confident she will be able to guide them as they make discoveries and ask questions. But in addition, she was not in a rush. She gave her students plenty of time to explore the problem, and made it clear that getting an answer was not the most important goal.

Another key ingredient to the curious classroom is openness to serendipity, the unexpected insight or accidental data. Most scientists agree that serendipity is an essential strand of good research (Merton and Barber 2006). But the scientist (or student) must be able to recognize the importance of an unanticipated datum; as Alan Baumeister puts it, she must be "sagacious"—attentive and clever—to build on what chance throws her way (2006).

For example, the social psychologist Saul Kassin describes the accidental observation that led him to decades of research on false confessions. He had been conducting research on how juries function, and was struggling to get his data "clean." He says, "It was clear that every case containing a confession yielded unanimous and consistent votes for conviction. The problem was so evident that in order to study the effects of various psychological factors on jury verdicts I had to edit out of my stimulus trials all references to confessions. Within my first year, I realized—wait, confessions are not a nuisance variable, they are of great interest in their own right—and oh by the way, are they really as infallible as evidence as we all assume them to be?" His ability to notice a small problem, and see that it was in fact an important source of data, led to his most important research (Kassin 2013).

In their study of the word "serendipity," Robert Merton and Elinor Barber point out that even among scientists, the value of attending to the unexpected is controversial. In telling that history, they refer to Alexander Fleming's discovery of penicillin, which Fleming himself described this way: "When I woke up just after dawn on September 28, 1928, I certainly didn't plan to revolutionise all medicine by discovering the world's first antibiotic, or bacteria killer. . . . But I suppose that was exactly what I did" (Haven 1994).

On September 3, 1928, Fleming returned to his lab after a summer vacation. Notoriously messy, he had left all of his staphylococci cultures stacked in a corner of the room. When he went over to take a look at them, he noticed that one culture was contaminated with a fungus. All the colonies of staphylococci that were close by had been destroyed, but the ones farther away were unaffected. Rather than return to his planned experiment with the staphylococci, he decided to follow up, by growing the mold deliberately. This led him to discover penicillin (Diggins 2003).

But as Merton and Barber argue, accidents are not enough; the good scientist seizes upon unanticipated discoveries. To bolster this point, they refer to Walter Cannon's account of Fleming (Cannon 1945). "In describing Fleming's discovery of penicillin [Cannon] tells us of the 'pregnant hint' that was given to Fleming when the culture he was working with underwent dissolution by accidental contamination with a mold—'A careless worker might have thrown the culture away'—but Fleming took the hint" (172). Most scientists probably agree that serendipity is key to their work. How, then, might we prepare students to discern the "pregnant hint" and make something of it? What does it take to encourage and accommodate serendipity and the work that must follow it, in a classroom?

Most of the time, when teachers want their students to learn something about laboratory research, they use a familiar experiment, one in which the results are pretty much guaranteed. But it's possible to approach things more authentically, if more riskily. Years after that conversation I had with the group of teachers who told me curiosity was their educational goal, we agreed that they should hire a young scientist to set up a lab at their elementary school. The idea was that someone who genuinely wanted an answer to a scientific question might engage the students more fully, and that students might actually learn more about how to do science by working alongside the scientist. The woman they hired had just finished her BA in ecology and was taking a few years off before heading to graduate school. She wanted to examine various aspects of marine life on the eastern end of Long Island. With help from her students she designed studies, collected and analyzed data, and wrote up her results. Along the way, several of the children developed their own questions about marine biology. Small groups undertook experiments and studies. Their questions included: "What is in our local water?" "Will flowers grow with acid on them?" "Can we make biodiesel to use at school?" "How much trash is there on the beach?" and "Are there different numbers and types of bugs in brackish ponds than in freshwater ponds?"

They, too, designed studies, collected and analyzed data, and reported their results. This way, science becomes a way of thinking and doing, rather than a body of circumscribed knowledge and procedures, ones that often don't ever follow the child outside the science room. As we know from Deanna Kuhn's research, this method for learning about the scientific method is a bit circuitous and time consuming—but also far more effective.

There is much more to learn about the development of curiosity, but researchers have already learned enough to conclude that the urge to find out should be fostered in schools. Furthermore, the research provides valuable ideas about how to put curiosity at the center of the classroom. Below, I offer four ways that educators can nurture and guide children's impulse to find out.

The first idea is to fill classrooms with the kinds of complexity that invite inquiry. Teachers should provide children with interesting materials, seductive details, and desirable difficulty. Instead of presenting children with material that has been made as straightforward and digested as possible, teachers should make sure their students encounter objects, texts, environments, and ideas that will draw them in and pique their curiosity.

FOUR SUGGESTIONS FOR THE CURIOUS CLASSROOM

Children need access to books with good language and complex characters, fish tanks, terrariums, complex machines and gadgets, and conversations about the unseen and unseeable. In her book "The Having of Wonderful Ideas," Eleanor Duckworth warned against the overly tidy, orderly classroom, suggesting that such a classroom probably would not contain children busily engaged in developing their own ideas. Along the same vein, I am not suggesting that children or teachers benefit from a chaotic environment, only that they need enough ambiguity to spark inquiry.

The second idea to emerge from the research is that question asking can become the goal of an educational activity, rather than a happy byproduct. Teachers can develop activities that invite or require students to figure out what they want to know and then seek answers. One way teachers can do this is by encouraging students to use the Internet to ask any question that occurs to them—or arises during class discussions or while doing schoolwork. Google can be a curious person's best friend. For instance, recently, in one afternoon, I used Google to answer the following unexpected questions that popped up during a range of activities: Which of Henry VIII's wives came after Anne Boleyn? What kind of milk is mozzarella made of? What does the city of Hyderabad look like? The ease with which we can look things up online is exhilarating—and it makes the urge to know feel good more often.

Children need to feel the satisfaction that comes from having the chance to satisfy curiosity, and get information, even when it is not in the service of a teacher-driven task, or one that will result in a grade.

On the other hand, a teacher who invites students to ask questions without helping them seek accurate answers or acquiring a robust body of knowledge would leave the educational task half done. In the best of circumstances, a child who is genuinely curious doesn't rest until he or she has satisfied the urge to know. So to cultivate students' curiosity, teachers need to give them both time to seek answers and guidance about various routes to getting answers, such as looking things up in reliable sources or testing hypotheses.

Along these same lines, teachers can encourage students to think about whether their original question has been answered to their satisfaction. Such techniques are the bread and butter of the autodidact, and can be made the figure, rather than the ground, of the educational process.

When I began doing research on curiosity, my dream was to come up with a measure that could be used in schools. That way, I figured, teachers and administrators could see whether curiosity was or wasn't being encouraged in their schools. I have yet to fulfill that dream (though there are several labs where researchers are currently trying to develop such measures). But teachers don't have to wait for standardized measures to borrow from the methods we've already developed, using various simple techniques to get a sense of whether curiosity pervades a particular classroom. One of the biggest obstacles to improving educational practices that might encourage curiosity is that curiosity is never the thing teachers measure (instead measuring things like vocabulary size, or computational skills). It doesn't mean much for educators to say they value a quality like curiosity in children if they never assess whether it's present. In his groundbreaking book *Better* (2007), physician Atul Gawande encourages people in the medical profession to "count something." He means that causal intuitions about what's happening in one's workplace can be misleading. This observation is as true of schools as it is of hospitals. Few teachers readily see that they're discouraging students' questions, just as few parents readily see that they're short-tempered with their children. Even the most thoughtful reflection at the end of the day does not provide the same information as actual recordings. Precise and methodical data collection enables teachers to learn things that are counterintuitive.

Teachers who watch themselves and count the number of questions students ask will see how much inquiry is being expressed in their classroom—and they'll learn how they respond to students' inquiries. To do this, teachers can audio-record lessons or conversations in their classrooms in order to count and categorize the questions their students ask. Video recording is another good tool for this kind of data collection. Teachers might regularly videotape activities in their classrooms and score one another's students (to increase objectivity and accuracy) on things like individual students' level of interest, the number of exploratory gestures students use when encountering materials or objects, and the duration of each student's engagement with one activity. Teachers who keep journals of their daily work with students might go through them at the end of the year to see how many occasions they created for students to figure out what they wanted to know—and pursue answers.

In classrooms where teachers are deliberately cultivating curiosity, they should see more of it in May than in September, they should see certain students learn to sustain their curiosity, while others simply become more ready to express it.

Finally, by simply by counting questions, a piece of the classroom dynamic that may have been invisible will become salient. Teachers can also use such data to discover what kinds of things individual students are curious about, who asks lots of questions, and who never asks even one. By attending to the quality of their students' questions, teachers can get ideas about how to help their students develop better questions. Finally, expressions of curiosity can serve as cues for thinking up new activities or topics to discuss.

One of the key findings of research is that children are heavily influenced not only by what adults say to them, but also by how the adults themselves behave. If schools value children's curiosity, they'll need to hire teachers who are curious. It is hard to fan the flames of a drive you yourself rarely experience. Many principals hire teachers who seem smart, who like children, and who have the kind of drive that supports academic achievement. They know that teachers who possess these qualities will foster the same in their students. Why not put curiosity at the top of the list of criteria for good teachers?

How do we judge whether someone is truly curious? A teacher's thirst for finding out should be evident in what he or she has done or in how he or she behaves. Sometimes a teacher with plenty of curiosity has done scientific research or spent years studying some topic of personal interest (such as butterflies or architecture). Sometimes teachers' curiosity is expressed as an urge to know more about their students. Often teachers of young children excel because of their unending interest in early development. Either way, the teacher who knows what the itch to find out feels like is in a better position to foster that itch in students.

This book began with a potato bug, and ends with an ant. When my eldest son Jake was a senior in college at Wesleyan University, he lived off campus with three friends. One of them, Ian, was working on an honor's thesis in physics. During that year, the four friends spent a lot of time talking about their respective projects in art, political science, American history, and physics. They probably spent a lot of time doing things I shouldn't describe in this book. But they also spent a fair amount of time dealing with a serious ant problem. The house, on the edge of the Middletown campus, was riddled with ants, and the four young men couldn't seem to get rid of them. One day, when they were sitting on their porch, drinking beer, and talking, yet again, about the ant problem, Ian said, "Yeah, no one seems to be able to tell me what kind of ant it is. And the weird thing is, when I tasted one, it emitted this black inky stuff." My son Jake put down his bottle of beer, taken aback. "What? What do you mean 'when you tasted one'? You put one of those ants in your mouth?" Ian answered offhandedly, "Yeah, you know, I put one in my mouth to see what they tasted like, and when I bit down, this inky black stuff squirted out." To Ian, such unconstrained experimentation was second nature. But why should Ian be among the lucky few whose hunger for knowledge remains robust?

Einstein was only partly right when he said, "Curiosity is a delicate little plant which, aside from stimulation, stands mainly in need of freedom." It turns out that like many delicate plants, in order to flourish, curiosity needs to be cultivated.

References

Ainsworth, M. S., and S. Bell. 1970. Attachment, exploration, and separation: Illustrated by the behavior of one-year-olds in a strange situation. *Child Development* 41(1): 49–67.

Alessandri, S. M., M. W. Sullivan, and M. Lewis, 1990. Violation of expectancy and frustration in early infancy. *Developmental Psychology* 26(5): 738.

Alter, A. 2013. The benefits of cognitive disfluency. *Current Directions in Psychological Science* 22(6): 437–442.

Anderson, R. C., P. T. Wilson, and L. G. Fielding, 1988. Growth in reading and how children spend their time outside of school. *Reading Research Quarterly* 23(3): 285–303.

Anglin, J. M. 1977. *Word, Object, and Conceptual Development.* New York: Norton.

Arend, R., F. Gove, and A. Sroufe. 1979. Continuity of individual adaptation from infancy to kindergarten: A predictive study of ego-resiliency and curiosity in preschoolers. *Child Development* 50(4): 950–959.

Arnone, M. P., and Grabowski, B. L. 1992. Effects on children's achievement and curiosity of variations in learner control over an interactive video lesson. *Educational Technology Research and Development* 40(1): 15–27.

Astuti, R. 2011. Death, ancestors, and the living dead: Learning without teaching in Madagascar. In *Children and Death: From Biological to Religious Conceptions,* edited by V. Talwar, P. L. Harris, and M. Schleifer, 1–18. Cambridge: Cambridge University Press.

Ayim, M. 1994. Knowledge through the grapevine: Gossip as inquiry. In *Good gossip,* edited by R. F. Goodman and A. Ben-Ze'ev, 85–99. Lawrence: University Press of Kansas.

Bamberg, M., and A. Georgakopoulou. 2008. Small stories as a new perspective in narrative and identity analysis. *Text and Talk: An Interdisciplinary Journal of Language, Discourse Communication Studies* 28(3): 377–396.

Bandura, A., and F. J. McDonald. 1963. Influence of social reinforcement and the behavior of models in shaping children's moral judgment. *Journal of Abnormal and Social Psychology* 67(3): 274.

Bandura, A., D. Ross, and S. A. Ross. 1963. Imitation of film-mediated aggressive models. *Journal of Abnormal and Social Psychology* 66(1): 3–11.

Banerjee, R. 2002. Audience effects on self-presentation in childhood. *Social Development* 11(4): 487–507.

Barbaranelli, C., G. Caprara, A. Rabasca, and C. Pastorelli. 2003. A questionnaire for measuring the Big Five in late childhood. *Personality and Individual Differences* 34:645–664.

Baron-Cohen, S., R. Knickmeyer, and M. Belmonte. 2005. Sex differences in the brain: Implications for explaining autism. *Science* 310:819–823.

Barron, F., and D. M. Harrington. 1981. Creativity, intelligence, and personality. *Annual Review of Psychology* 32(1): 439–476.

Bartlett, F. C. 2003. Remembering: A study in experimental and social psychology. In *The History of Psychology: Fundamental Questions*, edited by M. P. Munger, 430–446. New York: Oxford University Press.

Baumeister, A. A. 2006. Serendipity and the cerebral localization of pleasure. *Journal of the History of the Neurosciences* 15(2): 92–98.

Baumeister, R. F., L. Zhang, and K. D. Vohs. 2004. Gossip as cultural learning. *Review of General Psychology* 8(2): 111.

Beersma, B., and G. A. Van Kleef. 2012. Why people gossip: An empirical analysis of social motives, antecedents, and consequences. *Journal of Applied Social Psychology* 42(11): 2640–2670.

Begus, K., and V. Southgate. 2012. Infant pointing serves an interrogative function. *Developmental Science* 15(5): 611–617.

Ben-Ze'ev, A. 1994. The vindication of gossip. In *Good Gossip*, edited by R. F. Goodman and A. Ben-Ze'ev, 11–24. Lawrence: University Press of Kansas.

Berlyne, D. E. 1955. The arousal and satiation of perceptual curiosity in the rate. *Journal of Comparative Physiological Psychology* 48:238–246.

Berlyne, D. E. 1960. *Conflict, Arousal and Curiosity.* New York: McGraw Hill.

Bernstein, M. R. 1955. Relationship between interest and reading comprehension. *Journal of Educational Research* 49(4): 283–288.

Bianchi, S. M., and J. Robinson. 1997. What did you do today? Children's use of time, family composition, and the acquisition of social capital. *Journal of Marriage and the Family* 59(2): 332–344.

Bjork, R. A., and M. C. Linn. 2006. The science of learning and the learning of science. *APS Observer* 19(3): 1–2.

Blake, P. R. 2012. Personal communication with the author.

Blake, P. R., and K. McAuliffe. 2011. "I had so much it didn't seem fair": Eight-year-olds reject two forms of inequity. *Cognition* 120(2): 215–224.

Bloom, L. 1973. *One Word at a Time: The Use of Single-Word Utterances before Syntax.* Vol. 154. The Hague: Mouton.

Bonawitz, E., P. Shafto, H. Gweon, N. Goodman, E. Spelke, and L. Schulz. 2011. The double-edged sword of pedagogy: Instruction limits spontaneous exploration and discovery. *Cognition* 120:322–330.

Bower, T. G. 1974. *Development in Infancy.* New York: W. H. Freeman.

Bowlby, J. 1969. *Attachment and Loss.* London: Hogarth.

Brice-Heath, S. 1983. *Ways with Words.* Cambridge: Cambridge University Press.

Brown, A. 1997. Transforming schools into communities of thinking and learning about serious matters. *American Psychologist* 52(4): 399–413.

Brown, R. 1973. *A First Language: The Early Stages.* Cambridge, MA: Harvard University Press.

Bruner, J. 1966. *Toward a Theory of Instruction.* Cambridge, MA: Harvard University Press.

———. 1986. *Actual Minds, Possible Worlds.* Cambridge, MA: Harvard University Press.

———. 1990. *Acts of Meaning.* Cambridge, MA: Harvard University Press.

Campos, J., and C. Sternberg. 1981. Perception, appraisal, and emotion: The onset of social referencing. In *Infant Social Cognition: Empirical and Theoretical Considerations,* edited by M. Lamb and L. Sherrod, 273–314. Hillsdale, NJ: Lawrence Erlbaum.

Campos, J. J., D. I. Anderson, M. A. Barbu-Roth, E. M. Hubbard, M. J. Hertenstein, and D. Witherington. 2000. Travel broadens the mind. *Infancy* 1(2): 149–219.

Cannon, W. B. 1945. *The Way of an Investigator: A Scientist's Experiences in Medical Research.* New York: Norton.

Carey, S. 2009. *The Origins of Concepts.* New York: Oxford University Press.

Chafe, W. 1980. *The Pear Stories: Cultural, Cognitive, and Linguistic Aspects of Narrative Production.* Norwood, NJ: Ablex.

Chi, M. T. 1978. Knowledge structures and memory development. In *Children's Thinking: What Develops,* edited by R. Siegler, 73–96. Hillsdale, NJ: Lawrence Erlbaum.

Chouinard, M. M. 2007. Children's questions: A mechanism for development. *Monographs of the Society for Research in Child Development* 72(1).

Coie, J. D. 1974. An evaluation of the cross-situational stability of children's curiosity. *Journal of Personality* 42(1): 93–116.

Cook, C., N. Goodman, and L. Schulz. 2011. Where science starts: Spontaneous experiments in preschoolers' exploratory play. *Cognition* 120:341–349.

Csikszentmihalyi, M., and R. Larsen. 1984. *Being Adolescent: Conflict and Growth in the Adolescent Years.* New York: Basic Books.

Cuffaro, H. K. 1995. *Experimenting with the World: John Dewey and the Early Childhood Classroom.* New York: Teachers College Press.

Darwin, C. 1859/2003. *The Origin of Species.* New York: Signet Classics.

Dashiell, J. F. 1925. A quantitative demonstration of animal drive. *Journal of Comparative Psychology* 5(3): 205.

DeCasper, A. J., and W. P. Fifer. 1980. Of human bonding: Newborns prefer their mothers' voices. *Science* 208(4448): 1174–1176.

DeLoache, J. S., G. Simcock, and S. Macari. 2007. Planes, trains, automobiles—and tea sets: Extremely intense interests in very young children. *Developmental Psychology* 43(6): 1579.

Dewey, J. 1911. *The Child and the Curriculum.* Chicago: University of Chicago Press.

Diggins, F. 2003. The true history of the discovery of penicillin by Alexander Fleming. *Biomedical Scientist* (March), 246–249.

Dominus, S. 2013. Stephen King's family business. *New York Times*, July 31.

Dondi, M., F. Simion, and G. Caltran. 1999. Can newborns discriminate between their own cry and the cry of another newborn infant? *Developmental Psychology* 35(2): 418.

Duckworth, A. L., E. Tsukayama, and H. May. 2010. Establishing causality using longitudinal hierarchical linear modeling: An illustration predicting achievement from self-control. *Social Psychological and Personality Science* 1(4): 311–317.

Duckworth, E. 1972. The having of wonderful ideas. *Harvard Educational Review* 42(2): 217–231.

Dunbar, R., and R. I. M. Dunbar. 1998. *Grooming, Gossip and the Evolution of Language.* Cambridge, MA: Harvard University Press.

Dunbar, R. M., A. Marriott, and N. C. Duncan. 1997. Human conversational behavior. *Human Nature* 8(3): 231–246.

Dunn, J. 1988. *The Beginnings of Social Understanding.* Cambridge, MA: Harvard University Press.

Easterbrook, M. A., B. S. Kisilevsky, D. W. Muir, and D. P. Laplante. 1999. Newborns discriminate schematic faces from scrambled faces. *Canadian Journal of Experimental Psychology / Revue Canadienne de Psychologie Expérimentale* 53(3): 231.

Emler, N. 1994. Gossip, reputation, and social adaptation. In *Good Gossip*, edited by R. F. Goodman and A. Ben-Ze'ev, 117–138. Lawrence: University Press of Kansas.

Endsley, R. C., and S. A. Clarey. 1975. Answering young children's questions as a determinant of their subsequent question-asking behavior. *Developmental Psychology* 11(6).

Endsley, R. C., M. A. Hutcherson, A. P. Garner, and M. J. Martin. 1979. Interrelationships among selected maternal behaviors, authoritarianism, and preschool children's verbal and nonverbal curiosity. *Child Development* 50(2): 331–339.

Engel, S. 1995. *The Stories Children Tell: Making Sense of the Narratives of Childhood.* New York: W. H. Freeman, Times Books, Henry Holt.

Engel, S. 2011. Children's need to know: Curiosity in schools. *Harvard Educational Review* 84(4): 625–645.

Engel, S., and A. Li. 2004. Narratives, gossip, and shared experience: How and what young children know about the lives of others. In *The Development of the Mediated Mind: Sociocultural Context and Cognitive Development*, edited by J. M. Lucariello, J. A. Hudson, R. Fivush, and P. J. Bauer, 151–174. Mahwah, NJ: Lawrence Erlbaum.

Engelhard, G., Jr., and J. A. Monsaas. 1988. Grade level, gender, and school-related curiosity in urban elementary schools. *Journal of Educational Research* 82(1): 22–26.

Everett, D. 2009. *Don't Sleep, There Are Snakes.* New York: Vintage.

Fagan, J. 1974. Infant recognition memory: The effects of length of familiarization and type of discrimination task. *Child Development* 45(2): 351–356.

Fagan, J., and S. McGrath. 1981. Infant recognition memory and later intelligence. *Intelligence* 5(2): 121–130.

Fernald, A., V. A. Marchman, and A. Weisleder. 2013. SES differences in language-processing skill and vocabulary are evident at 18 months. *Developmental Science* 16(2): 234–248.

Fine, G. A. 1977. Social components of children's gossip. *Journal of Communication* 27(1): 181–185.

Fox, N., and H. Henderson. 1999. Does infancy matter? Predicting social behavior from infant temperament. *Infant Behavior and Development* 22(4): 445–455.

Fox, N. A., H. A. Henderson, K. Pérez-Edgar, and L. K. White. 2008. The biology of temperament: An integrative approach. In *Handbook of Developmental Cognitive Neuroscience,* 92nd ed., edited by C. A. Nelson and M. Luciana, 839–853. Cambridge, MA: MIT Press.

Frazier, B. N., S. A. Gelman, and H. M. Wellman. 2009. Preschoolers' search for explanatory information within adult-child conversation. *Child Development* 80(6): 1592–1611.

Fulton, C. 2009. The pleasure principle: The power of positive affect in information seeking. *Aslib Proceedings* 61(3): 245–261.

Garner, R., R. Brown, S. Sanders, and D. J. Menke. 1992. "Seductive details" and learning from text. In *The Role of Interest in Learning and Development,* edited by K. Renninger, S. Hidi, and A. Krapp, 239–254. Hillsdale, NJ: Lawrence Erlbaum.

Gauvain, M., R. L. Munroe, and H. Beebe. 2013. Children's questions in cross-cultural perspective: A four-culture study. *Journal of Cross-Cultural Psychology* 44(7): 1148–1165.

Gawande, A. 2007. *Better: A Surgeon's Notes on Performance.* New York: Picador.

Gleitman, H., D. Reisberg, and J. Gross. 2007. *Psychology,* 7th ed. New York: Norton.

Goodwin, M. H. 1980. He-said-she-said: Formal cultural procedures for the construction of a gossip dispute activity. *American Ethnologist* 7(4): 674–695.

Gopnik, A., A. Meltzoff, and P. Kuhl. 2000. *The Scientist in the Crib.* New York: William Morrow.

Grolnick, W. S., and R. M. Ryan. 1987. Autonomy in children's learning: An experimental and individual difference investigation. *Journal of Personality and Social Psychology* 52(5): 890.

Gyllstrom, K., and M. Moens. 2012. Surfin' Wikipedia: An analysis of the Wikipedia (nonrandom) surfer's behavior from aggregate access data. *Proceedings of the 4th Information Interaction in Context Symposium,* 155–163.

Harlow, H. F. 1958. The nature of love. *American Psychologist* 13(12): 673–685.

Harris, P. L. 2000. *The Work of the Imagination.* Malden, MA: Blackwell.

———. 2012. *Trusting What You're Told: How Children Learn from Others.* Cambridge, MA: Harvard University Press.

Hart, B., and T. R. Risley. 1992. American parenting of language-learning children: Persisting differences in family-child interactions observed in natural home environments. *Developmental Psychology* 28(6): 1096.

———. 1995. *Meaningful Differences in the Everyday Experience of Young American Children.* Baltimore: Paul H. Brookes Publishing.

Hart, R. 1979. *Children's Experience of Place.* Oxford: Irvington.

Haven, K. 1994. *Marvels of Science: 50 Fascinating Five-Minute Reads.* Littleton, CO: Libraries Unlimited.

Heath, S. B. 1983. *Ways with Words: Language, Life and Work in Communities and Classrooms.* Cambridge: Cambridge University Press.

Henderson, B. B. 1984. Parents and exploration: The effect of context on individual differences in exploratory behavior. *Child Development* 55(4): 1237–1245.

Henderson, B. B., and S. G. Moore. 1980. Children's responses to objects differing in novelty in relation to level of curiosity and adult behavior. *Child Development* 51:457–465.

Hepach, R., and G. Westermann. 2013. Infants' sensitivity to the congruence of others' emotions and actions. *Journal of Experimental Child Psychology* 115(1): 16–29.

Hickling, A. K., and H. M. Wellman. 2001. The emergence of children's causal explanations and theories: Evidence from everyday conversation. *Developmental Psychology* 37(5): 668.

Hill, V. A. 2007. *Children's Understanding of Gossip as It Relates to Reputation.* DeKalb: Northern Illinois University Press.

Hofferth, S. L., and J. F. Sandberg. 2001. How American children spend their time. *Journal of Marriage and Family* 63(2): 295–308.

Hrdy, S. 2009. *Mothers and Others: The Evolutionary Origins of Mutual Understanding.* Cambridge, MA: Harvard University Press.

Hudson, J., and K. Nelson. 1983. Effects of script structure on children's story recall. *Developmental Psychology* 19(4): 625.

Hunter, M. A., E. W. Ames, and R. Koopman. 1983. Effects of stimulus complexity and familiarization time on infant preferences for novel and familiar stimuli. *Developmental Psychology* 19(3): 338.

Hunter, M. A., H. S. Ross, and E. W. Ames. 1982. Preferences for familiar or novel toys: Effect of familiarization time in 1-year-olds. *Developmental Psychology* 18(4): 519.

Hutt, C. 1970. Curiosity in Young Children. *Science Journal* 6(2): 68–71.

Jirout, J., and D. Klahr. 2012. Children's scientific curiosity: In search of an operational definition of an elusive concept. *Developmental Review* 32(2): 125–160.

Johns, C., and R. C. Endsley. 1977. The effects of a maternal model on young children's tactual curiosity. *Journal of Genetic Psychology* 131(1): 21–28.

Kagan, J. 2002. *Surprise, Uncertainty, and Mental Structures.* Cambridge, MA: Harvard University Press.

Kagan, J., and N. Snidman. 2009. *The Long Shadow of Temperament.* New York: Belknap Books.

Kagan, J., N. Snidman, D. Arcus, and J. Reznick. 1994. *Galen's Prophecy: Temperament in Human Nature.* Basic Books.

Kang, M. J., M. Hsu, I. M. Krajbich, G. Loewenstein, S. M. McClure, J. T. Y. Wang, and C. F. Camerer. 2009. The wick in the candle of learning: Epistemic curiosity activates reward circuitry and enhances memory. *Psychological Science* 20(8): 963–973.

Kassin, S. 2013. Personal communication with author.

Kidd, D., and E. Castano. 2013. Reading literary fiction improves theory of mind. *Science* 342(6156): 377–380.

Klahr, D., and M. Nigam. 2004. The equivalence of learning paths in early science instruction effects of direct instruction and discovery learning. *Psychological Science* 15(10): 661–667.

Knobloch, S., G. Patzig, A. Mende, and M. Hastall. 2004. Affective news: Effects
of discourse structure in narratives on suspense, curiosity, and enjoyment
while reading news and novels. *Communication Research* 31(3): 259–287.

Kornell, N., and R. A. Bjork. 2008. Learning concepts and categories: Is spacing
the "enemy of induction"? *Psychological Science* 19(6): 585–592.

Kuhn, D., and V. Ho. 1980. Self-directed activity and cognitive development.
Journal of Applied Developmental Psychology 1(2): 119–133.

Kuhn, D., K. Iordanou, M. Pease, and C. Wirkala. 2008. Beyond control of variables: What needs to develop to achieve skilled scientific thinking? *Cognitive Development* 23(4): 435–451.

Kuo, F. E., and A. Taylor. 2004. A potential natural treatment for Attention-Deficit
/ Hyperactivity Disorder: Evidence from a national study. *American Journal
of Public Health* 94(9): 1580–1586.

Labov, W., and T. Labov. 1978. Learning the syntax of questions. In *Recent Advances in the Psychology of Language*, edited by R. N. Campbell and P. T.
Smith, 1–44. New York: Springer US.

Laosa, M. 1978. Maternal teaching strategies in Chicano families of varied educational and socioeconomic levels. *Child Development* 49(4): 1129–1135.

Laosa, L. M., and I. E. Sigel, eds. 1982. *Families as Learning Environments for
Children.* New York: Plenum.

Larson, R. W. 1990. The solitary side of life: An examination of the time people
spend alone from childhood to old age. *Developmental Review* 10(2): 155–183.

Levine, R., S. Levine, B. Schnell-Anzola, M. Rowe, and E. Dexter. 2012. *Literacy
and Mothering.* Oxford: Oxford University Press.

Lillard, A. S. 2008. *Montessori: The Science behind the Genius.* New York:
Oxford University Press.

Lillard, A. S., and D. C. Witherington. 2004. Mothers' behavior modifications
during pretense and their possible signal value for toddlers. *Developmental
Psychology* 40(1): 95.

Lindfors, J. W. 1987. *Children's Language and Learning.* Englewood Cliffs, NJ:
Prentice-Hall.

Loewenstein, G. 1994. The psychology of curiosity: A review and reinterpreta-
tion. *Psychological Bulletin* 116(1): 75–98.

Lowry, N., and D. W. Johnson. 1981. Effects of controversy on epistemic curiosity, achievement, and attitudes. *Journal of Social Psychology* 115(1): 31–43.

McDonald, K. L., M. Putallaz, C. L. Grimes, J. B. Kupersmidt, and J. D. Coie. 2007.
Girl talk: Gossip, friendship, and sociometric status. *Merrill-Palmer Quarterly* 53(3): 381–411.

Meichenbaum, D. H., K. S. Bowers, and R. R. Ross. 1968. Modification of classroom behavior of institutionalized female adolescent offenders. *Behaviour Research and Therapy* 6(3): 343–353.

Meichenbaum, D. H., and J. Goodman. 1971. Training impulsive children to talk
to themselves: A means of developing self-control. *Journal of Abnormal Psychology* 77(2): 115.

Meltzoff, A. 1995. Understanding the intentions of others: Re-enactment of intended acts by 18-month-old children. *Developmental Psychology* 31(5): 838–850.

Merton, R. K., and E. Barber. 2006. *The Travels and Adventures of Serendipity: A Study in Sociological Semantics and the Sociology of Science.* Princeton, NJ: Princeton University Press.

Mervis, C. B., and E. Rosch. 1981. Categorization of natural objects. *Annual Review of Psychology* 32(1): 89–115.

Michaels, S. 1981. "Sharing time": Children's narrative styles and differential access to literacy. *Language in Society* 10(3): 423–442.

———. 1991. The dismantling of narrative. In *Developing Narrative Structure,* edited by A. McCabe and C. Peterson, 303–351. Hillsdale, NJ: Lawrence Erlbaum.

Miller, G. A. 1956. The magical number seven, plus or minus two: Some limits on our capacity for processing information. *Psychological Review* 63(2): 81–97.

———. 1977. *Spontaneous Apprentices: Children and Language.* New York: Seabury Press.

Miller, G. A., E. Galanter, and K. Pribram. 1960. *Plans and the Structure of Behavior.* New York: Henry Holt.

Miller, P. J., J. Mintz, L. Hoogstra, H. Fung, and R. Potts. 1992. The narrated self: Young children's construction of self in relation to others in conversational stories of personal experience. *Merrill-Palmer Quarterly* 38(1): 45–67.

Miller, P. J., R. Potts, R., H. Fung, L. Hoogstra, and J. Mintz. 1990. Narrative practices and the social construction of self in childhood. *American Ethnologist* 17(2): 292–311.

Moore, S. G., and K. N. Bulbulian. 1976. The effects of contrasting styles of adult-child interaction on children's curiosity. *Developmental Psychology* 12(2): 171.

Moses, L. J., D. A. Baldwin, J. G. Rosicky, and G. Tidball. 2001. Evidence for referential understanding in the emotions domain at twelve and eighteen months. *Child Development* 72(3): 718–735.

Muentener, P., D. Friel, and L. Schulz. 2012. Giving the giggles: Prediction, intervention, and young children's representation of psychological events. *PloS one* 7(8): e42495.

Mullen, M., and S. Yi. 1995. The cultural context of talk about the past: Implications for the development of autobiographical memory. *Cognitive Development* 10(3): 407–419.

Nachman, P. A., D. N. Stern, and C. Best. 1986. Affective reactions to stimuli and infants' preferences for novelty and familiarity. *Journal of the American Academy of Child Psychiatry* 25(6): 801–804.

Neisser, U. 1988. Five kinds of self-knowledge. *Philosophical Psychology* 1(1): 35–59.

Nelson, K., and L. Gruendel. 1986. *Event Knowledge: Structure and Function in Development.* Hillsdale, NJ: Lawrence Erlbaum.

Newman, R. S. 2005. The cocktail party effect in infants revisited: Listening to one's name in noise. *Developmental Psychology* 41(2): 352.

Nishida, T. K., and A. S. Lillard. 2007. The informative value of emotional expressions: "Social referencing" in mother-child pretense. *Developmental Science* 10(2): 205–212.

O'Neill, D. K., R. M. Main, and R. A. Ziemski. 2009. I like Barney: Preschoolers' spontaneous conversational initiations with peers. *First Language* 29(4): 401–425.

Paley, V. G. 1984. *Boys and Girls: Superheroes in the Doll Corner.* Chicago: University of Chicago Press.

Parkhurst, J. T., and A. Hopmeyer. 1998. Sociometric popularity and peer-perceived popularity: Two distinct dimensions of peer status. *Journal of Early Adolescence* 18(2): 125–144.

Pellegrini, A. D., and L. Galda. 1990. The joint construction of stories by preschool children and an experimenter. In *Narrative Thought and Narrative Language,* edited by B. K. Britton and A. D. Pellegrini, 113–130. Hillsdale, NJ: Lawrence Erlbaum.

Pellicano, E., A. D. Smith, F. Cristino, B. M. Hood, J. Briscoe, and I. D. Gilchrist. 2011. Children with autism are neither systematic nor optimal foragers. *Proceedings of the National Academy of Sciences* 108(1): 421–426.

Pellow, S., P. Chopin, S. E. File, and M. Briley. 1985. Validation of open: Closed arm entries in an elevated plus-maze as a measure of anxiety in the rat. *Journal of Neuroscience Methods* 14(3): 149–167.

Perner, J. 1992. Grasping the concept of representation: Its impact on 4-year-olds' theory of mind and beyond. *Human Development* 35(3): 146–155.

Peters, R. A. 1978. Effects of anxiety, curiosity, and perceived instructor threat on student verbal behavior in the college classroom. *Journal of Educational Psychology* 70(3): 388.

Piaget, J. 1964a. *Development and Learning in Piaget Rediscovered.* Edited by R. E. Ripple and V. N. Rockcastle. New York: John Wiley.

———. 1964b. *The Early Growth of Logic in the Child.* London: Routledge and Kegan Paul.

Pidgeon, S. 2013. Rapturous research. *New York Times,* January 5.

Preece, A. 1987. The range of narrative forms conversationally produced by young children. *Journal of Child Language* 14(2): 353–373.

Raver, C. C., S. M. Jones, C. Li-Grining, F. Zhai, K. Bub, and E. Pressler. 2011. CSRP's impact on low-income preschoolers' preacademic skills: Self-regulation as a mediating mechanism. *Child Development* 82(1): 362–378.

Renninger, K. 1992. Individual interest and development: Implications for theory and practice. In *The Role of Interest in Learning and Development,* edited by K. A. Renninger, S. Hidi, and A. Krapp, 361–396. Hillsdale, NJ: Lawrence Erlbaum.

Richardson, R. D. 2007. *William James: In the Maelstrom of American Modernism.* Boston: Houghton Mifflin.

Rochat, P. 2001. *The Infant's World.* Cambridge, MA: Harvard University Press.

Rosch, E. 1978. Principles of categorization. In *Cognition and Categorization,* edited by Eleanor Rosch and Barbara B. Lloyd, 27–48. Hillsdale, NJ: Lawrence Erlbaum.

Rose, S. A., A. W. Gottfried, P. Melloy-Carminar, and W. H. Bridger. 1982. Familiarity and novelty preferences in infant recognition memory: Implications for information processing. *Developmental Psychology* 18(5): 704.

Russell, R., and J. Lucariello. 1992. Narrative, yes, narrative ad infinitum, no. *American Psychologist* 47(5): 671–672.

Sachs, J. 1983. Talking about the there and then: The emergence of displaced reference in parent-child discourse. *Children's Language* 4:1–28.

Saxe, R., and G. Stollak. 1971. *Child Development* 42:373–384.

Schafer, R. 1992. *Retelling a Life.* New York: Basic Books.

Schank, R., and R. Abelson. 1977. *Scripts, Plans, Goals, and Understanding: An Inquiry into Human Knowledge Structures.* New York: Psychology Press.

Schieche, M., and Spangler, G. 2005. Individual differences in bio-behavioral organization during problem-solving in toddlers: The influence of maternal behavior, infant-mother attachment and behavioral inhibition on the attachment-exploration balance. *Developmental Psychobiology* 46:293–306

Schulz, L. E., and E. B. Bonawitz. 2007. Serious fun: Preschoolers engage in more exploratory play when evidence is confounded. *Developmental Psychology* 43(4): 1045.

Schwartz, C., C. Wright, L. Shin, J. Kagan, and S. Rauch. 2003. Inhibited and uninhibited infants "grown up": Adult amygdalar response to novelty. *Science* 300(5627): 1952–1953.

Scribner, S., and M. Cole. 1978. Unpackaging literacy. *Social Science Information / Sur les Sciences Sociales* 17(1): 19–40.

Shirey, L. L., and R. E. Reynolds. 1988. Effect of interest on attention and learning. *Journal of Educational Psychology* 80(2): 159–166.

Shotwell, J., D. Wolf, and H. Gardner. 1979. Exploring early symbolization: Styles of achievement. In *Play and Learning,* edited by Brian Sutton-Smith, 127–156. New York: Gardner Press.

Siegler, R. S. 2000. Unconscious insights. *Current Directions in Psychological Science* 9(3): 79–83.

Silvia, P. 2006. *Exploring the Psychology of Interest.* New York: Oxford University Press.

Smith, F. 1998. *The Book of Learning and Forgetting.* New York: Teachers College Press.

Snow, C. E. 1983. Literacy and language: Relationships during the preschool years. *Harvard Educational Review* 53(2): 165–189.

———. 2010. Academic language and the challenge of reading for learning about science. *Science* (April 23): 450–452.

Sorce, J., R. Emde, J. Campos, and M. Klinnert. 1985. Maternal emotional signaling: Its effect on the visual cliff behavior of 1-year-olds. *Developmental Psychology* 21(1): 195–200.

Southgate, V., C. Van Maanen, and G. Csibra. 2007. Infant pointing: Communication to cooperate or communication to learn? *Child Development* 78(3): 735–740.

Spelke, E. S. 1999. Innateness, learning, and the development of object representation. Developmental *Science* 2:145–148.

Spence, D. P. 1983. Narrative persuasion. *Psychoanalysis and Contemporary Thought* 6(3): 457–481.

Stern, C., W. Stern, and T. J. Lamiell. 1999. *Recollection, Testimony, and Lying in Early Childhood.* Washington, DC: American Psychological Association.

Stern, W. 1924. *Psychology of Early Childhood.* New York: Henry Holt.

Stevenson, H. W., S. Lee, C. Chen, J. W. Stigler, C. Hsu, S. Kitamura, and G. Hatano. 1990. Contexts of achievement: A study of American, Chinese, and Japanese children. *Monographs of the Society for Research in Child Development* 55(1–2).

Stigler, J. W., and H. W. Stevenson. 1991. How Asian teachers polish each lesson to perfection. *American Educator* 15(1): 12–20.

Sully, J. 1895. *Studies of Childhood*. New York: Appleton.

Switzky, H. N., H. C. Haywood, and R. Isett. 1974. Exploration, curiosity, and play in young children: Effects of stimulus complexity. *Developmental Psychology* 10(3): 321.

Taylor, A. F., F. E. Kuo, and W. C. Sullivan. 2002. Views of nature and self-discipline: Evidence from inner city children. *Journal of Environmental Psychology* 22(1): 49–63.

Taylor, K., and D. Rohrer. 2010. The effects of interleaved practice. *Applied Cognitive Psychology* 24(6): 837–848.

Tizard, B., and M. Hughes. 1984. *Children Learning at Home and in School*. London: Fontana. *London*.

Tomasello, M. 1999. The human adaptation for culture. *Annual Review of Anthropology* 28:509–529.

Tough, P. 2011. The poverty clinic. *New Yorker*, March 21.

Trevarthen, C., and K. J. Aitken. 2001. Infant intersubjectivity: Research, theory, and clinical applications. *Journal of Child Psychology and Psychiatry* 42:3–48.

Ursache, A., C. Blair, and C. C. Raver. 2012. The promotion of self-regulation as a means of enhancing school readiness and early achievement in children at risk for school failure. *Child Development Perspectives* 6(2): 122–128.

Uzgiris, I. C., and J. V. Hunt. 1975. *Assessment in Infancy: Ordinal Scales of Psychological Development*. Champaign: University of Illinois Press.

van Schijndel, T. P., E. Singer, H. J. van der Maas, and M. J. Raijmakers. 2010. A sciencing programme and young children's exploratory play in the sandpit. *European Journal of Developmental Psychology* 7(5): 603–617.

Vygotsky, L. S. 1978. *Mind in Society: The Development of Higher Psychological Processes*. Cambridge, MA: Harvard University Press.

Walker-Andrews, A. S., and E. Lennon. 1991. Infants' discrimination of vocal expressions: Contributions of auditory and visual information. *Infant Behavior and Development* 14(2): 131–142.

Wallace, D. B., M. B. Franklin, and R. T. Keegan. 1994. The observing eye: A century of baby diaries. *Human Development* 37(1): 1–29.

Weisleder, A., and A. Fernald. 2013. Talking to children matters: Early language experience strengthens processing and builds vocabulary. *Psychological Science* 24(11): 2143–2152.

Wellman, H. M., A. K. Hickling, and C. A. Schult. 1997. Young children's psychological, physical, and biological explanations. *New Directions for Child and Adolescent Development* 75:7–26.

Wells, G. 1986. *The Meaning Makers: Children Learning Language and Using Language to Learn*. Portsmouth, NH: Heinemann Educational Books.

White, R. W., and R. A. Roth. 2009. Exploratory search: Beyond the query-response paradigm. *Synthesis Lectures on Information Concepts, Retrieval, and Services* 1(1): 1–98.

Whiten, A., and E. Flynn. 2010. The transmission and evolution of experimental microcultures in groups of young children. *Developmental Psychology* 46(6): 1694–1709.

Wilson, D. S., C. Wilczynski, A. Wells, and L. Weiser. 2000. Gossip and other aspects of language as group-level adaptations. In *The Evolution of Cognition*, edited by C. Heyes and L. Huber, 347–365. Cambridge, MA: MIT Press.

Wilson, R. 2013. Truth and beauty: Interview with Diane Sawyer. *Harper's Bazaar*, March 12, 22.

Winchester, S. 2003. *The Meaning of Everything: The Story of the Oxford English Dictionary.* New York: Oxford University Press.

———. 2012. The mongrel speech of the streets. *New York Review of Books*, March 8.

Wong, Scott. 2013. Department of History, Williams College, personal communication with author.

Wright, R. 1945. *Black Boy: A Record of Childhood and Youth.* New York: Harper and Brothers.

Wynn, K. 1998. Psychological foundations of number: Numerical competence in human infants. *Trends in Cognitive Sciences* 2(8): 296–303.

———. 2000. Findings of addition and subtraction in infants are robust and consistent: Reply to Wakeley, Rivera, and Langer. *Child Development* 71(6): 1535–1536.

Zimmerman, B. J., and E. O. Pike. 1972. Effects of modeling and reinforcement on the acquisition and generalization of question-asking behavior. *Child Development* 43(3): 892–907.

Acknowledgments

THE SPENCER FOUNDATION generously supported a number of my studies on curiosity. The Hedgebrook Writers' Residence provided me with heavenly time and space to write. I thank both wonderful organizations.

Several superb students at Williams carried out studies that were essential to my thinking and to this book: Hillary Hackmann, Alice Li, Elissa Brown, Kellie Randall, Prim Assarat, Madelyn Labella, Katrina Ferrara, Laura Corona, and Daniel Silver. They were a joy to work with.

Several friends, colleagues, and students read part or all of this manuscript and gave me invaluable feedback. I am deeply indebted to each of them: Marlene Sandstrom, Paul Harris, James Schulman, Hannah Hausman, Alex Jones, and two anonymous reviewers.

A number of people gave me good ideas along the way, told me about their childhoods, questioned my arguments, or in other ways nourished my understanding of curiosity: Scottie Mills, Verlyn Klinkenborg, Isa Catto Shaw, J. J. Abrams, Simon Winchester, Katherine Nelson, and Margery Franklin.

I thank Elizabeth Knoll, who enthusiastically shepherded the first stages of this book, as well as Joy Deng, Maria Ascher, Andrew Kinney, and Susan Wallace Boehmer at Harvard University Press and Brian Ostrander at Westchester Publishing Services, who skillfully stepped in and helped me with the last stages of it.

I thank the teachers, students, and families who have so tolerantly allowed me to watch, listen, and involve them in my research. This book is written with them in mind.

Finally, I thank my family. They're the ones who have heard me obsess about children's curiosity for over a decade now. They must be hoping I've become curious about a new topic.

Index